5-7-99

Christian

From Cheryl —
happy birthday!

DEVELOPING
A CHRISTIAN
IMAGINATION

DEVELOPING A CHRISTIAN IMAGINATION

An Interpretive Anthology

Compiled by
Warren W. Wiersbe

VICTOR BOOKS

A DIVISION OF SCRIPTURE PRESS PUBLICATIONS INC.
USA CANADA ENGLAND

Editor: Robert N. Hosack
Designer: Scott Rattray

Library of Congress Cataloging-in-Publication Data

Developing a Christian imagination: an interpretative anthology / compiled
by Warren W. Wiersbe.
    p.   m.
  ISBN: 1-56476-422-2
   1. Preaching. 2. Imagination—Religious aspects—Christianity.
 I. Wiersbe, Warren W.
BV4211.2.D39   1995
251–dc20   95-15356
                                           CIP

1 2 3 4 5 6 7 8 9 10 Printing/Year 99 98 97 96 95

Contents

Introduction

THE AIM OF this book is twofold: (1) to widen your views of the place of imagination in the ministry of the Word of God, and (2) to sharpen your skills in communicating the biblical truths creatively.

The material in this anthology is useful to anyone who wants to preach or teach the Bible more effectively, but it is especially designed as a companion volume to my *Preaching and Teaching with Imagination: The Quest for Biblical Ministry* (Victor Books, 1994).

That book grew out of a Doctor of Ministries course I have taught for various seminaries over the past few years. During the course, I asked the students to read many of the articles and sermons now compiled in this book. More than once, I wished that my handouts were assembled in one handy volume; and now they are.

I want to thank the writers and publishers who gave me permission to use their copyrighted material. I also want to thank my students for their insightful responses to this body of information. I always learn a great deal from students, and I'm grateful for the help they give me.

The first part of the book deals with the basics: what imagination is and how metaphor works in human speech. The second part presents sermons that illustrate in some way an effective use of imagination. The final part contains miscellaneous selections about imagination and preaching, some of them from pulpit masters of the past, others from contemporary writers and preachers.

For a bibliography on imagination, see *Preaching and Teaching with Imagination: The Quest for Biblical Ministry*, pages 383–89.

In this day of fast food, digests, and headline news bites, we who minister God's Word must learn to communicate it effectively to a busy and distracted video generation. I believe that reaching the imagination must be an important part of our strategy.

An Eastern proverb says, "The great teacher is the one who turns your ears into eyes so you can see the truth."

We all may not achieve that kind of greatness, but we can strive for greater effectiveness; and to that end this anthology is sent forth.

Warren W. Wiersbe

Part One

The Basics

Imagination involves three worlds: the world of creation around us (Emerson called it "Nature"), the world of pictures within us, and the world of words that bridges the two. The human mind is a picture gallery, language is pictorial, and the images for both come from the created world around us.

Metaphor isn't a way of using language, an embellishment; it's the way language works. Emerson points this out in "Language," and I illustrate it from Scripture in "What Hushai Knew: Words."

When John Bunyan published his *Pilgrim's Progress,* he included a defense of his allegorical/metaphorical approach, because the Puritans were suspect of anything other than "plain talk." They forgot that the Bible is saturated with metaphorical language and that Jesus used it frequently. Not every generation has been friendly toward the use of imagination.

The two selections from Spurgeon help us better understand why he was such an effective preacher. It's remarkable to see how much he agrees with Emerson.

If you want to pursue further your study of the technical aspects of metaphor and imagination, note the books mentioned in the notes to "What Hushai Knew: Words." I especially recommend Lakoff and Johnson, *Metaphors We Live By.*

1

"Language"
Ralph Waldo Emerson

THIS IS CHAPTER 4 of Emerson's first book, *Nature*, first published in 1836. After making certain generalizations about nature in chapter 1, Emerson then deals in subsequent chapters with the uses of nature: commodity, beauty, language, and discipline. "The word is emblematic," he writes. "Parts of speech are metaphors because the whole of nature is a metaphor of the human mind." That summarizes his view of nature and language.

"Language"

A third use which nature subserves to man is that of Language. Nature is the vehicle of thought, and in a simple, double, and three-fold degree.

1. Words are signs of natural facts.
2. Particular natural facts are symbols of particular facts.
3. Nature is the symbol of spirits.

1. Words are signs of natural facts. The use of natural history is to give us aid in supernatural history. The use of the outer creation is to give us language for the beings and changes of the inward creation. Every word which is used to express a moral or intellectual fact, if traced to its root, is found to be borrowed from some material appearance. *Right* originally means *straight; wrong* means *twisted. Spirit* primarily means *wind; transgression,* the crossing of a *line; supercilious,* the *raising of the eye-brow.* We say the *heart* to express emotion, the *head* to denote thought; and *thought* and *emotion* are, in their turn, words borrowed from sensible things, and now appropriated to spiritual nature. Most of the process by which this transformation is made, is hidden from us in the remote time when language was framed; but the same tendency may be daily observed in children. Children and savages use only nouns or names of things, which they continually convert into verbs, and apply to analogous mental acts.

2. But this origin of all words that convey a spiritual import—so conspicuous a fact in the history of language—is our least debt to nature. It is not words only that are emblematic; it is things which are emblematic. Every natural fact is a symbol of some spiritual fact. Every appearance in nature corresponds to some state of the mind, and that state of the mind can only be described by presenting that natural appearance as its picture. An enraged man is a lion, a cunning man is a fox, a firm man is a rock, a learned man is a torch. A lamb is innocence; a snake is subtle spite; flowers express to us the delicate affections. Light and darkness are our familiar expression for knowledge and ignorance; and heat for love. Visible distance behind and before us, is respectively our image of memory and hope.

Who looks upon a river in a meditative hour, and is not reminded of the flux of all things? Throw a stone into the stream, and the circles that propagate themselves are the beautiful type of all influence. Man is conscious of a universal soul within or behind his individual life, wherein, as in a firmament, the natures of Justice, Truth, Love, Freedom, arise and shine. This universal soul, he calls Reason: it is not mine or thine or his, but we are its; we are its property and men. And the blue sky in which the private earth is buried, the sky with its eternal calm, and full of everlasting orbs, is the type of Reason. That which, intellectually considered, we call Reason, considered in relation to nature, we call Spirit. Spirit is the Creator. Spirit hath life in itself. And man in all ages and countries, embodies it in his language, as the FATHER.

It is easily seen that there is nothing lucky or capricious in these analogies, but that they are constant, and pervade nature. These are not the dreams of a few poets, here and there, but man is an analogist, and studies relations in all objects. He is placed in the center of beings, and a ray of relation passes from every other being to him. And neither can man be understood without these objects, nor these objects without man. All the facts in natural history taken by themselves, have no value, but are barren like a single sex. But marry it to human history, and it is full of life. Whole Floras, all Linnæus' and Buffon's volumes, are but dry catalogs of facts; but the most trivial of these facts, the habit of a plant, the organs, or work, or noise of an insect, applied to the illustration of a fact in intellectual philosophy, or, in any way associated to human nature, affects us in the most lively and agreeable manner. The seed of a plant—to what affecting analogies in the nature of man, is that little fruit made use of, in all discourse, up to the voice of Paul, who calls the human corpse a seed—"It is sown a natural body; it is raised a spiritual body." The motion of the earth round its axis, and round the sun, makes the day, and the year. These are certain amounts of brute light and heat. But is there no intent of an analogy between man's life and the seasons? And do the seasons gain no grandeur or pathos from that analogy? The instincts of the ant are very unimportant considered as the ant's; but the moment a ray of relation is seen to extend from it to man, and the little drudge is seen to be a monitor, a little body with a mighty heart, then all its habits, even that said to be recently observed, that it never sleeps, become sublime.

Because of this radical correspondence between visible things and human thoughts, savages, who have only what is necessary, converse

in figures. As we go back in history, language becomes more picturesque, until its infancy, when it is all poetry; or, all spiritual facts are
represented by natural symbols. The same symbols are found to
make the original elements of all languages. It has moreover been
observed, that the idioms of all languages approach each other in
passages of the greatest eloquence and power. And as this is the first
language, so is it the last. This immediate dependence of language
upon nature, this conversion of an outward phenomenon into a
type of somewhat in human life, never loses its power to affect us. It
is this which gives that piquancy to the conversation of a strong-
natured farmer or back-woodsman, which all men relish.

Thus is nature an interpreter, by whose means man converses
with his fellow men. A man's power to connect his thought with its
proper symbol, and so utter it, depends on the simplicity of his
character, that is, upon his love of truth and his desire to communicate it without loss. The corruption of man is followed by the corruption of language. When simplicity of character and the sovereignty of ideas is broken up by the prevalence of secondary desires, the
desire of riches, the desire of pleasure, the desire of power, the
desire of praise — and duplicity and falsehood take place of simplicity
and truth, the power over nature as an interpreter of the will, is in a
degree lost; new imagery ceases to be created, and old words are
perverted to stand for things which are not; a paper currency is
employed when there is no bullion in the vaults. In due time, the
fraud is manifest, and words lose all power to stimulate the understanding or the affections. Hundreds of writers may be found in
every long-civilized nation, who for a short time believe, and make
others believe, that they see and utter truths, who do not of themselves clothe one thought in its natural garment, but who feed unconsciously upon the language created by the primary writers of the
country, those, namely, who hold primarily on nature.

But wise men pierce this rotten diction and fasten words again to
visible things; so that picturesque language is at once a commanding
certificate that he who employs it, is a man in alliance with truth and
God. The moment our discourse rises above the ground line of
familiar facts, and is inflamed with passion or exalted by thought, it
clothes itself in images. A man conversing in earnest, if he watches
his intellectual processes, will find that always a material image,
more or less luminous, arises in his mind, contemporaneous with

every thought, which furnishes the vestment of the thought. Hence, good writing and brilliant discourse are perpetual allegories. This imagery is spontaneous. It is the blending of experience with the present action of the mind. It is proper creation. It is the working of the Original Cause through the instruments he has already made.

These facts may suggest the advantage which the country-life possesses for a powerful mind, over the artificial and curtailed life of cities. We know more from nature than we can at will communicate. Its light flows into the mind evermore, and we forget its presence. The poet, the orator, bred in the woods, whose senses have been nourished by their fair and appeasing changes, year after year, without design and without heed—shall not lose their lesson altogether, in the roar of cities or the broil of politics. Long hereafter, amidst agitation and terror in national councils—in the hour of revolution—these solemn images shall reappear in their morning lustre, as fit symbols and words of the thoughts which the passing events shall awaken. At the call of a noble sentiment, again the woods wave, the pines murmur, the river rolls and shines, and the cattle low upon the mountains, as he saw and heard them in his infancy. And with these forms, the spells of persuasion, the keys of power are put into his hands.

3. We are thus assisted by natural objects in the expression of particular meanings. But how great a language to convey such peppercorn informations! Did it need such noble races of creatures, this profusion of forms, this host of orbs in heaven, to furnish man with the dictionary and grammar of his municipal speech? Whilst we use this grand cipher to expedite the affairs of our pot and kettle, we feel that we have not yet put it to its use, neither are able. We are like travelers using the cinders of a volcano to roast their eggs. Whilst we see that it always stands ready to clothe what we would say, we cannot avoid the question, whether the characters are not significant of themselves. Have mountains, and waves, and skies, no significance but what we consciously give them, when we employ them as emblems of our thoughts? The world is emblematic. Parts of speech are metaphors because the whole of nature is a metaphor of the human mind. The laws of moral nature answer to those of matter as face to face in a glass. "The visible world and the relation of its parts, is the dial plate of the invisible." The axioms of physics translate the laws of ethics. Thus, "the whole is greater than its part;"

"reaction is equal to action;" "the smallest weight may be made to lift the greatest, the difference of weight being compensated by time;" and many the like propositions, which have an ethical as well as physical sense. These propositions have a much more extensive and universal sense when applied to human life, than when confined to technical use.

In like manner, the memorable words of history, and the proverbs of nations, consist usually of a natural fact, selected as a picture or parable of a moral truth. Thus: A rolling stone gathers no moss; A bird in the hand is worth two in the bush; A cripple in the right way, will beat a racer in the wrong; Make hay whilst the sun shines; 'Tis hard to carry a full cup even; Vinegar is the son of wine; The last ounce broke the camel's back; Long-lived trees make roots first— and the like. In their primary sense these are trivial facts, but we repeat them for the value of their analogical import. What is true of proverbs, is true of all fables, parables, and allegories.

This relation between the mind and matter is not fancied by some poet, but stands in the will of God, and so is free to be known by all men. It appears to men, or it does not appear. When in fortunate hours we ponder this miracle, the wise man doubts, if, at all other times, he is not blind and deaf;

> _____ "Can these things be,
> And overcome us like a summer's cloud,
> Without our special wonder?"

for the universe becomes transparent, and the light of higher laws than its own, shines through it. It is the standing problem which has exercised the wonder and the study of every fine genius since the world began; from the era of the Egyptians and the Brahmins, to that of Pythagoras, of Plato, of Bacon, of Leibnitz, of Swedenborg. There sits the Sphinx at the roadside, and from age to age, as each prophet comes by, he tries his fortune at reading her riddle. There seems to be a necessity in spirit to manifest itself in material forms; and day and night, river and storm, beast and bird, acid and alkali, preexist in necessary Ideas in the mind of God, and are what they are by virtue of preceding affections, in the world of spirit. A Fact is the end or last issue of spirit. The visible creation is the terminus or the circumference of the invisible world. "Material objects," said a

French philosopher, ''are necessarily kinds of *scoriæ* of the substantial thoughts of the Creator, which must always preserve an exact relation to their first origin; in other words, visible nature must have a spiritual and moral side.''

This doctrine is abstruse, and though the images of ''garment,'' ''scoriæ,'' ''mirror,'' etc., may stimulate the fancy, we must summon the aid of subtler and more vital expositors to make it plain. ''Every Scripture is to be interpreted by the same spirit which gave it forth'' — is the fundamental law of criticism. A life in harmony with nature, the love of truth and of virtue, will purge the eyes to understand her text. By degrees we may come to know the primitive sense of the permanent objects of nature, so that the world shall be to us an open book, and every form significant of its hidden life and final cause.

A new interest surprises us, whilst, under the view now suggested, we contemplate the fearful extent and multitude of objects; since ''every object rightly seen, unlocks a new faculty of the soul.'' That which was unconscious truth, becomes, when interpreted and defined in an object, a part of the domain of knowledge — a new amount to the magazine of power.

Something to Do

1. Emerson began his career as a Unitarian minister. What references or allusions to Scripture can you find in this chapter?

2. Do you ever investigate the etymology of words as you study? What uses can be made of these facts?

3. Professor James Barr of Oxford says that ''the etymology of a word is not a statement about its meaning but about its history . . . and it is quite wrong to suppose that the etymology of a word is necessarily a guide either to its 'proper' meaning in a later period or to its actual meaning in that period.'' How might Emerson comment on what Barr said?

4. What is the Christian believer's proper approach to nature? How did Jesus relate to the natural world in His everyday life and His teaching ministry?

2

"What Hushai Knew: Words"
Warren W. Wiersbe

THIS IS CHAPTER 4 of my book *Preaching and Teaching with Imagination: The Quest for Biblical Ministry* (Wheaton, Ill.: Victor Books, 1994). The book begins with a study of the speeches of Ahithophel and Hushai to Absalom (2 Sam. 17:1-14) and explains how Hushai's imaginative approach won the day, humanly speaking. Because Hushai knew three things — how people think (pictures, not logic), how the world of nature illustrates truth, and how words convey pictures — he was able to convince Absalom to do what was utterly foolish for him to do. Ahithophel had the better counsel, but the poorer presentation. Ahithophel gave reasons; Hushai painted pictures.

Metaphors aren't the embellishments of speech; *they are the way speech works.* This chapter is a brief overview of the place of metaphor in communication.

Developing a Christian Imagination

"What Hushai Knew: Words"

"Inescapably, preaching is a work of metaphor."[1] David Buttrick says this in *Homiletic: Moves and Structures,* one of the most creative books on preaching that's been published since H. Grady Davis' *Design for Preaching.*[2] Buttrick goes on to say, "Theological meaning must always be embodied in images drawn from life."[3] Hushai had never read Buttrick's book, but he followed Buttrick's principles. That's why he talked to Absalom about bears, lions, sand, and dew. Ahithophel expressed only concepts while Hushai presented his concepts in *images.*

Theologian Sallie McFague writes: "Images 'feed' concepts; concepts 'discipline' images. Images without concepts are blind; concepts without images are sterile."[4] I suggest you read that statement again, ponder it, and then think about Ahithophel and Hushai. Ahithophel presented concepts without images, so his words were sterile. They failed to give birth to life-changing pictures in Absalom's mind. Hushai, on the other hand, combined concepts and images and won the contest.

One of the bridges between the world around us and the world within us is a system of symbols that we call language; and language is basically metaphorical. It communicates in *pictures.* God's creation is a theater and the human mind is a picture gallery, and we link the two by using *words.*

"Every word which is used to express a moral or intellectual fact, if traced to its root, is found to be borrowed from some material appearance," wrote Emerson in *Nature.* The word *right,* he points out, originated from *straight* (Latin, *rectus*); and *wrong* came from a root meaning "twisted" (from *wrong* to *wring* [twist]). He reminds us that the word *supercilious* is Latin for "raising the eyebrows," something that haughty people are prone to do when they disapprove of something.[5]

"Metaphor is a primary way in which we accommodate and assimilate information and experience to our conceptual organization of the world," writes philosopher Eva Feder Kittay. "In particular, it is the primary way we accommodate new experience. Hence it is at the source of our capacity to learn and at the center of our creative thought."[6] Since preachers want their people to learn, to think, and to have new and maturing experiences, they had better get ac-

20

quainted with this thing called *metaphor*.

Metaphor—the Way Language Works

Today we have an exploding literature on metaphor. When you start reading it, you soon discover that linguists and philosophers don't always agree on what constitutes a metaphor or how a metaphor actually works. But the linguists and philosophers seem to agree that the word *metaphor* comes from the two Greek words *meta* (trans, across) and *pherein* (to carry), and that together they mean "to carry across, to transfer." A metaphor is a "verbal transfer" that connects two seemingly unrelated things and creates from this union something new.

One scholar defines a metaphor as "a figure of speech whereby we speak about one thing in terms which are seen to be suggestive of another."[7] When Isaiah cried, "All flesh is grass!" he was using a metaphor and was inviting his listeners to ponder seriously the relationship between grass and people. Jesus spoke metaphorically when He said, "The seed is the word of God." His listeners knew what seeds were, but did they know the relationship between seeds and God's Word?

It's by using metaphorical language that you turn people's ears into eyes and help them see the truth. The task of the preacher is not unlike the task of the writer. Novelist Joseph Conrad said, "My task . . . is, by the power of the written word to make you hear, to make you feel—it is, before all, to make you see."[8] However, using metaphors means much more than following the principles of wise pedagogy and going from the known to the unknown. Metaphor is not simply a "function" of language; metaphor is the way language works. We don't use similes and metaphors to "embellish" our speech and impress people, the way eighteenth-century Britons put lace on their clothes and silver buckles on their shoes. Many scholars believe that metaphor is the fundamental way language is structured and that we use metaphorical expressions as we communicate simply because language is made that way. Like the man in Moliere's play who discovered he'd been speaking prose for forty years, we've been speaking metaphorically all our lives and perhaps didn't realize it.[9]

In their fascinating book *Metaphors We Live By*, Lakoff and Johnson give scores of examples of how metaphors are used in everyday

21

speech.[10] For example, when people talk about "half-baked ideas" or "warmed-over theories," they're comparing ideas to food. Ideas are also plants, as in statements such as "The idea died on the vine" or "The idea finally came to fruition." "I've lived life to the fullest" pictures life as a container, as does "I can't cram one more activity into my life." Each of these statements involves metaphors, even though we don't always recognize them. Metaphor is so much a part of everyday speech that we take it for granted.

I've already introduced you to the "conduit metaphor," which unfortunately seems to govern so much of our preaching and teaching. Questions such as "Am I coming across?" or "Am I getting through?" betray the fact that the speaker has the "conduit metaphor" in mind as he or she speaks. Many seemingly tame statements are really metaphors that belong to the "conduit" category. For example: "What are you trying to get into my head?" "What he says doesn't carry much weight." "That idea flew right past me." "Words just keep pouring out of her!" "Stop throwing out so many new ideas!" These statements picture ideas as "things" that are dropped into the conduit of speech and "delivered" (we hope) to the people listening.

Get the point? (Ideas are also like swords or arrows!) Even in our everyday conversations, we use metaphorical language, because *language is metaphorical*. "All language originated in metaphor. Literal language is a pruning away and a rationalization of our figurative thought."[11]

As far back as the third century before the birth of Christ, the Greeks were discussing metaphor, and Aristotle wrote in his *Poetics:*

It is a great thing, indeed, to make a proper use of these poetical forms, as also of compounds and strange words. But the greatest thing by far is to be a master of metaphor. It is the one thing that cannot be learned from others; and it is also a sign of genius, since a good metaphor implies an intuitive perception of the similarity in dissimilars.[12]

I agree with the great philosopher that we can't go to school and earn a master of metaphor degree; but I humbly disagree with him when he claims that the understanding and use of metaphors can't be learned. (The fact that Aristotle discussed metaphor in both his

Poetics and his *Rhetoric* suggests that he may have made that statement tongue-in-cheek.) Certainly, with every ability there must be an accompanying intuition that turns the skill into an art; and education alone can't supply that intuition. But since metaphor involves the use of the imagination, and imagination is a part of the divine image in men and women, then all of us must have within us the basic materials to work with to develop metaphorical skills. Preachers of the Word especially need to focus on mastering metaphor, for that's the way language is made, the way people think, and the way the Bible was written.

The Power Is in Showing, Not Telling

When I was pastoring the Moody Church in Chicago, I received an invitation to speak to a high school social studies class about "the biblical view of sex ethics." It was a glorious opportunity, but I turned it into an embarrassing disaster by making two mistakes. First, I took the "conduit" approach and unloaded a lot of theological baggage on them, most of which stayed in the conduit and was never picked up by the students. My second mistake was in presenting my case through argument, aiming at the left-brain students while the right-brain students—the majority—folded their mental tents and silently stole away.

A better approach would have been to show the teenagers the biblical pictures of what happened to people who practiced sex outside the boundaries established by God. Proverbs 5 pictures sanctified sexual love as a beautiful stream of refreshing water, and sex outside of marriage as a sewer running in the streets.[13] Proverbs 6 reminds us that sex is like fire: beautiful and powerful when kept under control, but destructive when out of bounds (vv. 27-29). Proverbs 7 presents a vivid picture of a young man *turning into an animal* and going to the slaughter as he falls into the traps of the prostitute (vv. 22-27). Nathan's "ewe lamb" story to David (2 Sam. 12:1-6) makes the point that sex outside of marriage turns people into thieves, and they end up robbing both themselves and others.[14]

So, according to Scripture, when it comes to the matter of sex, everybody must choose either the stream or the sewer, warmth and power or burning destruction, the human or the animal, investment or robbery. If, instead of lecturing, I had shared these pictures with the students, I might have made the kind of impact that would have stayed with them and made a difference in their lives.

C.S. Lewis said, "All our truth, or all but a few fragments, is won by metaphor."[15] And H. Richard Niebuhr believed that "we are far more image-making and image-using creatures than we usually think ourselves to be and . . . our processes of perception and conception, of organizing and understanding the signs that come to us . . . are guided and formed by images in our mind. Our languages, we are reminded, are symbolic systems."[16]

We have now reached a key question in our investigation: What is there about metaphorical language that gives it so much power? Contrary to popular belief, not every picture is worth a thousand words, but some words carry a dynamic that is greater than that of many pictures. When Sir Winston Churchill offered the people of Great Britain "blood, toil, tears, and sweat," why did they follow him instead of run him out of office? What is the secret, if there is one, of the power of metaphor?

Part of the answer is found, I think, in the fact that metaphors affect *the whole personality* and are not like routine concepts that touch only the mind. Metaphors challenge us and make us think. They arouse our curiosity and force us to adjust our perspective and try to see two things at one time. Then we have to figure out why the two things are put together when they are so different. Sallie McFague is right when she says that "good metaphors shock, they bring unlikes together, they upset conventions, they involve tension, and they are implicitly revolutionary."[17]

Notice the Puritan poet John Milton's use of this powerful device. When he received word that his friend Edward King had drowned in the Irish Sea, he wrote the elegy *Lycidas* in King's honor. In it, Milton wrestled with the problem of why a good man such as King died young while godless ministers lived long and prospered. He draws a vivid picture of the "false shepherds" of the seventeenth-century English church, calling them men who "for their bellies' sake creep and intrude, and climb into the fold," an obvious reference to John 10:1 and Philippians 3:19. But when, in line 119, Milton calls these false shepherds "blind mouths," we are immediately arrested. We stop and ask, "How can mouths be blind?" The metaphor has done its work![18]

I like Eva Kittay's statement that metaphors "rearrange the furniture of the mind."[19] When two seemingly contrary ideas such as "blindness" and "mouths" are brought together, the union creates a dynamic tension that excites the mind and arouses the emotions; and the will is held captive until the tension is either resolved or dismissed. The late physician-novelist Walker Percy wrote, "Metaphors are very strange because when you put two things together it's a way of discovering meanings which haven't been discovered before."[20] And Aristotle wrote in his *Rhetoric* that "strange words simply puzzle us; ordinary words convey only what we know already; it is from metaphor that we can best get hold of something fresh."[21]

Metaphors are something that we *experience.* Hearing a live metaphor and understanding it is a *transaction* that involves more than the intellect; and it can lead to a changed perspective on life. When that happens, our response to the preacher is, "Yes, now I *see* what you're saying!" And with this response comes an emotional and spiritual experience that makes the truth of the metaphor a part of our inner person. We may find ourselves echoing the words of the Emmaus disciples, "Were not our hearts burning within us while he talked with us on the road and opened the Scriptures to us?" (Luke 24:32)

In the last paragraph, I used the phrase "live metaphor," so I had better pause to explain it. Semantic scholars have decided that there are three kinds of metaphors: *live* or *vivid, sick* or *pale,* and *dead* or *faded.* Live metaphors are the kind that powerfully "connect" the mind and heart of the hearers so that they want to do something in response to what they learn. *Sick* or *pale* metaphors may affect the mind, but they have no effect on the emotions or the will. *Dead* or *faded* metaphors bore the mind and may even create a negative "So what?" response from the heart and will. Dead metaphors are clichés; and when we hear speakers use them, we respond negatively with boredom and with pity.[22]

One of the interesting things about metaphors is that they touch different people in different ways at different levels of life. The child's response to Psalm 23 is different from that of the veteran missionary; but both individuals can respond to the same metaphor, *and the response of each can be authentic and rewarding.* The people in our congregations come from different backgrounds, have different IQs and educational experiences, and are at different levels of emotional and spiritual maturity; yet each one of them can "plug into" a metaphor and be enriched spiritually. Metaphors are something like our Lord's seamless garment: people can even touch the hem of the garment and experience life-changing power.[23]

Notes

1. David Buttrick, *Homiletic: Moves and Structures* (Philadelphia: Fortress, 1987), 113.

2. H. Grady Davis, *Design for Preaching* (Philadelphia: Fortress, 1958). Both Buttrick and Davis were bold enough to abandon some of the classical homiletical armor and face the giant of sermon preparation using equipment meaningful to preachers ministering in the atomic age. Davis dared to develop a new vocabulary for homileticians, and Buttrick enlisted the aid of current communications theory. I can't conceive of a serious preacher of the Gospel ignoring these books.

3. Buttrick, *Homiletic,* 132.

4. Sallie McFague, *Metaphorical Theology* (London: SCM, 1983), 26. McFague presents an excellent discussion of both metaphors and models, and her documentary notes and bibliography are especially helpful.

5. Emerson, *Nature,* 32. I quote Emerson's examples even though I'm aware of James Barr's warning that "the etymology of a word is not a statement about its meaning but about its history." *The Semantics of Biblical Language* (London: SCM, 1983), 90. The fact that some people carry "word studies" too far certainly doesn't mean we should discard them completely.

6. Eva Feder Kittay, *Metaphor: Its Cognitive Force and Linguistic Structure* (Oxford: Clarendon, 1987), 39.

7. Janet Martin Soskice, *Metaphor and Religious Language* (Oxford: Clarendon, 1985), 15.

8. Cited in Leland Ryken, *The Liberated Imagination* (Wheaton, Ill.: Harold Shaw, 1989), 137. Conrad wrote this in the preface to his novel *The Nigger of the Narcissus.*

9. In the play, M. Jourdain asks his philosophy teacher: "What? when I say: 'Nicole, bring me my slippers, and give me my night-cap,' is that prose?" His teacher replies, "Yes, sir." Then M. Jourdain exclaims, "Good heavens! For more than forty years I have been speaking prose without knowing it." Moliere, *Le Bourgeois Gentilhomme,* act 2, sc. 4.

10. George Lakoff and Mark Johnson, *Metaphors We Live By* (Chicago: Univ. of Chicago Press, 1980). Though the book was written primarily to defend a semantic theory that the authors espouse, it is still one of the best introductions to the study of the place of metaphor in everyday life. Their second book, *More Than Cool Reason: A Field Guide to Poetic Metaphor* (Univ. of Chicago Press, 1989), explains how metaphor works in poetry and helps us understand what a poem means. *Women, Fire, and Dangerous Things,* by Lakoff (Univ. of Chicago Press, 1987), deals with metaphor, semantics, and psychology and is, I must confess, beyond me. (Now there's the conduit metaphor!) For a simple introduction to metaphor, see Terence Hawkes, *Metaphor* (London: Methuen, 1972).

11. Kittay, *Metaphor,* 5.

12. Aristotle, *Poetics,* in *The Works of Aristotle* in *The Great Books of the Western World,* vol. 9, 694 (Chicago: Encyclopedia Britannica, 1952).

13. It's worth noting that the word translated "captivated" in vv. 19-20 (NIV) can

also mean "intoxicated." The water has turned into wine! Is there some connection here with our Lord's first miracle at a marriage feast? (John 2)

14. Paul makes the same point in 1 Thes. 4:6, where "take advantage" (NIV) also means "to defraud." There are two ways to get money out of a bank. You can rob the bank, creating a whole new set of problems for yourself; or you can become a depositor, commit yourself to the bank, and have the privilege of making use of its assets. Sex outside of marriage is like robbing the bank. Marriage is the commitment that enriches life as husband and wife live together in the will of God.

15. Cited in McFague, *Metaphorical Theology*, 201. Lewis could write not only stimulating theological essays and novels but also captivating children's stories, the mark of a person with a healthy imagination.

16. H. Richard Niebuhr, *The Responsible Self* (San Francisco: Harper & Row, 1963), 151–52.

17. McFague, *Metaphorical Theology*, 17.

18. Bible students will recognize a reference to Ezekiel 34, where the prophet denounces the political leaders (shepherds) of the nation, who exploited the people and were blind to their needs.

19. See Kittay, *Metaphor*, 316ff. Sometimes it takes a metaphor to explain a metaphor.

20. Quoted in Eugene H. Peterson, *Answering God* (San Francisco: Harper & Row, 1989), 69.

21. See Aristotle *Rhetoric* 3.10.

22. The story is told about two farmers who met at the market one Monday morning. One asked, "What did your minister preach about yesterday?" The other replied, "Oh, the same old thing—ding-dong, ding-dong, ding-dong!" The first farmer smiled and said, "You're fortunate! All we ever get is ding-ding-ding-ding!"

23. See Mark 5:25-34.

Something to Do

1. Look up the following words in a good dictionary and find the word pictures buried in them: tribulation; pedigree; discipline; tactic; patriotism; jamboree.

2. Did you understand the statement by Sallie McFague quoted in the second paragraph? How does it especially apply to preaching and teaching the Bible? If we ignore this principle, what will probably happen to our preaching and teaching?

3. Rewrite Psalm 23 as prose.

4. In the light of what this chapter teaches, study Nathan's approach to David in 2 Samuel 12:1-4.

3

"The Conclusion" & "The Author's Apology for His Book"
John Bunyan

THE PURITANS PRACTICED plain speaking and plain living and were prone to be suspicious of "fine literature," especially if it dealt with religious themes. To write that way was to imitate the world, and imitating the world was the last thing a Puritan wanted to do. So, when he published the first part of *The Pilgrim's Progress,* Bunyan felt it necessary to defend his allegorical approach and to warn the reader to study carefully what he had written. This excerpt is from *The New Pilgrim's Progress,* notes by Warren W. Wiersbe (Grand Rapids: Discovery House, 1989), 193–200). Used by permission.

"The Conclusion"

Now, READER, I have told my dream to thee;
See if thou canst interpret it to me,
Or to thyself; or neighbor; but take heed
Of misinterpreting; for that, instead
Of doing good, will but thyself abuse:
By misinterpreting, evil ensues.

Take heed, also, that thou be not extreme,
In playing with the outside of my dream:
Nor let my figure or similitude
Put thee into a laughter or a feud.
Leave this for boys and fools; but as for thee,
Do thou the substance of my matter see.

Put by the curtains, look within my veil,
Turn up my metaphors, and do not fail,
There, if thou seekest them, such things to find,
As will be helpful to an honest mind.

What of my dross thou findest there, be bold
To throw away, but yet preserve the gold;
What if my gold be wrapped up in ore?
None throws away the apple for the core.
But if thou shalt cast all away as vain,
I know not but 'twill make me dream again.

"The Author's Apology for His Book"

When at the first I took my pen in hand
Thus for to write, I did not understand
That I at all should make a little book
In such a mode; nay, I had undertook
To make another; which, when almost done,
Before I was aware, I this begun.[1]

And thus it was: I, writing of the way
And race of saints, in this our gospel day,
Fell suddenly into an allegory
About their journey, and the way to glory,
In more than twenty things which I set down.
This done, I twenty more had in my crown;
And they again began to multiply,
Like sparks that from the coals of fire do fly,
Nay, then, thought I, if that you breed so fast,
I'll put you by yourselves, lest you at last
Should prove *ad infinitum*, and eat out
The book that I already am about.

Well, so I did; but yet I did not think
To show to all the world my pen and ink[2]
In such a mode; I only thought to make
I knew not what; nor did I undertake
Thereby to please my neighbor: no, not I;
I did it my own self to gratify.

Neither did I but vacant seasons spend
In this my scribble; nor did I intend
But to divert myself in doing this[3]
From worser thoughts which make me do amiss.

Thus I set pen to paper with delight,
And quickly had my thoughts in black and white.
For, having now my method by the end,
Still as I pulled, it came; and so I penned
It down: until it came at last to be,
For length and breadth, the bigness which you see.

Well, when I had thus put mine ends together,
I showed them others, that I might see whether
They would condemn them, or them justify:
And some said, Let them live; some, Let them die;
Some said, John, print it; others said, Not so;
Some said, I might do good; others said, No.

Developing a Christian Imagination

Now was I in a strait, and did not see
Which was the best thing to be done by me:
At last I thought, Since you are thus divided,
I print it will, and so the case decided.

For, thought I, some, I see, would have it done,
Though others in that channel do not run:
To prove, then, who advised for the best,
Thus I thought fit to put it to the test.

I further thought, if now I did deny
Those that would have it, thus to gratify;
I did not know but hinder them I might
Of that which would to them be great delight.

For those which were not for its coming forth,
I said to them, Offend you I am loath,
Yet, since your brethren pleased with it be,
Forbear to judge till you do further see.

If that thou wilt not read, let it alone;
Some love the meat, some love to pick the bone.
Yea, that I might them better palliate,
I did too with them thus expostulate.

May I not write in such a style as this?[4]
In such a method, too, and yet not miss
My end, thy good? Why may it not be done?
Dark clouds bring waters, when the bright bring none.
Yea, dark or bright, if they their silver drops
Cause to descend, the earth, by yielding crops,
Gives praise to both, and criticizes neither,
But treasures up the fruit they yield together;
Yea, so commixes both, that in her fruit
None can distinguish this from that: they suit
Her well when hungry; but, if she be full,
She spews out both, and makes their blessings null.

You see the ways the fisherman doth take

To catch the fish; what devices doth he make![5]
Behold! how he engageth all his wits;
Also his snares, lines, angles, hooks, and nets;
Yet fish there be, that neither hook, nor line,
Nor snare, nor net, nor device can make thine:
They must be groped for, and be tickled too,
Or they will not be catched, whate'er you do.

How doth the fowler seek to catch his game
By divers means! all which one cannot name:
His guns, his nets, his lime-twigs,[6] light, and bell;
He creeps, he goes, he stands; yea, who can tell
Of all his postures? Yet there's none of these
Will make him master of what fowls he please.
Yea, he must pipe and whistle to catch this;
Yet, if he does so, *that* bird he will miss.

If that a pearl may in a toad's head dwell,[7]
And may be found too in an oyster-shell;
If things that promise nothing do contain
What better is than gold; who will disdain,
That have an inkling of it, there to look
That they may find it? Now, my little book
(Though void of all these paintings that may make
It with this or the other man to take)
Is not without those things that do excel
What do in brave but empty notions dwell.

"Well, yet I am not fully satisfied,
That this your book will stand, when soundly tried."

Why, what's the matter? "It is dark."[8] What though?
"But it is feigned."[9] What of that? I trow
Some men, by feigned words, as dark as mine,
Make truth to spangle and its rays to shine.
"But they want solidness." Speak, man, thy mind.
"They drown the weak; metaphors make us blind."[10]

Solidity, indeed, becomes the pen

Of him that writeth things divine to men;
But must I needs want solidness, because
By metaphors I speak? Were not God's laws,
His gospel laws, in olden times held forth
By types, shadows, and metaphors? Yet loath
Will any sober man be to find fault
With them, lest he be found for to assault
The highest wisdom. No, he rather stoops,
And seeks to find out what by pins and loops,
By calves and sheep, by heifers and by rams,
By birds and herbs, and by the blood of lambs,
God speaketh to him; and happy is he
That finds the light and grace that in them be.

Be not too forward, therefore, to conclude
That I lack solidness, that I am rude;[11]
All things solid in show not solid be;
All things in parables despise not we,
Lest things most hurtful lightly we receive,
And things that good are, of our souls bereave.
My dark and cloudy words, they do but hold
The truth, as cabinets enclose the gold.

The prophets used much by metaphors
To set forth truth; yea, who so considers
Christ, his apostles too, shall plainly see,
That truths to this day in such garments be.

Am I afraid to say that holy writ,
Which for its style and phrase puts down[12] all wit,
Is everywhere so full of all these things —
Dark figures, allegories. Yet there springs
From that same book that lustre, and those rays
Of light, that turn our darkest nights to days.

Come, let my carper to his life now look,[13]
And find there darker lines than in my book
He findeth any; yea, and let him know,
That in his best things there are worse lines too.

May we but stand before impartial men,
To his poor one I dare adventure ten,
That they will take my meaning in these lines
Far better than his lies in silver shines.

Come, truth, although in swaddling clouts,[14] I find,
Informs the judgment, rectifies the mind;
Pleases the understanding, makes the will
Submit; the memory too it doth fill
With what doth our imaginations please;
Likewise it tends our troubles to appease.

Sound words, I know, Timothy is to use,[15]
And old wives' fables he is to refuse;[16]
But yet grave Paul him nowhere did forbid
The use of parables; in which lay hid
That gold, those pearls, and precious stones that were
Worth digging for, and that with greatest care.

Let me add one word more. O man of God,
Art thou offended? Dost thou wish I had
Put forth my matter in another dress?
Or that I had in things been more express?
Three things let me propound;[17] then I submit
To those that are my betters, as is fit.

1. I find not that I am denied the use
Of this my method, so I no abuse
Put on the words, things, readers; or be rude
In handling figure or similitude,
In application; but, all that I may,
Seek the advance of truth this or that way.
Denied, did I say? Nay, I have leave
(Example too, and that from them that have
God better pleased, by their words or ways,
Than any man that breatheth now-a-days)
Thus to express my mind, thus to declare
Things unto thee that excellentest are.

2. I find that men (as high as trees) will write
Dialogue-wise; yet no man doth them slight
For writing so: indeed, if they abuse
Truth, cursed be they, and the craft they use
To that intent; but yet let truth be free
To make her sallies upon thee and me,
Which way it pleases God; for who knows how,
Better than he that taught us first to plough,
To guide our mind and pens for his design?
And he makes base things usher in divine.

3. I find that holy writ in many places
Hath semblance with this method, where the cases
Do call for one thing, to set forth another;
Use it I may, then, and yet nothing smother
Truth's golden beams: nay, but this method may
Make it cast forth its rays as light as day.

And now before I do put up my pen,
I'll show the profit of my book, and then
Commit both thee and it unto that Hand
That pulls the strong down, and makes weak ones stand.

This book it chalketh out[18] before thine eyes
The man that seeks the everlasting prize[19]
It shows you whence he comes, whither he goes;
What he leaves undone, also what he does;
It also shows you how he runs and runs,
Till he unto the gate of glory comes.

It shows, too, who set out for life amain[20]
As if the lasting crown they would obtain;
Here also you may see the reason why
They lose their labour, and like fools do die.

This book will make a traveller of thee,[21]
If by its counsel thou wilt ruled be;
It will direct thee to the Holy Land,
If thou wilt its directions understand:

Yea, it will make the slothful active be;
The blind also delightful things to see.

Art thou for something rare and profitable?
Wouldest thou see a truth within a fable?
Art thou forgetful? Wouldest thou remember
From New Year's day to the last of December?
Then read my fancies; they will stick like burrs,[22]
And may be, to the helpless, comforters.

This book is writ in such a dialect
As may the minds of listless men affect:
It seems a novelty, and yet contains
Nothing but sound and honest gospel strains.

Wouldest thou divert thyself from melancholy?
Wouldest thou be pleasant, yet be far from folly?
Wouldest thou read riddles, and their explanation?
Or else be drowned in thy contemplation?
Dost thou love picking meat? Or wouldest thou see
A man i' the clouds, and hear him speak to thee?
Wouldest thou be in a dream, and yet not sleep?
Or wouldest thou in a moment laugh and weep?
Wouldest thou lose thyself and catch no harm,
And find thyself again without a charm?
Wouldest read thyself, and read thou knowest not what,
And yet know whether thou art blest or not,
By reading the same lines? Oh, then come hither,
And lay my book, thy head, and heart together.[23]

Notes

1. Bunyan felt it necessary in this poetic preface to explain how his book was written and why it was published. He did not want anyone to think he was being careless either in writing or in publishing. When he refers to "such a mode," he refers to the fact that it is an allegory, a form of literature in which persons, events, and objects have a deeper meaning than what is apparent in the story. His reference to "another" work probably refers to *The Heavenly Footman*, which was published after Bunyan's death. Based on 1 Cor. 9:24, this book has several ideas in it that parallel *The Pilgrim's Progress*. Some scholars think it was *The Strait Gate*, published in 1676.

Developing a Christian Imagination

2. Not only did he not intend to write this book, but he also did not intend to publish it. Bunyan had published at least a dozen books by 1678, when *The Pilgrim's Progress* came out, including *Grace Abounding to the Chief of Sinners* (1666). He was not sure that his allegory, quite unlike his other works, would be accepted or do any good.

3. Writing the book kept him occupied with spiritual thoughts while he was in jail.

4. Now he defends his style of writing by presenting several arguments. (1) Dark clouds in nature bring rain and fruitfulness. (2) Fishermen and hunters use "bait" to catch their game, and so must he if he is to catch the reader's interest. (3) Nature often puts jewels in unlikely places, and there are jewels in his book. (4) Other writers have used the same approach, including Bible writers, who present types, symbols, and metaphors. (5) Life itself often brings the light out of the darkness.

5. An allegory is merely a device to "catch" his prey.

6. Twigs that were smeared with bird lime, a sticky substance that held the birds fast.

7. An ancient superstition that there was a jewel (the "toadstone") hidden on, or in, the toad's head; that is, beauty in the midst of ugliness. Shakespeare mentions this in *As You Like It:* "Which, like a toad, ugly and venomous, wears yet a precious jewel in its head." He was wrong on both counts, for toads do not have jewels, nor are they poisonous.

8. Difficult to understand. See Prov. 1:6.

9. Made up, imaginary.

10. A kind of figurative language that uses one idea to suggest another. The purpose is to convey a much broader idea by using such a comparison. Eph. 4:14 is an example. An allegory is actually an extended metaphor.

11. Lacking solid truth and doctrine.

12. Luke 1:52.

13. The "carper" is the one finding fault with him, carping at him.

14. Swaddling clothes, such as babies were wrapped in. You do not reject the precious baby because the garments are humble.

15. 2 Tim. 1:13.

16. These were superstitions that only ignorant old women would accept. See 1 Tim. 4:7.

17. The three things: (1) I am not forbidden by God to use this approach, so long as I am telling truth. (2) If God so guided me, then let us accept His leading and "let truth be free." (3) The Bible uses this approach, and I am seeking to tell Bible truth.

18. Marks out, outlines a course to follow.

19. Phil. 3:14.

20. To begin suddenly, with great vigor. Several people in *The Pilgrim's Progress* made good beginnings but did not reach heaven.

21. This book will convert you and make you a pilgrim on the way to the Holy City. Bunyan's aim was not to entertain, but to evangelize.

22. By using imaginative pictures in his book, he helps us remember what he has said. We can easily forget sermons and lectures, but stories stick with us, like burrs.

23. Bunyan believed in a balanced Christian life, with the mind and the emotions involved. Truth ought to enlighten the mind, stir the emotions, and motivate the will. The Puritans did not believe in empty emotionalism; they wanted light as well as heat.

38

Something to Do

1. What similes and metaphors does Bunyan use in "The Conclusion" and "The Apology"?

2. In "The Conclusion," what does Bunyan mean by "playing with the outside of my dream"? If the reader doesn't learn to interpret Bunyan's allegory properly, what problems might arise?

3. What arguments does Bunyan give to defend his use of allegory and metaphor? Are they valid?

4. What biblical references and allusions are in "The Apology"? Does Bunyan use them accurately?

5. What twentieth-century writers, secular or religious, have used allegory successfully? Can it be used successfully in preaching God's truth?

4

"Everybody's Sermon"[1]
Charles Haddon Spurgeon

SPURGEON PREACHED THIS sermon on Sunday morning, July 25, 1858, to a great congregation in the Surrey Gardens Music Hall, the Park Street Chapel being too small to hold the crowds that wanted to hear him. He had turned twenty-four on June 19 and was already a phenomenon in the United Kingdom.

In the introduction, Spurgeon uses natural theology to illustrate and defend his sermonic proposition that "Providence is God's sermon." He makes it clear that the "messages" we see and hear in daily life, through God's providential working, should lead us to the truths of Scripture. Note that almost every illustration he gives is tied to a Bible text, though Spurgeon does not give the references.

In using this approach, Spurgeon declared that he did not believe that natural theology was sufficient of itself to convict the sinner or reveal the Savior. Nature can lead us to the Word, for God uses images from nature to reveal His truth and then the Spirit uses the Word to lead us to the Savior. The miraculous star led the magi to Jerusalem, but the prophecy from the Word led them to Bethlehem where they found the Savior.

"Every natural fact is a symbol of some spiritual fact," wrote Ralph Waldo Emerson in *Nature*.[2] Emerson would not have subscribed to Spurgeon's Calvinistic theology, but he would have agreed with Spurgeon that nature (God) teaches us valuable lessons if we will only open our eyes and see. "The moral influence of nature upon every individual," said Emerson, "is that amount of truth which it illustrates to him."[3] See "Charles Haddon Spurgeon on Nature" in chapter 5 of this book.

Spurgeon didn't linger long to discuss or explain the biblical images and references that he cited. He assumed that his listeners would easily recognize them and be able to interpret and apply them for themselves. He was probably right, for most church-going people in the Victorian Age had a basic knowledge of the Bible and would recognize the many references Spurgeon made to Scripture. Preachers today don't dare make that assumption about their listeners.

Spurgeon often used familiar and homey images, especially from nature, and sought to build a bridge from the image to the scriptural truth he was proclaiming.[4] If you want to read additional sermons of Spurgeon that take this approach, see *Farm Sermons* by C.H. Spurgeon (Pasadena, Texas: Pilgrim Publications, 1989).

Charles Haddon Spurgeon (1834–1892) was converted January 6, 1850, and soon after affiliated with the Baptists. He began distributing tracts and doing Sunday School work, but soon his gift of preaching opened doors for him in a wider area. In 1852 he became pastor of Waterbeach Chapel, Cambridge, and saw the work grow from a handful of people to over 400. In 1854, he accepted the call to the New Park Street Chapel in London, a church made famous by Benjamin Keach, who served there from 1668 to 1704, and John Gill, whose ministry there was from 1720 to 1771. In spite of its glorious history, the church was in serious decline, but the Lord would soon change that.

The work prospered and the chapel facilities were soon unable to accommodate the crowds that wanted to hear this remarkable young preacher. Spurgeon moved the services to Exeter Hall, and then to the Surrey Music Hall, which seated 10,000, and often he preached out-of-doors to great congregations. In March 1861, the great Metropolitan Tabernacle ("Spurgeon's Tabernacle") was opened with a seating capacity of about 5,000. Here Spurgeon preached for thirty years and saw 14,460 people baptized and received into membership.

Spurgeon died on January 31, 1892, leaving behind the record of a remarkable ministry that included not only the Tabernacle but also a Pastor's College, orphanages, alms houses, mission stations throughout London, a colportage association, and eventually sixty-three volumes of printed sermons that are still read and appreciated today.

Spurgeon's *Autobiography* was completed by his wife and secretary. Originally in four large volumes, it is now available (slightly condensed) in two volumes published by Banner of Truth. There are numerous biographies of Spurgeon, including one by his associate W.Y. Fullerton, reprinted in 1966 by Moody Press. One of the best of the recent biographies is *Spurgeon, Prince of Preachers,* by Lewis Drummond (Grand Rapids: Kregel, 1992).

Notes

1. From The New Park Street Pulpit, vol. 4 (London: Alabaster and Passmore, 1859), 331–36
2. Ralph Waldo Emerson, *Nature* (Boston: Beacon, 1985), 33. See the excerpt from *Nature* in chapter 1 of this book.
3. Ibid., 53.
4. See Jay E. Adams, *Sense Appeal in the Sermons of Charles Haddon Spurgeon* (Grand Rapids: Baker, 1975).

Developing a Christian Imagination

"Everybody's Sermon"

"I have multiplied visions, and used similitudes." — Hosea 12:10.

When the Lord would win his people Israel from their iniquities, he did not leave a stone unturned, but gave them precept upon precept, line upon line, here a little and there a little. He taught them sometimes with a rod in his hand, when he smote them with sore famine and pestilence, and invasion; at other times he sought to win them with bounties, for he multiplied their corn and their wine and their oil, and he laid no famine upon them. But all the teachings of his providence were unavailing, and whilst his hand was stretched out, still they continued to rebel against the Most High. He hewed them by the prophets. He sent them first one, and then another: the golden-mouthed Isaiah was followed by the plaintive Jeremy; while at his heels in quick succession, there followed many far-seeing, thunder-speaking seers. But though prophet followed prophet in quick succession, each of them uttering the burning words of the Most High, yet they would have none of his rebukes, but they hardened their hearts, and went on still in their iniquities. Among the rest of God's agencies for striking their attention and their conscience, was the use of similitudes. The prophets were accustomed not only to preach, but to be themselves as signs and wonders to the people. For instance, Isaiah named his child, Maher-shalal-hash-baz, that they might know that the judgment of the Lord was hastening upon them; and this child was ordained to be a sign, "for before the child shall have knowledge to cry, my father and my mother, the riches of Damascus and the spoil of Samaria shall be taken away before the king of Assyria." On another occasion, the Lord said unto Isaiah, "Go and loose the sackcloth from off thy loins, and put off thy shoe from thy foot. And he did so, walking naked and barefoot. And the Lord said, "Like as my servant Isaiah hath walked naked and barefoot three years for a sign and wonder upon Egypt and upon Ethiopia; so shall the king of Assyria lead away the Egyptians prisoners, and the Ethiopians captives young and old, naked and barefoot, to the shame of Egypt." Hosea, the prophet, himself had to teach the people by a similitude. You will notice in the first chapter a most extraordinary similitude. The Lord said to him, "Go, take unto thee a wife of whoredoms; for the land hath committed great whoredom,

44

departing from the Lord," and he did so; and the children begotten by this marriage, were made as signs and wonders to the people. As for his first son he was to be called Jezreel, "for yet a little while, and I will avenge the blood of Jezreel upon the house of Jehu." As for his daughter, she was to be called Lo-ruhamah, "for I will no more have mercy upon the house of Israel; but I will utterly take them away." Thus by divers significant signs, God made the people think. He made his prophets do strange things, in order that the people might talk about what he had done, and then the meaning which God would have them learn, should come home more powerfully to their consciences, and be the better remembered.

Now it struck me that God is every day preaching to us by similitudes. When Christ was on earth he preached in parables, and, though he is in heaven now, he is preaching in parables today. Providence is God's sermon. The things which we see about us are God's thoughts and God's words to us; and if we were but wise there is not a step that we take, which we should not find to be full of mighty instruction. O ye sons of men! God warns you every day by his own word; he speaks to you by the lips of his servants, his ministers; but, besides this, by similitudes he addresses you at every time. He leaves no stone unturned to bring his wandering children to himself, to make the lost sheep of the house of Israel return to the fold. In addressing myself to you this morning, I shall endeavour to show how every day, and every season of the year, in every place, and in every calling which you are made to exercise, God is speaking to you by similitudes.

I. EVERY DAY God speaks to you by similitudes. Let us begin with the *early morning*. This morning you awakened and you found yourselves unclothed, and you began to array yourselves in your garments. Did not God, if you would but have heard him, speak to you by a similitude? Did he not as much as say to thee, "Sinner, what will it be when thy vain dreams shall have ended, if thou shouldst wake up in eternity to find thyself naked? Wherewithal shalt thou array thyself? If in this life thou dost cast away the wedding garment, the spotless righteousness of Jesus Christ, what wilt thou do when the trump of the archangel shall awaken thee from thy clay-cold couch in the grave, when the heavens shall be blazing with lightnings, and the solid pillars of the earth shall quake with the terror of God's thunder? How wilt thou be able to dress thyself then?'' Canst thou confront thy Maker without a covering for thy nakedness? Adam dared not, and canst thou attempt it? Will he not affright thee with his terrors? Will he not cast thee to the tormentors that thou mayest be burned up with unquenchable fire, because thou didst forget the clothing of thy soul while thou wast in this place of probation?

Well, you have put on your dress, and you come down to your families, and your children gather round your table for the morning meal. If you have been wise *God has been preaching to you by a similitude then:* he seemed to say to thee—"Sinner, to whom should a child go but to his father? And where should be his resort when he is hungry but to his father's table?'' And as you feed your children, if you had an ear to hear, the Lord was speaking to you and saying, "How willingly would I feed you! How would I give you of the bread of heaven and cause you to eat angels' food! But thou hast spent thy money for that which is not bread, and thy labour for that which satisfieth not. Hearken diligently unto me, and eat ye that which is good, let thy soul delight itself in fatness.'' Did he not stand there as a Father, and say, "Come my child, come to my table. The precious blood of my Son has been shed to be thy drink, and he has given his body to be thy bread. Why wilt thou wander hungry and thirsty? Come to my table, O, my child, for I love my children to be there and to feast upon the mercies I have provided.''

You left your home and you went to your business. I know not in what calling your time was occupied—of that we will say more before we shall have gathered up the ends of your similitudes this morning—but you spend your time in your work; and surely, beloved, all the time that your fingers were occupied, God was speaking to your heart, if the ears of your soul had not been closed, so that you were heavy and ready to slumber, and could not hear his voice. And when the sun was shining in high heaven, and the hour of noon was reached, mightest thou not have lifted up thine eye and remembered that if thou hadst committed thy soul to God, thy path should have been as the shining light which shineth more and more unto the perfect day? Did he not speak to thee and say, "I brought the sun from the darkness of the east; I have guided him and helped him to ascend the slippery steeps of heaven, and now he standeth in his zenith, like a giant that hath run his race, and hath attained his goal. And even so will I do with thee. Commit thy ways unto me and

I will make thee full of light, and thy path shall be as brightness, and thy life shall be as the noon-day: thy sun shall not go down by day, but the days of thy mourning shall be ended, for the Lord God shall be thy light, and thy salvation."

And the sun began to set, and the shadows of evening were drawing on, and did not the Lord then remind thee of thy death? Suns have their setting, and men have their graves. When the shadows of the evening were stretched out, and when the darkness began to gather, did he not say unto thee, "O man, take heed of thine eventide, for the light of the sun shall not endure forever? There are twelve hours wherein a man shall work, but when they are past there is no work nor device in the night of that grave whither we are all hastening. Work while ye have the light, for the night cometh wherein no man can work. Therefore, whatsoever thine hand findeth to do, do it with all thy might." Look I say to the sun at his setting, and observe the rainbow hues of glory with which he paints the sky, and mark how he appears to increase his orb as he nears the horizon. O man kneel down and learn this prayer—"Lord, let my dying be like the setting of the sun; help me, if clouds and darkness are round about me, to light them up with splendour; surround me, O my God, with a greater brightness at my death than I have shown in all my former life. If my death-bed shall be the miserable pallet, and if I expire in some lone cot, yet nevertheless, grant, O Lord, that my poverty may be gilded with the light that thou shalt give me, that I may exhibit the grandeur of a Christian's departure at my dying hour." God speaketh to thee, O man, by similitude, from the rising to the setting of the sun.

And now, thou hast lit thy candle and thou sittest down; thy children are about thee, and the Lord sends thee a little preacher to preach thee a sermon, if thou wilt hear. It is a little gnat, and it flieth round and round about thy candle, and delighteth itself in the light thereof, till, dazzled and intoxicated, it begins to singe its wings and burn itself. Thou seekest to put it away, but it dashes into the flame, and having burned itself it can scarcely fan itself through the air again. But as soon as it has recruited its strength again, mad-like it dashes to its death and destruction. Did not the Lord say to thee, "Sinner, thou art doing this also; thou lovest the light of sin; oh! that thou wert wise enough to tremble at the fire of sin, for he who delights in the sparks thereof, must be consumed in the burning!"

Did not thy hand seem to be like the hand of thy Almighty, who would put thee away from thine own destruction, and who rebukes and smites thee by his providence, as much as to say to thee, "Poor silly man, be not thine own destruction." And whilst thou seest perhaps with a little sorrow the death of the foolish insect, might not that forewarn thee of thine awful doom, when, after having been dazzled with the giddy round of this world's joys, thou shalt at last plunge into the eternal burning and lose thy soul, so madly, for nothing but the enjoyments of an hour? Doth not God preach to thee thus?

And now it is time for thee to retire to thy rest. Thy door is bolted, and thou hast fast closed it. Did not that remind thee of that saying, "When once the master of the house is risen up, and hath shut-to the door, and ye begin to stand without, and to knock at the door, saying, 'Lord, Lord, open unto us;' and he shall answer and say unto you, 'I know not whence you are?' " in vain shall be your knocking then, when the bars of immutable justice shall have fast closed the gates of mercy on mankind; when the hand of the Almighty Master shall have shut his children within the gates of Paradise, and shall have left the thief and the robber in the cold chilly darkness, the outer darkness, where there shall be weeping and wailing and gnashing of teeth. Did he not preach to thee by similitude? Even then, when thy finger was on the bolt, might not his finger have been on thy heart?

And at night time thou wast startled. The watchman in the street awoke thee with the cry of the hour of the night, or his tramp along the street. O man, if thou hadst ears to hear, thou mightest have heard in the steady tramp of the policeman the cry, "Behold, the bridegroom cometh; go ye out to meet him." And every sound at midnight that did awaken thee from thy slumber and startle thee upon thy bed, might seem to forewarn thee of that dread trump of the archangel which shall herald the coming of the Son of Man, in the day he shall judge both the quick and the dead, according to my gospel. O that ye were wise, that ye understood this, for all the day long from dewy morning till the darkness of the eventide, and the thick darkness of midnight, God evermore doth preach to man—he preacheth to him by similitudes.

II. And now we turn the current of our thoughts, and observe that ALL THE YEAR round God doth preach to man by similitudes. It was but a little while ago that we were sowing our seeds in our garden, and scattering the corn over the broad furrows. God had sent the seed time, to remind us that we too are like the ground, and that he is scattering seed in our hearts each day. And did he not say to us, "Take heed, O man, lest thou shouldest be like the high-way whereon the seed was scattered, but the fowls of the air devoured it. Take heed that thou be not like the ground that had its basement on a hard and arid rock, lest this seed should spring up and by-and-bye should wither away when the sun arose, because it had not much depth of earth. And be thou careful, O son of man, that thou art not like the ground where the seed did spring up, but the thorns sprang up and choked it; but be thou like the good ground whereon the seed did fall, and it brought forth fruit, some twenty, some fifty, and some a hundred fold."

We thought, when we were sowing the seed, that we expected one day to see it spring up again. Was there not a lesson for us there? Are not our actions all of them as seeds? Are not our little words like grains of mustard-seed? Is not our daily conversation like a handful of the corn that we scatter over the soil? And ought we not to remember that our words shall live again, that our acts are as immortal as ourselves, that after having laid a little while in the dust to be matured, they shall certainly arise? The black deeds of sin shall bear a dismal harvest of damnation; and the right deeds which God's grace has permitted us to do, shall, through his mercy and not through our merit, bring forth a bounteous harvest in the day when they who sow in tears shall reap in joy. Doth not seed-time preach to thee, O man, and say, "Take heed that thou sowest good seed in thy field."

And when the seed sprang up, and the season had changed, did God cease then to preach? Ah! no. First the blade, then the ear, and then the full corn in the ear, had each its homily. And when at last the harvest came, how loud the sermon which it preached to us! It said to us, "O Israel, I have set a harvest for thee. Whatsoever a man soweth that shall he also reap. He that soweth to the flesh shall of the flesh reap corruption, and he that soweth to the Spirit shall of the Spirit reap life everlasting." If you have an opportunity to journey into the country during the next three weeks, you will, if your heart is rightly attuned, find a marvellous mass of wisdom couched in a cornfield. Why, I could not attempt for a moment to open the mighty mines of golden treasure which are hidden there. Think, beloved, of the joy of the harvest. How does it tell us of the joy of the redeemed, if we, being saved, shall at last be carried like shocks of corn fully ripe into the garner. Look at the ear of corn when it is fully ripe, and see how it bendeth toward the earth! It held its head erect before, but in getting ripe how humble does it become! And how does God speak to the sinner, and tell him, that if he would be fit for the great harvest he must drop his head and cry, "Lord have mercy upon me a sinner." And when we see the weeds spring up amongst wheat, have we not our Master's parable over again of the tares among the wheat; and are we not reminded of the great day of division, when he shall say to the reaper, "Gather first the tares and bind them in bundles, to burn them; but gather the wheat into my barn." O yellow field of corn, thou preachest well to me, for thou sayest to me, the minister, "Behold, the fields are ripe already to the harvest. Work thou thyself, and pray thou the Lord of the harvest to send forth more labourers into the harvest." And it preaches well to thee, thou man of years, it tells thee that the sickle of death is sharp, and that thou must soon fall, but it cheers and comforts thee, for it tells thee that the wheat shall be safely housed, and it bids thee hope that thou shalt be carried to thy Master's garner to be his joy and his delight for ever. Hark, then, to the rustling eloquence of the yellow harvest.

In a very little time, my beloved, you will see the birds congregated upon the housetops in great multitudes, and after they have whirled round and round and round, as if they were taking their last sight of Old England, or rehearsing their supplications before they launched away, you will see them, with their leader in advance, speed across the purple sea to live in sunnier climes, while winter's cold hand shall strip their native woods. And doth not God seem to preach to you, sinners, when these birds are taking their flight? Do you not remember how he himself puts it? "Yea, the stork in the heaven knoweth her appointed times; and the turtle, and the crane, and the swallow, observe the time of their coming; but my people know not the judgment of the Lord." Doth he not tell us that there is a time of dark winter coming upon this world; a time of trouble, such as there has been none like it, neither shall be any more; a time, when all the joys of sin shall be nipped and frost-bitten, and when the summer of man's estate shall be turned into the dark winter of his disappointment! And does he not say to you, "Sinner, fly away—away—away to the goodly land, where Jesus dwells! Away from self and sin! Away from the city of destruction! Away from the whirl of pleasures, and from the tossing to and fro of trouble! Haste thee, like a bird to its rest! Fly thou across the sea of repentance and faith, and build thy nest in the land of mercy, that when the great day of vengeance shall pass o'er this world, thou mayest be safe in the clefts of the rock."

I remember well, how once God preached to me by a similitude in the depth of winter. The earth had been black, and there was scarcely a green thing or a flower to be seen. As you looked across the field, there was nothing but blackness—bare hedges and leafless trees, and black, black earth, wherever you looked. On a sudden God spake, and unlocked the treasures of the snow, and white flakes descended until there was no blackness to be seen, and all was one sheet of dazzling whiteness. It was at that time that I was seeking the Saviour, and it was then I found him; and I remember well that sermon which I saw before me: "Come now, and let us reason together; though your sins be as scarlet they shall be as snow, though they be red like crimson they shall be whiter than wool." Sinner! thy heart is like that black ground; thy soul is like that black tree and hedgerow, without leaf or blossom; God's grace is like the white snow—it shall fall upon thee till thy doubting heart shall glitter in whiteness of pardon, and thy poor black soul shall be covered with the spotless purity of the Son of God. He seems to say to you, "Sinner, you are black, but I am ready to forgive you; I will wrap thy heart in the ermine of my Son's righteousness, and with my Son's own garments on, thou shalt be holy as the Holy One."

And the *wind* of today, as it comes howling through the trees—many of which have been swept down—reminds us of the Spirit of the Lord, which "bloweth where it listeth," and when it pleaseth; and it tells us to seek earnestly after that divine and mysterious influence, which alone can speed us on our voyage to heaven; which shall cast down the trees of our pride, and tear up by the roots the goodly cedars of our self-confidence; which shall shake our refuges of lies about our ears, and make us look to Him who is the only covert from the storm, the only shelter when "the blast of the terrible ones is as a storm against the wall."

Ay, and when the *heat* is coming down, and we hide ourselves beneath the shadow of the tree, an angel standeth there, and whispereth, "Look upwards, sinner, as thou hidest thyself from the burning rays of Sol beneath the tree; so there is One who is like the apple tree among the trees of the wood, and he bids thee come and take shadow beneath his branches, for he will screen thee from the eternal vengeance of God, and give thee shelter when the fierce heat of God's anger shall beat upon the heads of wicked men."

III. And now again, EVERY PLACE to which you journey, every *animal* that you see, every *spot* you visit, has a sermon for you. Go into your farmyard, and your ox and your ass shall preach to you. "The ox knoweth his owner, and the ass his master's crib; but Israel doth not know, my people doth not consider." The very dog at your heels may rebuke you. He follows his master; a stranger will he not follow, for he knows not the voice of a stranger, but ye forsake your God and turn aside unto your crooked ways. Look at the chicken by the side of younder pond, and let it rebuke your ingratitude. It drinks, and every sip it takes it lifts its head to heaven and thanks the giver of the rain for the drink afforded to it; while thou eatest and drinkest, and there is no blessing pronounced at thy meals, and no thanksgiving bestowed upon thy Father for his bounty. The very horse is checked by the bridle, and the whip is for the ass; but thy God hath bridled thee by his commandments, and he hath chastened by his providence, yet art thou more obstinate than the ass or the mule; still thou wilt not run in his commandments, but thou turnest aside, wilfully and wickedly following out the perversity of thine own heart. Is it not so? Are not these things true of you? If you are still without God and without Christ, must not these things strike your conscience? Would not any one of them lead you to tremble before the most High, and beg of him that he would give you a new heart and a right spirit, and that no longer you might be as the beasts of the field, but might be a man full of the Divine Spirit, living in obedience to your Creator.

And in *journeying,* you have noticed how often the road is rough with stones, and you have murmured because of the way over which you have to tread; and have you not thought that those stones were helping to make the road better, and that the worst piece of road when mended with hard stones would in time become smooth and fit to travel on? And did you think how often God has mended you; how many stones of affliction he has cast upon you; how many wagon-loads of warnings you have had spread out upon you, and you have been none the better, but have only grown worse; and when he comes to look on you to see whether your life has become smooth, whether the highway of your moral conduct has become more like the king's highway of righteousness, how might he say, "Alas! I have repaired this road, but it is none the better; let it alone until it becomes a very bog and quagmire, until he who keeps it thus ill shall have perished in it himself."

And thou hast gone by the seaside, and has not the sea talked to thee? Inconstant as the sea art thou, but thou art not one-half so obedient. God keeps the sea, the mountain-waved sea, in check with a belt of sand; he spreads the sand along the seashore, and even the sea observes the landmark. "Fear ye not me? saith the Lord: will ye not tremble at my presence, which have placed the sand for the bound of the sea by a perpetual decree, that it cannot pass it: and though the waves thereof toss themselves, yet can they not prevail; though they roar, yet can they not pass over it?" It is so. Let thy conscience prick thee. The sea obeys Him from shore to shore, and yet thou wilt not have him to be thy God, but thou sayest, "Who is the Lord that I should fear him? Who is Jehovah that I should acknowledge his sway?"

Hear the *mountains* and the *hills,* for they have a lesson. Such is God. He abideth for ever, think not that he shall change.

And now, sinner, I entreat thee to open thine eyes as thou goest home today, and if nothing that I have said shall smite thee, perhaps God shall put into thy way something that shall give thee a text, from which thou mayest preach to thyself a sermon that never shall be forgotten. Oh! if I had but time, and thought, and words, I would bring the things that are in heaven above, and in the earth beneath, and in the waters under the earth, and I would set them all before thee, and they should every one give their warning before they had passed from thine inspection, and I know that their voice would be, "Consider the Lord thy Creator and fear and serve him, for he hath made thee, and thou hast not made thyself;" we obey him, and we find it is our beauty to be obedient, and our glory ever to move according to his will; and thou shalt find it to be the same." Obey him while thou mayest, lest haply when this life is over all these things shall rise up against thee, and the stone in the street shall clamour for thy condemnation, and the beam out of the wall shall bear witness against thee, and the beasts of the field shall be thine accusers, and the valley and hill shall begin to curse thee. O man, the earth is made for thy warning. God would have thee be saved. He hath set hand-posts everywhere in nature and in providence, pointing thee the way to the City of Refuge, and if thou art but wise thou needest not miss thy way; it is but thy wilful ignorance and thy neglect that shall cause thee to run on in the way of error, for God hath made the way straight before thee and given thee every encouragement to run therein.

IV. And now, lest I should weary you, I will just notice that every man in his CALLING has a sermon preached to him.

The *farmer* has a thousand sermons; I have brought them out already; let him open wide his eye, and he shall see more. He need not go an inch without hearing the songs of angels, and the voice of spirits wooing him to righteousness, for all nature round about him has a tongue given to it, when man hath an ear to hear.

There are others, however, engaged in a business which allows them to see but very little of nature, and yet even there God has provided them with a lesson. There is the *baker* who provides us with our bread. He thrusts his fuel into the oven, and he causeth it to glow with heat, and puts bread therein. Well may he, if he be an ungodly man, tremble as he stands at the oven's mouth, for there is a text which he may well comprehend as he stands there: "For the day cometh that shall burn as an oven, and all the proud and they that do wickedly shall be as stubble; they shall be consumed." Men ingather them in bundles and cast them into the fire, and they are burned. Out of the oven's mouth comes a hot and burning warning, and the man's heart might melt like wax within him if he would but regard it.

Then see the *butcher*. How doth the beast speak to him? He sees the lamb almost lick his knife, and the bullock goes unconsciously to the slaughter. How might he think every time that he smites the unconscious animal, (who knows nothing of death), of his own doom. Are we not, all of us who are without Christ, fattening for the slaughter? Are we not more foolish than the bullock, for doth not the wicked man follow his executioner, and walk after his own destroyer into the very chambers of hell? When we see a drunkard pursuing his drunkenness, or an unchaste man running in the way of licentiousness, is he not as an ox going to the slaughter, until a dart smite him through the liver? Hath not God sharpened his knife and made ready his axe that the fatlings of this earth may be killed, when he shall say to the fowls of the air and the beasts of the field, "Behold, I have made a feast of vengeance for you, and ye shall feast upon the blood of the slain, and make yourselves drunken with the streams thereof?" Ay, butcher, there is a lecture for you in your trade; and your business may reproach you.

And ye whose craft is to sit still all day, making shoes for our feet, the lapstone in your lap may reproach you, for your heart, perhaps, is as hard as that. Have you not been smitten as often as your lapstone, and yet your heart has never been broken or melted? And what shall the Lord say to you at last, when your stony heart being still within you, he shall condemn you and cast you away because you would have none of his rebukes and would not turn at the voice of his exhortation?

Let the *brewer* remember that as he brews he must drink. Let the *potter* tremble lest he be like a vessel marred upon the wheel. Let the *printer* take heed, that his life be set in heavenly type, and not in the black letter of sin. *Painter,* beware! for paint will not suffice, we must have unvarnished realities.

Others of you are engaged in business where you are continually using scales and measures. Might you not often put yourselves into those scales? Might you not fancy you saw the great Judge standing by with his Gospel in one scale and you in the other, and solemnly looking down upon you, saying, "*Mene, mene, tekel*—thou art weighed in the balances and found wanting." Some of you use the measure, and when you have measured out, you cut off the portion that your customer requires. Think of your life too, it is to be of a certain length, and every year brings the measure a little farther, and at last there come the scissors that shall clip off your life, and it is done. How knowest thou when thou art come to the last inch? What is that disease thou hast about thee, but the first snip of the scissors? What that trembling in thy bones, that failing in thy eyesight, that fleeing of thy memory, that departure of thy youthful vigour, but the first rent? How soon shalt thou be rent in twain, the remnant of thy days past away, and thy years all numbered and gone, misspent and wasted forever!

But you say you are engaged as a *servant* and your occupations are diverse. Then diverse are the lectures God preaches to you. "A servant waits for his wages and the hireling fulfilleth his day." There is a similitude for thee, when thou hast fulfilled thy day on earth, and shalt take thy wages at last. Who then is thy master? Art thou serving Satan and the lusts of the flesh, and wilt thou take out thy wages at last in the hot metal of destruction? or art thou serving the fair prince Emmanuel, and shalt thy wages be the golden crowns of heaven? Oh! happy art thou if thou servest a good master, for according to thy master shall be thy reward; as is thy labour such shall the end be.

Or thou art one that *guideth the pen*, and from hour to hour wearily thou writest. Ah! man, know that thy life is a writing. When thy hand is not on the pen, thou art a writer still; thou art always writing upon the pages of eternity; thy sins thou art writing or else thy holy confidence in him that loved thee. Happy shall it be for thee, O writer, if thy name is written in the Lamb's book of life, and if that black writing of thine, in the history of thy pilgrimage below, shall have been blotted out with the red blood of Christ, and thou shalt have written upon thee the fair name of Jehovah, to stand legible for ever.

Or perhaps thou art a *physician* or a *chemist*; thou prescribest or preparest medicines for man's body. God stands there by the side of thy pestle and thy mortar, and by the table where thou writest thy prescriptions, and he says to thee, "Man, thou art sick; I can prescribe for thee. The blood and righteousness of Christ, laid hold of by faith, and applied by the Spirit, can cure thy soul. I can compound a medicine for thee that shall rid thee of thy ills and bring thee to the place where the inhabitants shall no more say 'I am sick.' Wilt thou take my medicine or wilt thou reject it? Is it bitter to thee, and dost thou turn away from it? Come, drink my child, drink, for thy life lieth here; and how shalt thou escape if thou neglect so great salvation?" Do you cast iron, or melt lead, or fuse the hard metals of the mines? then pray that the Lord may melt thine heart and cast thee in the mould of the gospel? Do you make garments for men? oh, be careful that you find a garment for yourself forever.

Are you busy in *building* all day long, laying the stone upon its fellow and the mortar in its crevice? Then remember thou art building for eternity too. Oh that thou mayest thyself be built upon a good foundation! Oh that thou mayest build thereon, not wood, hay, or stubble, but gold, and silver, and precious stones, and things that will abide the fire! Take care man lest thou shouldest be God's scaffold, lest thou shouldest be used on earth to be a scaffolding for building his church, and when his church is built thou shouldest be cast down and burned up with fire unquenchable. Take heed that thou art built upon a rock, and not upon the sand, and that the vermillion cement of the Saviour's precious blood unites thee to the foundation of the building, and to every stone thereof.

Art thou a *jeweller,* and dost thou cut thy gem and polish the diamond from day to day? Would to God thou wouldest take warning from the contrast which thou presentest to the stone on which thou dost exercise thy craft. Thou cuttest it, and it glitters the more thou dost cut it; but though thou hast been cut and ground, though thou hast had cholera and fever, and hast been at death's door many a day, thou art none the brighter, but the duller, for alas! thou art no diamond. Thou art but the pebble-stone of the brook, and in the day when God makes up his jewels he shall not enclose thee in the casket of his treasures; for thou art not one of the precious sons of Zion, comparable unto fine gold. But be thy situation what it may, be thy calling what it may, there is a continual sermon preached to thy conscience. I would that thou wouldest now from this time forth open both eye and ear, and see and hear the things that God would teach thee.

And now, dropping the similitude while the clock shall tick but a few times more, let us put the matter thus—Sinner, thou art as yet without God and without Christ; thou art liable to death every hour. Thou canst not tell but that thou mayst be in the flames of hell before the clock shall strike ONE today. Thou art today "condemned already," because thou believest not in the Son of God. And Jesus Christ saith to thee this day, "Oh, that thou wouldest consider thy latter end!" He cries to thee this morning, "How often would I have gathered thee as a hen gathereth her chickens under her wings, but ye would not." I entreat you, consider your ways. If it be worth while to make your bed in hell, do it. If the pleasures of this world are worth being damned to all eternity for enjoying them, if heaven be a cheat and hell a delusion, go on in your sins. But, if there be hell for sinners and heaven for repenting ones, and if thou must dwell a whole eternity in one place or the other, without similitude, I put a plain question to thee—Art thou wise in living as thou dost, without thought—careless, and godless? Wouldest thou ask now the way of salvation? It is simply this—"Believe on the Lord Jesus Christ and thou shalt be saved." He died; he rose again; thou art to believe him to be thine. Thou art to believe that he is able to save unto the uttermost them that come unto God by him. But, more than that, believing that to be a fact, thou art to cast thy soul upon that fact and trust to him, sink or swim. Spirit of God! help us each to do this; and by similitude, or by providence, or by thy prophets, bring us each to thyself and save us eternally, and unto thee shall be the glory.

Something to Do

1. List the biblical references that Spurgeon alludes to in this sermon. Does his use of any text take it out of context?

2. Which of the images and vocations in the sermon do not mean as much to contemporary congregations as they did to congregations in Spurgeon's day? With what images or vocations would you replace them?

3. If we took this approach today, what barriers, if any, must we overcome so that the modern listener would understand the message?

4. Do you agree with the views of nature held by Emerson and Spurgeon? Of what value is this interpretation to the preaching of the Word of God?

5

"Nature"
Charles Haddon Spurgeon

THIS BRIEF EXCERPT is from *Lectures to My Students* (London: Marshall, Morgan and Scott, reprint 1965), 405–6. It's part of a lecture Spurgeon gave on where to find illustrations for sermons. Note how his view of nature compares with that of Emerson.

Developing a Christian Imagination

"Nature"

Well now, supposing that you have exhausted all the illustrations to be found in current history, in local history, in ancient and modern history, and in religious history—which I do not think you will do unless you are yourselves exhausted—you may then turn to *natural history*, where you will find illustrations and anecdotes in great abundance; and you need never feel any qualms of conscience about using the facts of nature to illustrate the truths of Scripture, because there is a sound philosophy to support the use of such illustrations. It is a fact that can easily be accounted for, that people will more readily receive the truth of revelation if you link it with some kindred truth in natural history, or anything that is visible to the eye, than if you give them a bare statement of the doctrine itself. Besides, there is this important fact that must not be forgotten, the God who is the Author of revelation, is also the Author of creation, and providence, and history, and everything else from which you ought to draw your illustrations. When you use natural history to illustrate the Scriptures, you are only explaining one of God's books by another volume that He has written.

It is just as if you had before you two works by one author, who had, in the first place, written a book for children; and then, in the second place, had prepared a volume of more profound instruction for persons of riper years, and higher culture. At times, when you found obscure and difficult passages in the work meant for the more advanced scholars, you would refer to the little book which was intended for the younger folk, and you would say, "We know that this means so-and-so, because that is how the matter is explained in the book for beginners." So creation, providence, and history, are all books which God has written for those to read who have eyes, written for those who have ears to hear his voice in them, written even for carnal men to read, that they may see something of God therein. But the other glorious Book is written for you who are taught of God, and made spiritual and holy. Oftentimes, by turning to the primer, you will get something out of that simple narrative which will elucidate and illustrate the more difficult classic, for that is what the Word of God is to you.

There is a certain type of thought which God has followed in all things. What He made with His Word has a similarity to the Word itself by which He made it; and the visible is the symbol of the invisible, because the same thought of God runs through it all. There is a touch of the divine finger in all that God has made; so that the things which are apparent to our senses have certain resemblances to the things which do not appear. That which can be seen, and tasted, and touched, and handled, is meant to be to us the outward and visible sign of a something which we find in the Word of God, and in our spiritual experience, which is the inward and the spiritual grace; so that there is nothing forced and unnatural in bringing nature to illustrate grace; it was ordained of God for that very purpose. Range over the whole of creation for your similes; do not confine yourself to any particular branch of natural history. The congregation of one very learned doctor complained that he gave them spiders continuously by way of illustration. It would be better to give the people a spider or two occasionally, and then to vary the instruction by stories, and anecdotes, and similes, and metaphors drawn from geology, astronomy, botany, or any of the other sciences which will help to shed a side light upon the Scriptures.

Something to Do

1. How does Spurgeon's view of nature compare with that of Emerson?

Part Two

Sermons

AS BEAUTY IS in the eye of the beholder, so creativity is often in the imagination of the editor; therefore, I cannot guarantee that you will agree with me that the sermons I've selected show imagination. However, I think they do. I found each of them revealing a preacher whose imagination was at work as he studied the text and sought to relate it to his congregation.

"Christ and the Imagination," by George Morrison, and "Listening to God," by Hugh Black, deal with imagination itself and how it relates to the Christian life. They form a fitting introduction to this section.

"You may master a catechism unimaginatively," says Morrison, "but you will never master the Bible unimaginatively." A Scotsman of the old school—which means a man in touch with God, humanity, and nature—and a former associate of that imaginative pulpit genius Alexander Whyte, Morrison preached messages based on solid Christian doctrine but "packaged" with imagination and creativity. His messages are a joy to read; they are nourishing, interesting, and original. I recommend you secure his books of sermons, now being reprinted by Kregel Publications, as well as the superb anthology of forty sermons, *The Incomparable Christ*, selected by George M. Docherty and published in 1959 by Hodder and Stoughton.

"The highest truths are not reached by analysis," says Black. "The deepest appeal is not made to logic but to imagination, not to intellect but to heart." This from a long-time seminary professor who would be expected to emphasize left-brain competence! He summarizes his convictions in this terse weighty sentence: "We do not find the deep truths of life; they find us."

The two sermons on the rainbow (Gen. 9:13-16) give you opportunity to compare and contrast the work of two master preachers, George H. Morrison and Charles Haddon Spurgeon. Notice how the poet comes through in Morrison and the Calvinistic theologian in Spurgeon.

The next three sermons all deal with that fascinating "eagle text" from Deuteronomy 32:11-12; and this time we join Spurgeon, Alexander Maclaren, and G. Campbell Morgan, all of them pulpit giants. It's like attending a seminar in homiletics to read these sermons and discover how each of these men deals with the imagery in the text and applies its truths to everyday life. If nothing else, we learn to be true to our own gifts and not to imitate another speaker, no matter how gifted he or she may be. "Preach your own message!" was Alexander Whyte's advice to an associate who was beginning to imitate his master; and that advice is still good today.

The remaining sermons were selected simply as examples of interesting approaches to texts by recognized pulpit masters. Please note that my selections were made from preachers who are no longer with us, men whose reputations have been made and are not likely to be altered. The creative preaching of contemporary preachers is easily available in print or on cassettes. I want to introduce you to some of the giants of the past, and I hope you will get to know them better. Like Isaac, we need to dig again the old wells our fathers dug.

6

"Christ and the Imagination"
George H. Morrison

GEORGE MORRISON (1866–1928) was one of Scotland's most famous preachers, and his books of sermons are classics that should be in every preacher's library to be read and studied.

After completing his university work, Morrison served for a time as an assistant to Sir James Murray, architect of the great *Oxford English Dictionary*. He then prepared for ministry at the Free Church College in Glasgow, graduating in 1893. He became assistant to Alexander Whyte in Edinburgh, then pastored in Thurso and Dundee. In 1902, he became pastor of the distinguished Wellington Presbyterian Church on University Avenue in Glasgow, on the university campus, and remained there until his untimely death in 1928.

Morrison's preaching was the rare combination of a pastor's heart, a theologian's mind, and a poet's soul.

65

His Sunday morning messages were expository and dealt with the great themes of the Christian faith, but the Sunday evening messages were popular (in the best sense) and appealed to the imagination of his hearers. At Wellington Church, people queued up an hour before the Sunday evening service to be assured of seats in the large auditorium. No doubt some of them were attracted by sermon titles such as "The Deceptions of God," "Wasted Gains," and "The Intolerance of Jesus."[1]

"Christ and the Imagination" is taken from *The Return of the Angels* (London: Hodder and Stoughton, 1909), 179–89. Kregel Publications is reprinting all of George H. Morrison's books, and I enthusiastically recommend them to you.

Notes

1. The texts for these three messages are Jer. 20:7, Prov. 12:27, and Matt. 12:30. Look them up and read them.

"Christ and the Imagination"

That imagination plays a great part in practical life is a truth which no observer can dispute. Few powers are more determinative of a man's career than the power of imaginatively grasping a situation. Hazlitt, indeed, in his *Table Talk* asserts that to succeed in business one must be unimaginative. The only possible truth in that is this, that imagination unchecked by will may foster cowardice. On every other reasonable ground, Hazlitt's assertion is beside the mark, for every leader, whether in war or commerce, reveals the gift of constructive imagination. A great bridge is a work of imagination just as certainly as a great poem. A successful campaign demands as much imagination, to say the least of it, as a successful novel. To the upbuilding of our modern civilisation there has gone far more than intellect and will; there has gone at every step of the advance, what we describe as imaginative power.

But imagination is something more than that; it is also a religious power of the highest order. How fully that is allowed in Christianity will be evident from one or two considerations.

66

"Christ and the Imagination"

Think, for example, of the sustained appeal which the Bible makes to the imagination. From its first page of creation to its last of vision the Bible calls for imaginative handling. You have not explained the secret of the Bible when you have dwelt on its power over the human intellect. You have not exhausted its enduring charm when you have told how it appeals to feeling. In psalm and in love-song, in vision and in prophecy, the Bible appeals to the imagination, and it takes a trained and sanctified imagination to make it in all its parts a living book. You may master a catechism unimaginatively, but you will never master the Bible unimaginatively. A creed gets at the heart through the intelligence, but the Bible enters through a wider door. And that is one reason why the Bible is so much more powerful than any catechism, that by its gleams and shadowings and silences it makes such a pictorial appeal. Now the very fact that the word of God does that, reveals God's judgment of imagination. The Bible would never dare to use that faculty, unless it was a faculty which God honoured. And when we find it so constantly employed in matters of the most sublime importance, we begin to see how in the eyes of God it is a religious power of the highest order.

The same thing is very evident, again, from the use which Christ made of the imagination. If there is one word to describe the form His teaching took, is it not just that word 'imaginative'? Like a true teacher, Christ touched on many chords; like a true teacher, He knocked at many doors. In His passionate desire to get home, He would try every gateway to the soul. But one would be amazed, were it not so familiar, how often in matters of tremendous import the gateway to which He traveled first was 'the ivory gate and golden.' You never find Jesus teaching syllogistically. It is all pictorial and poetic. Every parable is an imaginative masterpiece, proving nothing and yet conveying everything. And my point is that this would be intolerable, and a degradation of the teacher's office, unless the imagination, in Christ's eyes, was a religious power of the highest order.

The same thing is witnessed in another way—in the emphasis which Jesus put on childhood. The child, as we all freely recognise, is the type of the citizen in Jesus' kingdom. Now we must not over-strain that perfect thought, nor tease it out into minute detail. It is well to leave it largely unanalysed, and rich in a certain indefinite suggestion. And yet if there be one thing in the child which is of the

very essence of its being, it is the sway of the imagination. That is
the time, as Henry Vaughan writes in *The Retreat* —

> When on some gilded cloud or floure
> My gazing soul would dwell an houre;
> And in those weaker glories spy
> Some shadows of eternity.

Sir George Trevelyan in his Life of Lord Macaulay[1] tells us how
young Macaulay played on Clapham common, and how its gorse
bushes and poplar groves and gravel pits were to him a region of
inexhaustible romance. A slight ridge, which no one above eight
years old would notice, was dignified with the title of the Alps; while
a little hillock covered with shrubs was regarded with infinite awe as
Mount Sinai. You do not require a doll that costs a guinea to turn a
little girl into a mother. The failure of expensive toys is this, that
they leave nothing to the imagination. A bundle of rags will serve the
purpose better, and be loved and nursed and cradled till it sleeps,
and though the child does not know it, she loves the worst dolls
best, because they leave everything to the imagination. Now the
point which I wish to emphasise is this, that that is of the genius of
childhood. Whatever may come to us in after years, we are all little
Macaulays in our infancy. And unless in the eyes of Christ there had
been ample room for imagination in the Christian character, Christ
never would have thought to make the child the parable and picture
of the Christian. All this, then, serves to make plain to us the religious power of the imagination — its place in the Bible; its constant
use by Christ; its sway in the life of every little child. And now I want
to ask how does it work, and in what way does it aid religious life. I
think we can discern three lines of service.

In the first place, it revivifies the past, and clothes it in all the
freshness of reality. In the *Memoir* of Lord Tennyson[2] by his son
there is a remarkable statement of John Richard Green. Mr. Green
was one of the greatest of historians, and one of the most diligent
and accurate of investigators. Yet he says that Tennyson's tragedy of
Becket gave him more real insight into King Henry II. and his court,
than he had gained from all his researches. That is a very remarkable
testimony to the vivifying power of the imagination. Most of us, I
fancy, in our own small way have had something of a like experi-

ence. For all that we ever learned, in school or college, of some particular period of the past, never brought it quite so near to us as a play of Shakespeare, or a novel of Sir Walter. Now ours is a historical religion. That is the strength and that the glory of it. It is not begotten of any dim abstraction; it is born of a historic revelation. Anything, then, that takes these facts of history, and brings them near us, and makes them real and living, is doing a mighty service to the faith. That is just what imagination does. It answers the heart-cry "Sir, we would see Jesus." It takes us to Calvary and to Gethsemane, and withdrawing the veil, it says, "Behold the man." And so our faith is strengthened and refreshed because the past, in which our faith is rooted, leaps up in life, like the bones of Elisha's vision, under the power of imagination.

Then again, it is a religious power because of its efficacy to quicken sympathy. There are few powers so helpful to compassion as is the power of the imagination. The fact is that there are many faults which we commonly assign to lack of love, while all the time it is not lack of love, it is lack of imagination, which creates them. A vast deal of men's callousness and cruelty, and of their censorious or unkindly judgment, does not arise so much from want of heart, as from failure to understand imaginatively. A person who has no imagination is certain to be a tactless person. A person who has no imagination is always an unsympathetic person. For at the back of sympathy and tact there is the power to grasp another's situation; the faculty that can realise another's thought, or the secret pressure of another's burden. Now it is not love which realises that. Love's work begins when it *is* realised. The power that helps us to share another's feelings is largely the imaginative power. Hence every dramatist and every novelist who reaches and reveals us to ourselves, is a man pre-eminently of imagination. Now, brethren, whatever else our faith be, it is the faith of brotherhood and love. There is no religion, whether of East or West, which makes such urgent summons for compassion. And if at the back of all the truest sympathy there lies the power of the imagination, you see, do you not? how the imagination is a religious power of the highest order.

But not only is it an aid to love. It is also an aid to faith in the unseen. Some of you may recall a word of insight which was uttered by that man of genius Horace Bushnell. When God made man, said Horace Bushnell, He looked on His work, and behold, it was very good. But God considered His work and said, 'Man is not finished yet. There is no door large enough to let Me in. I will open in him the great door of imagination, that I may go to him and he may come to Me.' What Bushnell meant was that in imagination unseen realities draw very near. Like a breath of wind it plays upon the mists, till they scatter, and show the everlasting hills. And so imagination, which is an aid to love, is also an aid to faith in the invisible, for it draws into something of visionary clearness the objects on which faith must always rest. Imagination is not faith, any more than it is love. But imagination may be their foster-mother from whose breast they draw the nourishment which strengthens. For faith is the whole manhood turning Godwards, and coming to rest in the eternal certainties, while of that manhood the imagination is only a particular faculty or power. No man is saved by his imagination. It is a question if any man is saved without it. Without its vivifying and realising help, the task of faith is simply overwhelming. And therefore, because it wakes the sleeping past — because it helps to brotherhood — because it helps to God, I want you to realise that the imagination is a religious power of the highest order.

In closing, may I say a word or two on the influence of Christianity on the imagination? I should expect to find that influence to be great, just because ours is a Gospel for the poor. Shut off as the poor are from many joys, and from the influences of broad and varied life; chained to the spot where they exercise their calling, with few opportunities of culture or of travel, the poor are more dependent than the rich on the quiet ministry of the imagination; more certain to be blessed when it is pure, and to be ruined when it is corrupt. To quicken the imagination of the poor, till it moves with delight in high and tender scenes, is one of the noblest and truest services to those whose lives are cabined and confined. And if it be a mark of Christianity that it is the benefactor of the poor, I should expect to find it mighty in that service. Is it the case, then, that the Christian faith has quickened the imagination of mankind? Let me point you to Italy in confirmation.[3]

Well, the ancient Romans, whatever were their virtues, were not pre-eminently an imaginative people. Their genius was of that practical order which embodied itself in organisation. The creative imagination of the artist, which was so splendidly conspicuous in Greece, was never to any great extent a leading character of ancient

Rome. The strange thing is that at a later day Italy shone unrivalled in that sphere. All that was noblest in poetry and painting, came to its fulness in that storied land. And above all other powers that were at work, there stands confessedly the power of Christianity, in changing the practical and busy Roman into the imaginative child of Italy. How much was loss, and how much gain in that, is not the question which I am discussing here. What we want to find is on the stage of history the influence of Christ on the imagination. And that is found in Dante and in Petrarch, in Michelangelo and Leonardo, men who interpret and register the change that had passed on Italy since the old days of Rome. Whatever else has happened in the interval, something has kindled the imagination. Whatever has been lost, this has been gained, this marvellous imaginative power. And I think that no historian will dispute that whatever other causes were at work, the mightiest cause of all was nothing else than the influence of the gospel of Christ Jesus.

Brethren, among all the services of Christ to a world which He has redeemed and is redeeming, there are not many more notable and blessed, than His quickening of the imagination. It would be much had He taught us perfect truth; but He has done more, He has shown us perfect beauty. He has given us a vision of such grace that it haunts the heart and will not let it go. It is that figure, so tender and so loving, so brave and patient, so silent, so unselfish, which has cast a spell on the imagination, and through the imagination reached the heart. No worse curse can fall upon a man than to have a corrupt imagination. There is no greater purifying power than an imagination that is pure. And he who dwells in the fellowship of Christ has such a vision of what is fair and lovely, that things unclean and bestial and base steal away into the forests of the night.

Notes

1. *Life and Letters of Lord Macaulay, i.* (1880), 29.
2. *Memoir,* xxxi. (1899), 580.
3. This is treated of at length in Church, *On Some Influences of Christianity upon National Character, ii.*

Something to Do

1. What does Morrison mean by the Bible's "gleams and shadowing and silences"? How does this relate to what the poetess Emily Dickinson wrote in her Poem #1129?

> Tell all the Truth, but tell it slant —
> Success in circuit lies
> Too bright for our infirm Delight
> The Truth's superb surprise.

2. What images of the imagination are used in this sermon?

3. Have you ever read a short story or novel that penetrated your imagination and gave you deeper insights into truth?

4. Morrison says, "A person who has no imagination is always an unsympathetic person." Do you agree?

5. How would a "corrupt imagination" affect a person's life adversely? How is the corrupt imagination cleansed?

7

"Listening to God"
Hugh Black

FROM 1896 to 1906, Hugh Black
(1868–1953) served as associate to
Alexander Whyte at Free St. George's
in Edinburgh. More liberal in his
thinking and less of a Puritan than
Whyte, Dr. Black drew large congregations in his own church and wherever he preached. It was jestingly
said in Edinburgh that Whyte black-
ened the saints in the morning service while Black whitewashed the
sinners in the evening service. Dr.
Black became Professor of Homiletics at Union Theological Seminary in
New York, retiring in 1938.

This message is taken from *Listening to God*, published in 1906 by
Fleming H. Revell Company.

Developing a Christian Imagination

"Listening to God"

I will incline mine ear to a parable — Psalm 49:4.

In this Psalm the subject is the great and dark problem of divine providence, the old problem that troubled so many Old Testament saints, why the wicked sometimes succeed and the righteous suffer. The Psalmist tells us in his introduction that he will open the dark saying, the riddle, on the harp. By his poetic and spiritual intuition he pierces through the surface of things to declare the utter vanity of life without God, no matter what appearance of success there may be. He tells us frankly that it is not by argument he arrives at this certitude, but by inspiration. He is stating a fact that must be, in spite of all seeming facts that contradict it. He has learned this from his own inner experience. His mouth is going to speak of wisdom; but with the beautiful figure of our text he suggests the only true attitude for one who is dealing with the great problem of human life. He does not say that he will open his mouth to speak a parable, but that he will incline his ear to a parable; as if he bends to hear and simply repeats what he thus learns. The method is intuition, not induction. He the Teacher is giving out what he has learned. "I will incline mine ear," as a man who listens to truth from above that he may give it out to others. He asks for attention because he himself has attended. He can be God's interpreter to others because he himself has listened to God. Through insight into the true foundation of life, he assumes the right to proclaim his message to all. He has listened to the wisdom that is from above, and so has truth to declare. This is the attitude of a true Teacher, that he is a Learner, opens his ear morning by morning to receive the right impressions; as Isaiah says, "He wakeneth mine ear morning by morning to hear as a learner." He who is sent to teach gets not the tongue of a master but the tongue of a disciple. The secret of the golden tongue is the open ear.

A great preacher used to say that in preaching the thing of least importance was the sermon. I suppose what he meant was that it is not what he says but *himself* that counts most. Not the fine expressions and the logical marshalling of the thoughts, but the spiritual atmosphere he creates, the indefinable impression of earnestness and seriousness and conviction — this is the great instrument of persuasion. You have been awed and influenced by speech, not one word of which you can remember. It was not important that you should remember anything, but it was of infinite importance that you should be impressed by the reality of the particular truth, and most of all assured of the reality of the spiritual world. In all prophetic speech there is a subtle spirit which communicates itself to disciples, and which the teacher himself will lose if he forgets his true attitude. Perhaps this explains some of the ultimate failures in the ministry and in all teachers, failures of men who at one time had power and influence and moved others. The teacher must ever be a learner, simple and humble and sincere. It is not what we say but the spirit of our saying it. And this is true in the final judgment not only of speech but of all life. It is not what you do but the spirit of your doing it—the spiritual qualities that lie behind and colour every word and action.

Real growth is far more of a passive thing than we usually imagine, the reception of great influences, opening ourselves humbly to the forces that will mould us. The Psalmist when he asks people to give ear to him says as his qualification for speaking, "I will incline mine ear." He must be attuned in spirit before he can open his dark saying on the harp to any purpose and teach others by his song. This passive attitude is the preparation for all true activity and the condition of all true growth. We become by attending, by inclining ear and heart, by listening, by being open to great formative influences. Wordsworth tells how the inspiration of Nature enters a maiden's heart and leaves its sweet mark on every feature.

> She shall lean her ear
> In many a secret place,
> Where rivulets dance their wayward round
> And beauty born of murmuring sound
> Shall pass into her face.

In the higher reaches of all truth a moment of insight is of more worth than a year of laborious learning. The two are not contradictory; indeed are usually found together, provided the labour is accompanied by a sincere mind and a humble heart. Certainly in religion no door is opened except to those who bend, who wait, who incline their ear.

That is why the child is the type of the Kingdom of Heaven, the mind that is open to the daily lesson, that morning by morning receives its portion, that sweetly accepts the teaching of the Master, the life that waits on God patiently and appropriates each lesson humbly, ever susceptible to divine influence, ever responsive to the touch of God, ever obedient to the voice of God — of such, not of the proud, the arrogant, the self-assertive, but of such simple, inquiring, humble souls, is the Kingdom. We think sorrowfully of the contrast between this and our common attitude, the pitiful conceit that mars so much of our best work, the self-willed pride that disfigures our lives, the poor ambitions of pre-eminence, the brazen-throated assertion of our superior claims, the loud calling of intellectual wares in the market, the advertisement of capacity to instruct. The secret of wisdom and power and knowledge is humility. The secret of influence is simplicity. We learn to speak the high language of the soul as a child learns. We must be receptive and listen, and repeat what we hear. "I will incline mine ear to a parable," catch the story whose faint accents can only be heard in the silence, and then echo it to others, if perchance they too may incline their ear and listen. "I will hear what God the Lord will speak," says another Psalmist. To desire to hear, to be willing to listen, to incline the ear, is the first step to the great experience.

There is a moment which came to the prophets and to men called to exceptional work, a moment when the world is dissolved, when earth has faded and heaven has opened and reveals the eternal, a moment when in all the universe there seems nothing but God and the human soul. That moment altered the perspective of everything afterwards; they read everything in the light of that moment, and when in the future they were brought up against seemingly impassable difficulties and things that seemed irreconcilable with their faith, they simply fell back on God; for they knew that, whatever else might be false, that great experience must be true. We each in our degree can have something of the same assurance, the same certitude; and the method of acquiring it is to incline the ear and the heart.

It is the old story, you say, a plea for faith? Yes, a plea for faith. But be sure you know what faith is before you dismiss it contemptuously. Faith is not shutting the eyes to believe something which is not true. It is opening them, opening eye and ear and heart and the whole nature, and submitting them to that for which they were made. It is to have the ear of a learner, the heart of a child, to listen to the Father's voice. Faith is not the acceptance of propositions, an intellectual apprehension of truths. It is an attitude of soul, listening to catch the faint echoes of the eternal song, an attitude of patient waiting and of eager desire to know God's will and way. It is the temper of the disciple who says by his expectant attitude, "I will incline mine ear."

The highest truths are not reached by analysis. The deepest appeal is not made to logic but to imagination, not to intellect but to heart. This is true not only in religion, but also in everything. To know and love nature is a simpler and higher thing than to know the geology of the rocks and the chemistry of the trees. To know and love flowers is a simpler and higher thing than to understand the botany of flowers. And to know and love Christ is a simpler and higher thing than to understand Christology, the theology of His person and work. Science can dissect and dissolve and analyse, and get at many a hidden secret by the way; but *the* secret has vanished. The life and meaning and vital breath and flavour elude the microscope. When science has done its best or its worst, we need the poet, the prophet, the seer, to interpret nature to us, not by analysis but by constructive imagination. "Nature exists," says George Macdonald, "primarily for her face, her look, her appeals to the heart and the imagination, her simple service to human need, and not for the secrets to be discovered in her and turned to man's use. What in the name of God is our knowledge of the elements of the atmosphere to our knowledge of the elements of Nature? What are its oxygen, its hydrogen, its nitrogen, its carbonic acid, its ozone, and all the possible rest, to the blowing of the wind on our faces? What is the analysis of water to the babble of a running stream? . . . I would not be supposed to depreciate the labours of science, but I say its discoveries are unspeakably less precious than the merest gifts of Nature, those which from morning to night we take unthinking from her hands."

Let us not kill the poet in us for lack of listening and looking, the poet that dies so young in most of us. Let us cherish the passive, receptive mood with its simple intuitions and its high inspirations. We do not find the deep truths of life: they find us. Our part is only to incline the ear and open the heart. As rain and sunshine and balmy air fertilise the waiting earth, gracious influences envelop our soul if we are responsive. This is how the contemplative life breeds in men a rich wisdom, mellower, sweeter than all worldly activities, however varied, can achieve. Surrender is the first word and the last word in this process. That surrender is faith.

It is hard for human pride to submit, to make the surrender. How often it is pride alone which stands in the way of communion, pride of intellect, pride of heart, or the garish pride of life. We will not bend: we will not incline our ear: we will not open the door: we go on our self-willed and wayward path, and refuse to wait that we may see and hear. We disdain the simplicity of faith. We neglect the great, pleading, prophetic word, "Ho, every one that thirsteth, come. . . . Incline your ear and come unto me: hear, and your soul shall live; and I will make an everlasting covenant with you, even the sure mercies of David."

If you live through this mysterious life on this mysterious earth with no outlook on the unseen and eternal, if spiritual truth sounds like an idle tale, if you act as if there were nothing to hear and nothing to learn, no secrets which God can whisper in your ear, if the great words of religion are as figures of speech; if, above all, you do not feel Christ's imperious claims and see His transcendent beauty and hear His insistent appeal, what is to be said but that seeing you see and do not perceive, and hearing you hear and do not understand? Is that not for you the judgment?

Nay, but I yield: I will incline mine ear to the parable. "I will hear what God the Lord will speak: He will speak peace unto His people, but let them not return unto folly." He speaks that message of peace through righteousness by many voices, and not one of them without signification — in nature and grace, in providence and love, in history and experience, and in the face of Jesus Christ. If He spoke in the thunder and the whirlwind and the tempest, all the earth might keep silence for a startled moment. But not thus is the secret of His peace conveyed. You cannot hear that still small voice, unless you are still and incline your ear and submit your heart. The Lord Christ speaks to us not only by what He said, but by what He was and what He did. He speaks peace to us by His words of heavenly beauty and His deeds of gentle love, and by the blood and the tears and the passion and the cross. I will incline mine ear to that wondrous parable of the eternal love of God.

"Listening to God"

"He that hath ears to hear, let him hear."

Something to Do

1. Do Morrison and Black agree in their views of imagination and the Christian life? Where do they disagree? Is their disagreement of vital importance?

2. What does Black mean by the "moment of insight [that] is of more worth than a year of laborious learning"? Is this statement anti-intellectual? How does one achieve this insight, and how important is study?

3. Black defines faith as "opening eye and ear and heart and the whole nature, and submitting them to that for which they were made." How might Emerson respond to that definition?

4. How do we "kill the poet in us"?

5. What conditions must be met before we can hear God's voice? How does Black's answer apply to the preparation of sermons and Bible lessons?

8

"Sinners in the Hands of an Angry God"
Jonathan Edwards

THIS IS PROBABLY the best known, most criticized, and least read sermon in all American preaching history. Jonathan Edwards (1703–1758) first preached it at Enfield, Massachusetts, July 8, 1741; and according to one of his editors, it was "attended with remarkable impressions on many of the hearers." The Great Awakening (1734–1744) was then moving across New England, and many were coming to saving faith in Christ.

Edwards possessed one of the greatest intellects America has ever produced. Before he was thirteen, he knew Latin, Greek, and Hebrew; and he graduated from Yale with highest honors before he was seventeen. He pastored the Congregational Church in Northampton for twenty-three years, but was forced to resign because of doctrinal differences with the leadership of the church. He then pastored in Stockbridge and ministered to the Indians, and in 1757 was elected president of Princeton College. Five weeks after his installation, he died of smallpox.

The sermon is taken from *The Works of Jonathan Edwards*, vol. 2 (reprint; Carlisle, Pa.: Banner of Truth, 1976). It is found in many sermon anthologies and various collections of Edwards' works.

"Sinners in the Hands of an Angry God"

Deuteronomy 32:35.
Their foot shall slide in due time.

In this verse is threatened the vengeance of God on the wicked unbelieving Israelites, who were God's visible people, and who lived under the means of grace; but who, notwithstanding all God's wonderful works towards them, remained (as v. 28) void of counsel, having no understanding in them. Under all the cultivations of Heaven, they brought forth bitter and poisonous fruit; as in the two verses next preceding the text. The expression I have chosen for my text, *Their foot shall slide in due time,* seems to imply the following things, relating to the punishment and destruction to which these wicked Israelites were exposed.

1. That they were always exposed to *destruction;* as one that stands or walks in slippery places is always exposed to fall. This is implied in the manner of their destruction coming upon them, being represented by their foot sliding. The same is expressed, Psalm 73:18. "Surely thou didst set them in slippery places; thou castedst them down into destruction."

2. It implies, that they were always exposed to sudden unexpected destruction. As he that walks in slippery places is every moment liable to fall, he cannot foresee one moment whether he shall stand or fall the next; and when he does fall, he falls at once without warning: which is also expressed in Psalm 73:18-19. "Surely thou didst set them in slippery places; thou castedst them down into destruction: how are they brought into desolation as in a moment?"

3. Another thing implied is, that they are liable to fall *of themselves,* without being thrown down by the hand of another; as he that stands or walks on slippery ground needs nothing but his own weight to throw him down.

4. That the reason why they are not fallen already, and do not fall now, is only that God's appointed time is not come. For it is said that when that due time, or appointed time, comes, *their foot shall slide.* Then they shall be left to fall, as they are inclined by their own weight. God will not hold them up in these slippery places any longer, but will let them go; and then, at that very instant, they shall fall into destruction; as he that stands in such slippery declining ground, on the edge of a pit, he cannot stand alone, when he is let go he immediately falls and is lost.

The observation from the words that I would now insist upon is this — "There is nothing that keeps wicked men at any one moment out of hell, but the mere pleasure of God." By the *mere* pleasure of God, I mean his *sovereign* pleasure, his arbitrary will, restrained by no obligation, hindered by no manner of difficulty, any more than if nothing else but God's mere will had in the least degree, or in any respect whatsoever, any hand in the preservation of wicked men one moment. The truth of this observation may appear by the following considerations.

1. There is no want of *power* in God to cast wicked men into hell at any moment. Men's hands cannot be strong when God rises up: the strongest have no power to resist him, nor can any deliver out of his hands. He is not only able to cast wicked men into hell, but he can most easily do it. Sometimes an earthly prince meets with a great deal of difficulty to subdue a rebel, who has found means to fortify himself, and has made himself strong by the numbers of his followers. But it is not so with God. There is no fortress that is any defence from the power of God. Though hand join in hand, and vast multitudes of God's enemies combine and associate themselves, they are easily broken in pieces. They are as great heaps of light chaff before the whirlwind; or large quantities of dry stubble before devouring flames. We find it easy to tread on and crush a worm that we see crawling on the earth; so it is easy for us to cut or singe a slender thread that any thing hangs by: thus easy is it for God, when he pleases, to cast his enemies down to hell. What are we, that we should think to stand before him, at whose rebuke the earth trem-

bles, and before whom the rocks are thrown down?

2. They *deserve* to be cast into hell; so that divine justice never stands in the way, it makes no objection against God's using his power at any moment to destroy them. Yea, on the contrary, justice calls aloud for an infinite punishment of their sins. Divine justice says of the tree that brings forth such grapes of Sodom, "Cut it down, why cumbereth it the ground?" Luke 13:7. The sword of divine justice is every moment brandished over their heads, and it is nothing but the hand of arbitrary mercy, and God's mere will, that holds it back.

3. They are already under a sentence of *condemnation* to hell. They do not only justly deserve to be cast down thither, but the sentence of the law of God, that eternal and immutable rule of righteousness that God has fixed between him and mankind, is gone out against them, and stands against them; so that they are bound over already to hell. John 3:18. "He that believeth not is condemned already." So that every unconverted man properly belongs to hell: that is his place; from thence he is, John 8:23. "Ye are from beneath," and thither he is bound; it is the place that justice, and God's word, and the sentence of his unchangeable law, assign to him.

4. They are now the objects of that very same *anger* and wrath of God, that is expressed in the torments of hell. And the reason why they do not go down to hell at each moment, is not because God, in whose power they are, is not then very angry with them; as he is with many miserable creatures now tormented in hell, and there feel and bear the fierceness of his wrath. Yea, God is a great deal more angry with great numbers that are now on earth; yea, doubtless with many that are now in this congregation, who it may be are at ease, than he is with many of those who are now in the flames of hell. So that it is not because God is unmindful of their wickedness, and does not resent it, that he does not let loose his hand and cut them off. God is not altogether such a one as themselves, though they imagine him to be so. The wrath of God burns against them, their damnation does not slumber; the pit is prepared, the fire is made ready, the furnace is now hot, ready to receive them; the flames do now rage and glow. The glittering sword is whet, and held over them, and the pit hath opened its mouth under them.

5. The *devil* stands ready to fall upon them, and seize them as his

own, at what moment God shall permit him. They belong to him; he has their souls in his possession, and under his dominion. The Scripture represents them as his goods, Luke 11:12. The devils watch them; they are ever by them, at their right hand; they stand waiting for them, like greedy hungry lions that see their prey, and expect to have it, but are for the present kept back. If God should withdraw his hand, by which they are restrained, they would in one moment fly upon their poor souls. The old serpent is gaping for them; hell opens its mouth wide to receive them; and if God should permit it, they would be hastily swallowed up and lost.

6. There are in the souls of wicked men those hellish *principles* reigning, that would presently kindle and flame out into hell-fire, if it were not for God's restraints. There is laid in the very nature of carnal men, a foundation for the torments of hell. There are those corrupt principles, in reigning power in them, and in full possession of them, that are seeds of hell-fire. These principles are active and powerful, exceeding violent in their nature, and if it were not for the restraining hand of God upon them, they would soon break out, they would flame out after the same manner as the same corruptions, the same enmity, does in the hearts of damned souls, and would beget the same torments as they do in them. The souls of the wicked are in Scripture compared to the troubled sea, Isaiah 57:20. For the present, God restrains their wickedness by his mighty power, as he does the raging waves of the troubled sea, saying, "Hitherto shalt thou come, and no further;" but if God should withdraw that restraining power, it would soon carry all before it. Sin is the ruin and misery of the soul; it is destructive in its nature; and if God should leave it without restraint, there would need nothing else to make the soul perfectly miserable. The corruption of the heart of man is immoderate and boundless in its fury; and while wicked men live here, it is like fire pent up by God's restraints, whereas if it were let loose, it would set on fire the course of nature; and as the heart is now a sink of sin, so, if sin was not restrained, it would immediately turn the soul into a fiery oven, or a furnace of fire and brimstone.

7. It is no security to wicked men for one moment, that there are no visible means of death at hand. It is no security to a natural man, that he is now in health, and that he does not see which way he should now immediately go out of the world by any accident, and

that there is no visible danger in any respect in his circumstances. The manifold and continual experience of the world in all ages, shows this is no evidence, that a man is not on the very brink of eternity, and that the next step will not be into another world. The unseen, unthought of ways and means of persons going suddenly out of the world are innumerable and inconceivable. Unconverted men walk over the pit of hell on a rotten covering, and there are innumerable places in this covering so weak that they will not bear their weight, and these places are not seen. The arrows of death fly unseen at noon-day; the sharpest sight cannot discern them. God has so many different unsearchable ways of taking wicked men out of the world and sending them to hell, that there is nothing to make it appear, that God had need to be at the expense of a miracle, or go out of the ordinary course of his providence, to destroy any wicked man, at any moment. All the means that there are of sinners going out of the world, are so in God's hands, and so universally and absolutely subject to his power and determination, that it does not depend at all the less on the mere will of God, whether sinners shall at any moment go to hell, than if means were never made use of, or at all concerned in the case.

8. Natural men's prudence and care to preserve their own lives, or the care of others to preserve them, do not secure them a moment. To this, divine providence and universal experience does also bear testimony. There is this clear evidence that men's own wisdom is no security to them from death; that if it were otherwise we should see some difference between the wise and politic men of the world, and others, with regard to their liableness to early and unexpected death: but how is it in fact? Ecclesiastes 2:16. "How dieth the wise man? even as the fool."

9. All wicked men's pains and *contrivance* which they use to escape hell, while they continue to reject Christ, and so remain wicked men, do not secure them from hell one moment. Almost every natural man that hears of hell, flatters himself that he shall escape it; he depends upon himself for his own security; he flatters himself in what he has done, in what he is now doing, or what he intends to do. Every one lays out matters in his own mind how he shall avoid damnation, and flatters himself that he contrives well for himself, and that his schemes will not fail. They hear indeed that there are but few saved, and that the greater part of men that have

86

died heretofore are gone to hell; but each one imagines that he lays out matters better for his own escape than others have done. He does not intend to come to that place of torment; he says within himself, that he intends to take effectual care, and to order matters so for himself as not to fail.

But the foolish children of men miserably delude themselves in their own schemes, and in confidence in their own strength and wisdom; they trust to nothing but a shadow. The greater part of those who heretofore have lived under the same means of grace, and are now dead, are undoubtedly gone to hell; and it was not because they were not as wise as those who are now alive; it was not because they did not lay out matters as well for themselves to secure their own escape. If we could speak with them, and inquire of them, one by one, whether they expected, when alive, and when they used to hear about hell, ever to be the subjects of that misery, we, doubtless, should hear one and another reply, "No, I never intended to come here: I had laid out matters otherwise in my mind; I thought I should contrive well for myself: I thought my scheme good. I intended to take effectual care; but it came upon me unexpected: I did not look for it at that time, and in that manner; it came as a thief: Death outwitted me: God's wrath was too quick for me. O my cursed foolishness! I was flattering myself, and pleasing myself with vain dreams of what I would do hereafter; and when I was saying, Peace and safety, then sudden destruction came upon me."

10. God has laid himself under *no obligation,* by any promise, to keep any natural man out of hell one moment. God certainly has made no promises either of eternal life, or of any deliverance or preservation from eternal death, but what are contained in the covenant of grace, the promises that are given in Christ, in whom all the promises are yea and amen. But surely they have no interest in the promises of the covenant of grace who are not the children of the covenant, who do not believe in any of the promises, and have no interest in the Mediator of the covenant.

So that, whatever some have imagined and pretended about promises made to natural men's earnest seeking and knocking, it is plain and manifest, that whatever pains a natural man takes in religion, whatever prayers he makes, till he believes in Christ, God is under no manner of obligation to keep him a moment from eternal destruction.

So that thus it is that natural men are held in the hand of God over the pit of hell; they have deserved the fiery pit, and are already sentenced to it; and God is dreadfully provoked, his anger is as great towards them as to those that are actually suffering the executions of the fierceness of his wrath in hell, and they have done nothing in the least to appease or abate that anger, neither is God in the least bound by any promise to hold them up one moment: the devil is waiting for them, hell is gaping for them, the flames gather and flash about them, and would fain lay hold on them, and swallow them up; the fire pent up in their own hearts is struggling to break out; and they have no interest in any Mediator, there are no means within reach that can be any security to them. In short, they have no refuge, nothing to take hold of; all that preserves them every moment is the mere arbitrary will, and uncovenanted, unobliged forbearance, of an incensed God.

Application

The use of this awful subject may be for awakening unconverted persons in this congregation. This that you have heard is the case of every one of you that are out of Christ. That world of misery, that lake of burning brimstone, is extended abroad under you. There is the dreadful pit of the glowing flames of the wrath of God; there is hell's wide gaping mouth open; and you have nothing to stand upon, nor any thing to take hold of; there is nothing between you and hell but the air; it is only the power and mere pleasure of God that holds you up.

You probably are not sensible of this; you find you are kept out of hell, but do not see the hand of God in it; but look at other things, as the good state of your bodily constitution, your care of your own life, and the means you use for your own preservation. But indeed these things are nothing; if God should withdraw his hand, they would avail no more to keep you from falling, than the thin air to hold up a person that is suspended in it.

Your wickedness makes you as it were heavy as lead, and to tend downwards with great weight and pressure towards hell; and if God should let you go, you would immediately sink and swiftly descend and plunge into the bottomless gulf; and your healthy constitution, and your own care and prudence, and best contrivance, and all your righteousness, would have no more influence to uphold you and keep you out of hell, than a spider's web would have to stop a falling rock. Were it not for the sovereign pleasure of God, the earth would not bear you one moment; for you are a burden to it: the creation groans with you; the creature is made subject to the bondage of your corruption, not willingly; the sun does not willingly shine upon you to give you light to serve sin and Satan; the earth does not willingly yield her increase to satisfy your lusts; nor is it willingly a stage for your wickedness to be acted upon; the air does not willingly serve you for breath to maintain the flame of life in your vitals, while you spend your life in the service of God's enemies. God's creatures are good, and were made for men to serve God with, and do not willingly subserve to any other purpose, and groan when they are abused to purposes so directly contrary to their nature and end. And the world would spew you out, were it not for the sovereign hand of him who hath subjected it in hope. There are the black clouds of God's wrath now hanging directly over your heads, full of the dreadful storm, and big with thunder; and were it not for the restraining hand of God, it would immediately burst forth upon you. The sovereign pleasure of God, for the present, stays his rough wind; otherwise it would come with fury, and your destruction would come like a whirlwind, and you would be like the chaff of the summer threshing-floor.

The wrath of God is like great waters that are dammed for the present; they increase more and more, and rise higher and higher, till an outlet is given; and the longer the stream is stopped, the more rapid and mighty is its course, when once it is let loose. It is true, that judgment against your evil works has not been executed hitherto; the floods of God's vengeance have been withheld; but your guilt in the mean time is constantly increasing, and you are every day treasuring up more wrath; the waters are constantly rising, and waxing more and more mighty; and there is nothing but the mere pleasure of God, that holds the waters back, that are unwilling to be stopped, and press hard to go forward. If God should only withdraw his hand from the flood-gate, it would immediately fly open, and the fiery floods of the fierceness and wrath of God would rush forth with inconceivable fury, and would come upon you with omnipotent power; and if your strength were ten thousand times greater than it is, yea, ten thousand times greater than the strength of the stoutest, sturdiest devil in hell, it would be nothing to withstand or endure it.

The bow of God's wrath is bent, and the arrow made ready on the string, and justice bends the arrow at your heart, and strains the bow, and it is nothing but the mere pleasure of God, and that of an angry God, without any promise or obligation at all, that keeps the arrow one moment from being made drunk with your blood. Thus all you that never passed under a great change of heart, by the mighty power of the Spirit of God upon your souls; all you that were never born again, and made new creatures, and raised from being dead in sin, to a state of new, and before altogether unexperienced, light and life, are in the hands of an angry God. However you may have reformed your life in many things, and may have had religious affections, and may keep up a form of religion in your families and closets, and in the house of God, it is nothing but his mere pleasure that keeps you from being this moment swallowed up in everlasting destruction. However unconvinced you may now be of the truth of what you hear, by and by you will be fully convinced of it. Those that are gone from being in the like circumstances with you, see that it was so with them; for destruction came suddenly upon most of them; when they expected nothing of it, and while they were saying, Peace and safety: now they see, that those things on which they depended for peace and safety, were nothing but thin air and empty shadows.

The God that holds you over the pit of hell, much as one holds a spider, or some loathsome insect, over the fire, abhors you, and is dreadfully provoked: his wrath towards you burns like fire; he looks upon you as worthy of nothing else, but to be cast into the fire; he is of purer eyes than to bear to have you in his sight; you are ten thousand times more abominable in his eyes, than the most hateful venomous serpent is in ours. You have offended him infinitely more than ever a stubborn rebel did his prince: and yet, it is nothing but his hand that holds you from falling into the fire every moment. It is to be ascribed to nothing else, that you did not go to hell the last night; that you was suffered to awake again in this world, after you closed your eyes to sleep. And there is no other reason to be given, why you have not dropped into hell since you arose in the morning, but that God's hand has held you up. There is no other reason to be given why you have not gone to hell, since you have sat here in the house of God, provoking his pure eyes by your sinful wicked manner of attending his solemn worship. Yea, there is nothing else that is to be given as a reason why you do not this very moment drop down into hell.

O sinner! consider the fearful danger you are in: it is a great furnace of wrath, a wide and bottomless pit, full of the fire of wrath, that you are held over in the hand of that God, whose wrath is provoked and incensed as much against you, as against many of the damned in hell. You hang by a slender thread, with the flames of divine wrath flashing about it, and ready every moment to singe it, and burn it asunder; and you have no interest in any Mediator, and nothing to lay hold of to save yourself, nothing to keep off the flames of wrath, nothing of your own, nothing that you ever have done, nothing that you can do, to induce God to spare you one moment. And consider here more particularly,

1. *Whose* wrath it is: it is the wrath of the infinite God. If it were only the wrath of man, though it were of the most potent prince, it would be comparatively little to be regarded. The wrath of kings is very much dreaded, especially of absolute monarchs, who have the possessions and lives of their subjects wholly in their power, to be disposed of at their mere will. Proverbs 20:2. ''The fear of a king is as the roaring of a lion: whoso provoketh him to anger, sinneth against his own soul.'' The subject that very much enrages an arbitrary prince, is liable to suffer the most extreme torments that human art can invent, or human power can inflict. But the greatest earthly potentates, in their greatest majesty and strength, and when clothed in their greatest terrors, are but feeble, despicable worms of the dust, in comparison of the great and almighty Creator and King of heaven and earth. It is but little that they can do, when most enraged, and when they have exerted the utmost of their fury. All the kings of the earth, before God, are as grasshoppers; they are nothing, and less than nothing; both their love and their hatred is to be despised. The wrath of the great King of kings, is as much more terrible than theirs, as his majesty is greater. Luke 12:4-5. ''And I say unto you, my friends, Be not afraid of them that kill the body, and after that have no more that they can do. But I will forewarn you whom ye shall fear: Fear him, which after he hath killed, hath power to cast into hell; yea, I say unto you, Fear him.''

2. It is the *fierceness* of his wrath that you are exposed to. We often read of the fury of God; as in Isaiah. 59:18. ''According to their deeds, accordingly he will repay fury to his adversaries.'' So Isaiah

66:15. "For behold, the Lord will come with fire, and with his chariots like a whirlwind, to render his anger with fury, and his rebuke with flames of fire." And in many other places. So, Revelation 19:15. we read of "the wine-press of the fierceness and wrath of Almighty God." The words are exceeding terrible. If it had only been said, "the wrath of God," the words would have implied that which is infinitely dreadful: but it is "the fierceness and wrath of God." The fury of God! the fierceness of Jehovah! O how dreadful must that be! Who can utter or conceive what such expressions carry in them? But it is also "the fierceness and wrath of *Almighty* God." As though there would be a very great manifestation of his almighty power in what the fierceness of his wrath should inflict; as though omnipotence should be as it were enraged, and exerted, as men are wont to exert their strength in the fierceness of their wrath. Oh! then, what will be the consequence! What will become of the poor worm that shall suffer it! Whose hands can be strong? and whose heart can endure? To what a dreadful, inexpressible, inconceivable depth of misery must the poor creature be sunk who shall be the subject of this!

Consider this, you that are here present, that yet remain in an unregenerate state. That God will execute the fierceness of his anger, implies, that he will inflict wrath without any pity. When God beholds the ineffable extremity of your case, and sees your torment to be so vastly disproportioned to your strength, and sees how your poor soul is crushed, and sinks down, as it were, into an infinite gloom; he will have no compassion upon you, he will not forbear the executions of his wrath, or in the least lighten his hand; there shall be no moderation or mercy, nor will God then at all stay his rough wind; he will have no regard to your welfare, nor be at all careful lest you should suffer too much in any other sense, than only that you shall *not suffer beyond what strict justice requires.* Nothing shall be withheld, because it is so hard for you to bear. Ezekiel 8:18. "Therefore will I also deal in fury; mine eye shall not spare, neither will I have pity; and though they cry in mine ears with a loud voice, yet I will not hear them." Now God stands ready to pity you; this is a day of mercy; you may cry now with some encouragement of obtaining mercy. But when once the day of mercy is past, your most lamentable and dolorous cries and shrieks will be in vain; you will be wholly lost and thrown away of God, as to any regard to your welfare. God will have no other use to put you to, but to suffer misery; you shall be continued in being to no other end; for you will be a vessel of wrath fitted to destruction; and there will be no other use of this vessel, but to be filled full of wrath. God will be so far from pitying you when you cry to him, that it is said he will only "laugh and mock," Proverbs 1:25-26.

How awful are those words, Isaiah 63:3. which are the words of the great God, "I will tread them in mine anger, and will trample them in my fury, and their blood shall be sprinkled upon my garments, and I will stain all my raiment." It is perhaps impossible to conceive of words that carry in them greater manifestations of these three things, *viz.* contempt, and hatred, and fierceness of indignation. If you cry to God to pity you, he will be so far from pitying you in your doleful case, or showing you the lest regard or favour, that, instead of that, he will only tread you under foot. And though he will know that you cannot bear the weight of omnipotence treading upon you, yet he will not regard that, but he will crush you under his feet without mercy; he will crush out your blood, and make it fly, and it shall be sprinkled on his garments, so as to stain all his raiment. He will not only hate you, but he will have you in the utmost contempt; no place shall be thought fit for you, but under his feet, to be trodden down as the mire of the streets.

3. The misery you are exposed to is that which God will inflict to that end, that he might show what that wrath of Jehovah is. God hath had it on his heart to show to angels and men, both how excellent his love is, and also how terrible his wrath is. Sometimes earthly kings have a mind to show how terrible their wrath is, by the extreme punishments they would execute on those that would provoke them. Nebuchadnezzar, that mighty and haughty monarch of the Chaldean empire, was willing to show his wrath when enraged with Shadrach, Meshech, and Abednego; and accordingly gave order that the burning fiery furnace should be heated seven times hotter than it was before: doubtless, it was raised to the utmost degree of fierceness that human art could raise it. But the great God is also willing to show his wrath, and magnify his awful majesty and mighty power, in the extreme sufferings of his enemies. Romans 9:22. "What if God, willing to show his wrath, and to make his power known, endured with much long-suffering the vessels of wrath fitted to destruction?" And seeing this is his design, and what he has

determined, even to show how terrible the unrestrained wrath, the fury and fierceness, of Jehovah is, he will do it to effect. There will be something accomplished and brought to pass that will be dreadful with a witness. When the great and angry God hath risen up and executed his awful vengeance on the poor sinner, and the wretch is actually suffering the infinite weight and power of his indignation, then will God call upon the whole universe to behold that awful majesty and mighty power that is to be seen in it. Isaiah 33:12-14. "And the people shall be as the burnings of lime, as thorns cut up shall they be burnt in the fire. Hear, ye that are afar off, what I have done; and ye that are near, acknowledge my might. The sinners in Zion are afraid; fearfulness hath surprised the hypocrites."

Thus it will be with you that are in an unconverted state, if you continue in it; the infinite might, and majesty, and terribleness of the omnipotent God shall be magnified upon you, in the ineffable strength of your torments. You shall be tormented in the presence of the holy angels, and in the presence of the Lamb; and when you shall be in this state of suffering, the glorious inhabitants of heaven shall go forth and look on the awful spectacle, that they may see what the wrath and fierceness of the Almighty is; and when they have seen it, they will fall down and adore that great power and majesty. Isaiah 66:23-24. "And it shall come to pass, that from one new moon to another, and from one sabbath to another, shall all flesh come to worship before me, saith the Lord. And they shall go forth and look upon the carcasses of the men that have transgressed against me; for their worm shall not die, neither shall their fire be quenched, and they shall be an abhorring unto all flesh."

4. It is *everlasting* wrath. It would be dreadful to suffer this fierceness and wrath of Almighty God one moment; but you must suffer it to all eternity. There will be no end to this exquisite horrible misery. When you look forward, you shall see a long forever, a boundless duration before you, which will swallow up your thoughts, and amaze your soul; and you will absolutely despair of ever having any deliverance, any end, any mitigation, any rest at all. You will know certainly that you must wear out long ages, millions of millions of ages, in wrestling and conflicting with this almighty merciless vengeance; and then when you have so done, when so many ages have actually been spent by you in this manner, you will know that all is but a point to what remains. So that your punish-

ment will indeed be infinite. Oh who can express what the state of a soul in such circumstances is! All that we can possibly say about it, gives but a very feeble, faint representation of it; it is inexpressible and inconceivable: for "who knows the power of God's anger?"

How dreadful is the state of those that are daily and hourly in danger of this great wrath and infinite misery! But this is the dismal case of every soul in this congregation that has not been born again, however moral and strict, sober and religious, they may otherwise be. Oh that you would consider it, whether you be young or old! There is reason to think, that there are many in this congregation now hearing this discourse, that will actually be the subjects of this very misery to all eternity. We know not who they are, or in what seats they sit, or what thoughts they now have. It may be they are now at ease, and hear all these things without much disturbance, and are now flattering themselves that they are not the persons, promising themselves that they shall escape. If we knew that there was one person, and but one, in the whole congregation, that was to be the subject of this misery, what an awful thing would it be to think of! If we knew who it was, what an awful sight would it be to see such a person! How might all the rest of the congregation lift up a lamentable and bitter cry over him! But, alas! instead of one, how many is it likely will remember this discourse in hell! And it would be a wonder, if some that are now present should not be in hell in a very short time, even before this year is out. And it would be no wonder if some persons, that now sit here, in some seats of this meeting-house, in health, quiet and secure, should be there before tomorrow morning. Those of you that finally continue in a natural condition, that shall keep out of hell longest, will be there in a little time! your damnation does not slumber; it will come swiftly, and, in all probability, very suddenly, upon many of you. You have reason to wonder that you are not already in hell. It is doubtless the case of some whom you have seen and known, that never deserved hell more than you, and that heretofore appeared as likely to have been now alive as you. Their case is past all hope; they are crying in extreme misery and perfect despair; but here you are in the land of the living, and in the house of God, and have an opportunity to obtain salvation. What would not those poor damned, hopeless souls give for one day's opportunity such as you now enjoy!

And now you have an extraordinary opportunity, a day wherein

Christ has thrown the door of mercy wide open, and stands in calling, and crying with a loud voice to poor sinners; a day wherein many are flocking to him, and pressing into the kingdom of God. Many are daily coming from the east, west, north, and south; many that were very lately in the same miserable condition that you are in, are now in a happy state, with their hearts filled with love to him who has loved them, and washed them from their sins in his own blood, and rejoicing in hope of the glory of God. How awful it is to be left behind at such a day! To see so many others feasting, while you are pining and perishing! To see so many rejoicing and singing for joy of heart, while you have cause to mourn for sorrow of heart, and howl for vexation of spirit! How can you rest one moment in such a condition? Are not your souls as precious as the souls of the people at Suffield [a town in the neighborhood], where they are flocking from day to day in Christ?

Are there not many here who have lived long in the world, and are not to this day born again? and so are aliens from the common-wealth of Israel, and have done nothing ever since they have lived, but treasure up wrath against the day of wrath? Oh, Sirs, your case, in an especial manner, is extremely dangerous. Your guilt and hardness of heart is extremely great. Do not you see how generally persons of your years are passed over and left, in the present remarkable and wonderful dispensation of God's mercy? You had need to consider yourselves, and awake thoroughly out of sleep. You cannot bear the fierceness and wrath of the infinite God. And you, young men and young women, will you neglect this precious season which you now enjoy, when so many others of your age are renouncing all youthful vanities, and flocking to Christ? You especially have now an extraordinary opportunity; but if you neglect it, it will soon be with you as with those persons who spent all the precious days of youth in sin, and are now come to such a dreadful pass in blindness and hardness. And you, children, who are unconverted, do not you know that you are going down to hell, to bear the dreadful wrath of that God, who is now angry with you every day and every night? Will you be content to be the children of the devil, when so many other children in the land are converted, and are become the holy and happy children of the King of kings?

And let every one that is yet out of Christ, and hanging over the pit of hell, whether they be old men and women, or middle aged, or young people, or little children, now harken to the loud calls of God's word and providence. This acceptable year of the Lord, a day of such great favour to some, will doubtless be a day of as remarkable vengeance to others. Men's hearts harden, and their guilt increases apace, at such a day as this, if they neglect their souls; and never was there so great danger of such persons being given up to hardness of heart and blindness of mind. God seems now to be hastily gathering in his elect in all parts of the land; and probably the greater part of adult persons that ever shall be saved, will be brought in now in a little time, and that it will be as it was on the great out-pouring of the Spirit upon the Jews in the apostles' days, the election will obtain, and the rest will be blinded. If this should be the case with you, you will eternally curse this day, and will curse the day that ever you was born, to see such a season of the pouring out of God's Spirit, and will wish that you had died and gone to hell before you had seen it. Now undoubtedly it is, as it was in the days of John the Baptist, the axe is in an extraordinary manner laid at the root of the trees, that every tree which brings not forth good fruit, may be hewn down, and cast into the fire.

Therefore, let every one that is out of Christ, now awake and fly from the wrath to come. The wrath of Almighty God is now undoubtedly hanging over a great part of this congregation. Let every one fly out of Sodom: "Haste and escape for your lives, look not behind you, escape to the mountain, lest you be consumed."

Something to Do

1. Read the sermon again and do two things: (1) count the number of times Edwards uses the word "hell"; (2) mark all the images he uses of divine judgment.

2. How do you think this vivid imagery would be received by congregations today? What makes it difficult to preach about hell today?

3. How then can we effectively preach about eternal punishment?

4. What images does Edwards use to break down the false confidence of sinners? Could they be used effectively today?

5. How does the sermon present Jesus Christ?

9

"The Rainbow"
Charles Haddon Spurgeon

"The Message of the Rainbow"
George H. Morrison

BY READING THESE two sermons on the same basic text, you can see how two pulpit giants used their imaginations and produced two different approaches.

The Spurgeon sermon is from volume 9 of *The Metropolitan Tabernacle Pulpit*, 361–72. He preached it at the Metropolitan Tabernacle on Sunday morning, June 28, 1863. The Morrison sermon is from his book *Flood-Tide: Sunday Evenings in a City Pulpit*, published in 1904 by Hodder and Stoughton, London.

"The Rainbow"

"And the bow shall be in the cloud; and I will look upon it, that I may remember the everlasting covenant between God and every living creature of all flesh that is upon the earth"—Genesis 9:16.

The story of Noah's preservation in the ark, is a suggestive representation of salvation by our Lord Jesus Christ. It is, we think, especially intended to depict that part of our salvation which lies in the washing of regeneration. In the same way as baptism is the outward symbol of regeneration, so also is the ark, "wherein few, that is, eight souls were saved by water." The ark was immersed in those dreadful rains and awful cataracts which deluged the earth, and Noah's family were buried in that ark to all the world; but by this burial they were floated out of the old condemned world, into the new world of life and grace. Death to the world, and burial in the ark, were the means of their safety. "The like figure whereunto," saith the apostle Peter (1 Peter 3:21), "even baptism doth also now save us (not the putting away the filth of the flesh, but the answer of a good conscience toward God,) by the resurrection of Jesus Christ." Baptism is a most significant picture of regeneration, but it is in no sense the cause of the new birth; and the blunder of the Puseyites lies in considering the outward manifestation of an accomplished fact, as though it were the means of creating that fact. Baptism saves no one, except, as Peter says, *in figure;* but as a figure, it is eminently full of divine teaching, for it sets forth the great truth that the believer, standing today in the old world, is buried to that world, "buried with Jesus Christ by baptism into death;" and his rising from the liquid tomb, is the figure of his resurrection in Christ, into a new world, as a new man, "that like as Christ was raised up from the dead by the glory of the Father, even so we also should walk in newness of life." (Romans 6:4.) Would to God that we thought more of being dead with Christ, buried with him and risen with him. Brethren, let Noah in his ark preach the work of righteousness within the heart to all of us this morning.

Do you not think, dear friends, that the history of Noah, when he left the ark, in all its items, may be viewed as typical and instructive? Noah came out of the ark—no longer cooped up and penned within its narrow limits, he walked abroad, and the whole world was before him where to choose. Was not that a picture of the freedom of the believer who has been "buried with Christ," and enjoys the possession of God's free Spirit? For him there is no spirit of bondage, he is free as a child in his father's house; all things are his, by gift of God, to use and to enjoy; he has learned the liberty wherewith Christ makes men free, and if the Son make us free, we are free indeed. When Noah slew the bullock and the other clean beasts, and offered them upon the altar, did he not show forth the believer's employment? for we also offer acceptable sacrifices of prayer and praise unto God, and we ourselves are living sacrifices unto God. Did he not as much as say to all generations of saints, "You being thus delivered from a death which you deserve, are to spend your lives as priests unto your God?" When the Lord was pleased on that day to bless Noah and his family, bidding them be fruitful, did he not therein set forth the fruitfulness which belongeth unto believers, so that, abiding in Christ, they "bring forth much fruit?" May not that benediction teach us how earnestly we should seek to be spiritually the parents of immortal souls, travailing in birth till Christ be formed in them? When the Divine Father gave them dominion over the fowl of the air, and the fish of the sea, and over all cattle, did not this pourtray the power which believers have over lust, and sin, and evil, and did it not prophesy the subjugation of all things by the power of their faith, so that they who become "priests" in sacrifice become also "kings," by virtue of the charter of dominion which the heavenly Father bestows upon them? What think ye, brethren? When he enlarged the grant of food, and permitted them to eat flesh, did he not set forth that food on which true believers feed, who now eat *his* flesh and drink *his* blood who has become the spiritual food of our souls? Is it straining the allegory, is it carrying it too far, if I close these spiritualisings by observing that the very same security which God then gave to Noah and his descendants is that security under which *we* stand. He gave them a covenant — a covenant embellished with a divine symbol, and ratified with his own signature written out in all the colours of beauty; we too stand under a covenant which has its own faithful witness in heaven, more transcendantly illustrious and beautiful than the rainbow — the Person of Christ Jesus our Lord.

Leaving, however, all those points, which I have only started to excite thought among you, we come to this. We have scriptural reason for asserting, that this venerable covenant, that the world shall no more be destroyed by a flood, is typical of a yet more ancient compact, which God made with Christ, that he would be unto his people a God, and they should be his chosen ones, world without end. In the fifty-fourth chapter of Isaiah we find such language as this: "In a little wrath I hid my face from thee for a moment; but with everlasting kindness will I have mercy on thee, saith the Lord thy Redeemer. For this is as the waters of Noah unto me: for as I have sworn that the waters of Noah should no more go over the earth; so have I sworn that I would not be wroth with thee, nor rebuke thee. For the mountains shall depart, and the hills be removed; but my kindness shall not depart from thee. neither shall the covenant of my peace be removed, saith the Lord that hath mercy on thee." The covenant of Noah, then, is typical of the great covenant made with Christ on the behalf of his people; and the rainbow, as the symbol of the covenant with Noah, is typical of our Lord Jesus, who is the Lord's witness to the people. You read in the fourth chapter of the book of Revelation, in the third verse, "there was a rainbow round about the throne;" showing that the bow is not a temporary symbol for earth only, but is a symbol of everlasting and heavenly things; and in the tenth chapter of the book of Revelation, if I mistake not, in the first verse, you will find that the mighty angel with the book in his right hand, who shall put one foot upon the sea, and another upon the land, is described as having his head crowned with a rainbow. In this place our Lord Jesus Christ, in his mediatorial capacity, wears the symbol of the covenant about his brow; and in the other passage our Lord, as King, is represented as sitting upon the throne, surrounded with the insignia of the covenant of grace which encompasses the throne; so that there are no goings forth of his majesty and his power and his grace, except in a covenant way and after a covenant sort, since the rainbow must be passed, before the bright rays of his power and love can reach the sons of men.

This brings us now into the centre of our discourse. We have to talk of two things—first, the *tenor* of the covenant, and secondly, the *token* of it—running a parallel all the way through between the two covenants. The tenor of Noah's covenant is the tenor of the covenant of grace—just as the rainbow represents, and in some sense *is,* the token of the covenant of grace also.

I. First, then, the covenant itself: WHAT IS ITS TENOR?

We reply, that it is a covenant of *pure grace.* There was nothing in Noah why God should make a covenant with *him.* He was a sinner — and proved himself to be so in a most shocking manner within a few days; he *needed* a sacrifice, for he afterwards became drunken. He was one of the best of men; but the best of men are but men at the best, and can have no claim upon the favour of God. He was saved by faith as the rest of us must be, and faith we all know is inconsistent with any claim of merit. At least one of his sons we must set down as being an open and abandoned sinner, and in him there could have been no ground why God should make a covenant with him. We have no reason to imagine that Noah ever *sought* this covenant. He did offer a sacrifice; but we do not know that he ventured to indulge the idea that God would enter into bonds with him not to destroy the earth. We imagine that the very first cloud which swept across the sky would excite the patriarch's alarm; the first drop which fell would damp his comfort. As a preacher of righteousness he understood well enough that on grounds of justice he had no claim upon the Most Holy God, and he would not venture to plead any merit of his own. But out of pure favor — just as out of the mountain's side the sparkling fountain gushes freely without the labour or art of man, so this covenant of sparing mercy sprang spontaneously from the overflowing, ever bounteous and loving heart of God. Certainly it is so with that greater covenant, whereof we strive to speak; for this was made with Christ, "or ever the earth was;" and as there were no *men* to supplicate, it could not have been possible that it was due to their intercession; as there were no men to merit anything it could not be bought by their worthiness, and as divine foreknowledge well knew that man would be evil — "only evil, and that continually from his youth up," no foresight of human goodness could have suggested it. And yet, because he "will have mercy on whom he *will* have mercy, and will have compassion on whom he *will* have compassion," he, the gracious God, whose heart was swelling like the deep sea with flood-tides of lovingkindness, was pleased to strike hands with Christ, our covenant and federal head, and from grace and grace alone to enter into engagements with him on our account.

The covenant, we note, in the next place, was all *of promise.* You will be struck, if you read these verses, how it runs over and over again "I *establish*" — "it *shall* come to pass" — "I *will*" — "it *shall*" — "I *will.*" He who knows the difference between "*thou shalt*" and "*I will*" is a good theologian. The old covenant of works is "*thou shalt.*" "Thou shalt not commit adultery; thou shalt not kill; thou shalt not steal." Death always comes to us by that covenant of command; but the new covenant is "*I will,*" and life comes to us by its promises. The covenant of grace runs on this wise: "*I will* sprinkle clean water upon you, and ye shall be clean; from all your iniquities *will I* save you." If there be a "*you shall,*" it is not by way of command, but by way of promise. "*I will,*" and "*you shall!*" O dear friends, one's heart rejoices to think of those potent *shalls* and *wills* — those immoveable pillars which death and hell cannot shake — the *shalls* and *wills* of a God who "speaks and it is done;" who "commands, and it stands fast." I do not see an *if,* nor a *but,* nor yet the shadow of a shade of a ghost of a *peradventure* in it. It is all "*I will, I will, I will,*" from beginning to end. And so when God covenanted with Christ, it was not, "*I will* save my people *if* they do this," but "*I will,*" and "they *shall,* from first to last.

'Tis like a living spring of waters, sweet and clear;
There's not an *if* to foul the stream nor peradventure here.
Grace is its fountain head, the source from whence it came;
In *wills* and *shalls* of Gospel grace, eternally the same.

The apostle Paul is very clear upon this. In that most blessed epistle to the Galatians he calls this "the covenant of promise," and marks the difference between Ishmael, "the son of the bondwoman," according to nature, and according to works, and Isaac, "who is the child of the promise, and the gift of God, *above* nature — not according to the efficacy and energy of the creature, but according to the will and power and truthfulness of the Most High. You and I do not stand today under a covenant which demands anything of us. Unconditional favours, unlimited mercies, made sure to all the seed by the oath and promise, the *shall* and *will* of God!

Further, I would have you observe that this covenant *has hitherto been faithfully kept.* It cheered my heart, when thinking this matter over, to remember that although *I* depend upon covenant faithfulness, I am not alone in that dependance, for every living thing upon the face of the earth lives by virtue of the immutable covenant of

God. Covenant engagements preserve the world from flood; were it not for that covenant, the tops of the mountains might be covered tomorrow. So that a covenant tenure is a very sure one, seeing that these thousands of years the world has never been destroyed by a flood. Ask ye, read ye, ask your sires, go back to ancient histories, and see whether since the deluge God has ever again swept away the race of man with water, and ye shall not even dare to hint that such a thing has been. No, the earth standing in the water and out of the water, since the fathers fell asleep, according to the testimony of scoffers themselves, abideth still the same; and so does the covenant of grace; it has never been removed or altered, nor have its promises been broken. O saint, ye dwell in tabernacles which shall never be taken down! God has never failed his people, nor cast away his chosen; not one promise hath lost its fulfilment, nor one word its faithfulness.

> This cov'nant of grace all blessing secures;
> Believer, rejoice, for all things are yours,
> And God from his purpose shall never remove,
> But love thee and bless thee and rest in his love.

Beloved, there is this about Noah's covenant, and about the covenant of grace, that *it does not depend in any degree at all upon man;* for, if you will notice, the bow is put in the cloud, but it does not say, "And when *ye* shall look upon the bow, and *ye* shall remember my covenant, *then* I will not destroy the earth," but it is gloriously put not upon *our* memory, which is fickle and frail, but upon *God's* memory, which is infinite and immutable. "The bow shall be in the cloud; and *I* will look upon it, that *I* may remember the everlasting covenant." Oh! it is not *my* remembering God, it is God's remembering *me;* it is not *my* laying hold of his covenant, but his covenant laying hold on me. Glory be to God! the whole of the bulwarks are secured, and even the minor-towers which we may fancy might have been left to man, are guarded by divine strength. Even the remembrance of the covenant is not left to our memories, for we might forget, but our Lord cannot, will not forget the saints, whom he has graven on the palms of his hands. It is with us today as it was with Israel in Egypt. The blood was upon the lintel and upon the two side-posts; but God did not say, "When *you* see the blood I will pass over you;" no, no, but "When *I* see the blood I will pass over you." My looking to Jesus brings me joy and peace, but it is God's looking to Jesus which secures my salvation and that of all his elect; for it is impossible for our God to look at Christ, our bleeding Surety, and then to be angry with us for sins already punished in him. No, dear friends, it is not left with *us* for sins already punished in him. No, dear friends, it is not left with *us* even to be saved by remembering the covenant. There's no linsey-wolsey here—not a single thread of the creature mars the fabric. Here we have the pure gold, and not an atom of alloy. It is not of man, neither by man, but of the Lord alone. We *should* remember the covenant, and we *shall* do it, through divine grace; but the hinge of the matter does not lie there; it is God's remembering *us,* not our remembering *him.*

And hence—for all these reasons it is *an everlasting covenant.* We know that as long as there is day and night, and summer and winter, and these shall be so long as the earth standeth, the proud waves can never cover the earth. *For ever* has God established this covenant in heaven. Even so the covenant of grace is not intended to be fleeting and temporary. "For ever, O Lord, thy word is settled in heaven." "He hath made with us an everlasting covenant, ordered in all things and sure." "He will ever be mindful of his covenant." If it concerns *you* today, it is "the same yesterday, today and for ever;" if the covenant blesses you at this hour, it shall bless you in old age, in the article of death, at resurrection, and throughout eternity. No *time* can change one of its stipulations. Ye may walk the centuries and fly adown the ages far into eternity, but ye can never discover such a thing as the change or failure of one single article of the covenant of grace, its jots and tittles are sure to all the seed.

> He lov'd the world of his elect,
>   With love surpassing thought;
> Nor will his mercy e'er neglect
>   The souls his Son has bought.
>
> The warm affections of his breast
>   Towards his chosen burn;
> And in this love he'll ever rest
>   Nor from his oath return.

Still to confirm his oath of old,
　　See in the heavens his bow,
No fierce rebukes, but love untold,
　　Awaits his children now.

Would to God you and I studied more the doctrine of this covenant of grace. Our old Puritanic forefathers were wont to preach
much about it. Those Scotch Theologians, who were a second band
of Puritans, Erskine and the men of his day, were always dwelling
upon the covenants. Good Witsins has left us a marvellously learned
and potent treatise on the same, and Fisher's Marrow of Theology is
a valuable exposition of the matter. He who studies the doctrines of
the covenant is not very likely to make a mingle-mangle of his ministry, or to preach a yea and nay gospel. My dear friends, when you
think of the covenant of law and the covenant of grace, and
remember that they are contrary the one to the other, and can never
mingle, can never be united, so that the one can dilute the other, it
must come out forcibly before you that we may address the gospel
to the sinner *as* a sinner, without a fitness on his part; that we may
still believe in God's love to the saint, even *though* he has sinned,
and that notwithstanding all the misbehaviour of any of the chosen
people, since they are under the covenant of grace and not of
works, their salvation is *never* in jeopardy, *never* at hazard, so far as
God's will and God's power are concerned; but he that vowed to
save them, and loved them in Christ, and has given them faith,
which is the token of his grace, will most assuredly save them and
bring them to glory. The earth shall be destroyed, with water, long
before one of God's elect shall be damned; it *shall* be destroyed,
with fire we know, but when "the mountains depart" and the hills
are removed," the covenant of his grace shall still stand, and He will
be mindful of all who have an interest in it.

So much, then, concerning the tenor of the covenant itself. My
soul! search, and look, and see whether *thou* hast an interest in that
covenant. Canst *thou* say from thy heart—

My hope is fixed on nothing less
Than Jesu's blood and righteousness!

Then, my soul, that everlasting covenant is thine, and thou art safe
beyond risk of harm.

II. Secondly, THE TOKEN OF THE COVENANT.

The covenant needs no token, as far as *God* is concerned; tokens are given for *us,* because of our littleness of heart, our unbelief, our constant forgetfulness of God's promise. The rainbow is the symbol of Noah's covenant; and Jesus Christ, who *is* the covenant, is also the symbol of that covenant to *us.* He *is* the Faithful Witness in heaven.

1. Briefly, upon this part of the subject let us notice *when we may expect to see the token of the covenant.*

The rainbow is only to be seen painted upon a *cloud.* Expect no tokens, except when thou needest them. The Lord Jesus, when he *can,* will trust us to our faith; for it is, on the whole, more healthy, more strengthening to us, to "walk by faith, and not by sight." Tokens are helps for our childhood; they would be unnecessary to us were we men. Tokens, to men whose faith is in vigorous order, would be as crutches to a man who is not lame, or as glasses to those whose eyes are perfect. The Lord is pleased to give tokens when tokens are wanted, I say; and hence he gives them, as he gives rainbows, when there is a cloud. When the greatest cloud which ever gathered upon earth, had covered Calvary with blackness, when the sun himself had suffered eclipse, when human sin and divine wrath had made a tempest so black and terrible that all the earth was in affright, then on that black cloud was painted the rainbow—for Jesus was lifted up, and amidst that thick darkness *he,* the expiation and the atonement, offered up himself, and poured forth his blood. When the sinner's conscience is dark with clouds, when he remembers his past sin, when he mourneth and lamenteth before God, Jesus Christ is revealed to him as the covenant Rainbow, speaking peace; and to the believer, when his trials surround him, when temptations beset him, when he suffers depression of spirits, then how sweet it is to behold the person of our Lord Jesus Christ—to see him bleeding for us, offered up for guilty men—God's rainbow, hung over the cloud of all our sins, our sorrows and our woes. Look, believer, when thou hast a cloud—look for a token, and be not satisfied without it. The ancient Church said upon one occasion, "We see not our signs;" and you and I have sometimes to say the same; but let us hasten to the Rock of our Salvation, and beseech him to bestow upon us a comfortable sight of Jesus, who shall will the covenant to our souls again.

Nor does a *cloud* alone give a rainbow; There must be *rain*. There can be no rainbows, unless there be the crystal drops, to reflect the light of the sun. So, beloved, our sorrows, must not only threaten, but they must really fall upon us. There had been no Christ for us if the vengeance of God had been merely a threatening cloud. It must fall in terrible drops upon him. Christ, who sets forth to us the vengeance and the love of God at the same time, had not come to us, unless there had been a *real* vengeance, and a *real* punishment of sin: until there is a *real* anguish in the sinner's conscience, there is no Christ for him; and until the chastisement which you feel becomes grievous to you — till the big drops bespatter you, and you feel it is not a threatening, but a real infliction of sorrow upon you, you cannot expect to see Jesus Christ. Perhaps, dear brethren, some of us have but slight views of Christ, and few have visits from him, because we have so few troubles; and the reason why the most of saints in these days do not live so near to Jesus as they were wont to do in the centuries gone by, may be because we have not so many of those showers of persecution which fell at that season. Why, when, in the reign of Dioclesian, and in the preceding centuries, believers were stoned, and dragged into the amphitheatre, or hacked to death with knives, they saw the glory of Jesus as the rainbow painted on the black cloud of persecution, while the raindrops fell upon them. It makes us even long to suffer as they suffered, that we may behold Jesus as they beheld him. But the day is coming when the world shall "hear of wars and rumours of wars." The earth shall rock and reel, and the pillars of heaven shall be shaken; the stars shall fall, the moon shall be turned into a clot of blood, and the sun shall be black as sackcloth of hair. Ah! then how glorious will that rainbow shine to all the people of God, when over the conflagrations of earth, and the destruction of men, and the melting of empires, and the blazing of earth, there shall be seen Christ the Mediator, securing all his people, and ratifying still the covenant of Grace. There must be drops of rain, or else no rainbow; some fallings of vengeance, or else no sight of Christ.

But then, there must be *a sun;* for clouds and drops of rain make not rainbows, unless the sun shineth. Beloved, our God, who is as the sun to us, always shines, but we do not always see him; clouds hide his face; but no matter what drops may be falling, or what clouds may be threatening, if *he* does but shine, there will be a rainbow at once. When the blessed Spirit "sheds abroad the love of God in our hearts"—when we can say, "Abba, Father," and a Father's love and a Father's peace are breathed upon us, then we see Jesus Christ, beholding the Father in the person of his Son.

It is said, that when we see the rainbow, that particular shower is over. So good Bishop Hall tells us in his "Contemplations." Certain it is, that when Christ comes, our troubles are over; when we behold Jesus, our sins are gone—our doubts and fears subside at his command; when *he* walks the waters of the sea, there will be a calm. But others say that the rainbow is the showery arch, and heralds bad weather. And probably this is quite as true. Certainly, whenever you get a love-token from Christ, you may expect some trouble; for he brings his people into the banqueting house either before a battle, or after it. Melchisedec came to meet Abraham when the kings had all been slaughtered; but sometimes our Melchisedec brings the bread and wine just before the battle is to commence. We are not *always* to be living upon love-tokens; our beloved Jesus would rather make us live by simple faith, and therefore we "walk in darkness, and see no light." Still, rainbows are delightful sights, and a vision of Jesus is rapturous and transporting, but ye cannot expect to see him, I say, unless it is when the storm is over, or when another storm is coming on, or when the cloud is there, or the drops are falling, or the light of God's countenance is especially shining upon you.

We will say no more about *when* this token is seen, but we will now notice briefly, what this token *is*.

2. *What do we see in our Covenant Witness in heaven?* We see in him what we see in the rainbow. In the rainbow we see *transcendant glory and beauty*. As one of the works of God, it is worthy to be sought out by them that have pleasure therein. One might stand and gaze on the rainbow with wonder and admiration, and never be weary. I do not know whether you have noticed paintings of rainbows—did you ever see a good one? *Will* you ever see a good one? There are one or two in the Royal Academy this year—I am no judge of paintings, but I can judge that they are as much *un*like rainbows as they well could be. Rainbows cannot be painted; the thing is impossible; there is such a melting and blending of colours, that human art shall never be able to rival the art of God. The Master Painter, with the black cloud for his palette, and the

110

sun's rays for his pencil, painteth so that no artist shall rival him. If you should gather together a heap of all the glittering gems and jewels which adorn an Oriental prince and build therewith a glorious arch, ye could not make such glitter and brightness of glory as in the rainbow, which is the simple work of a drop of rain and a ray of light. But shall I compare my Lord Jesus to the rainbow? I do him an injustice.

"All human beauties, all divine, in my beloved meet and shine."

You never saw a picture of *his* face which satisfied you, and you never will. You shall go all over the Continent, and see some of the marvelous productions of the masters put up as altar pieces; and you will say when you see them, "*That* is not like Jesus Christ." They can paint Judas; there are some fine heads of Peter; sweet guesses at John—John the Baptist to the life, all but that little bit of a cockle-shell in his hand; they can paint Mary Magdalen if you will, but never Jesus Christ; they can never paint him; no artist that ever lived can catch his expression of countenance, much less put it on canvas. And as to the beauty of his character, must we not burst out with the spouse in the Canticles, "He is altogether lovely?"

"The spacious earth, the swelling flood,
Proclaim the wise and powerful God;
And thy rich glories from afar,
Sparkle in every rolling star.

But in *his* looks a glory stands,
The noblest labour of thine hands:
God, in the person of his Son,
Hath all his mightiest works outdone."

The rainbow has been recognised by ancient poets and bards as an appointed messenger of God. Homer calls it the messenger of the gods, and the old mythologies speak of it as the Iris, the messenger of Juno. They knew not who had sent it, nor what was the errand on which it came. Still they recognised it as a divine ambassador. And surely such is Christ, the messenger of the covenant whom we delight in, God's great ambassador, who is "our peace," "the desire of all nations," who shall yet come, and shall be hailed as "King of kings, and Lord of lords." O blessed rainbow! Jesus! when shall thy beauties be beheld by mortal eyes? When shall *all* kings fall down before thee, and yield their sceptres and their crowns to thee?

Again: in the rainbow, and in Christ, I see *vengeance satisfied*. Is not the bow the symbol of the warrior's power? With far-reaching arrows he draws the string, and woe unto his enemies; but when a hero hangs up his bow upon the wall, what meaneth he but that warfare is over, and peace is proclaimed? When he looseneth the bow, and leaveth it without the string and without an arrow, it means that he will go no more out to hunt his adversaries; his arrows shall be no more "drunk with the blood of the slain;" he layeth the bow aside, hangeth it up on high, and leaveth it unstrung, without an arrow. Such is the rainbow. A bow, it is true, but a bow hung up—a bow without string or arrow. And such is Christ, God's bow. "*Thine* arrows are sharp in the heart of the king's enemies, whereby the people fall under thee." When *he* takes the "rod of iron," he breaks his enemies in pieces "like a potter's vessel." "Who is this that cometh from Edom, with dyed garments from Bozrah, travelling in the greatness of his strength?" Jesus, the arrow of God, the polished shaft in the quiver of the Most High. But *there* I see him: a bow still—still mighty to destroy—but yet a bow without a string. He threw *that* away, when he came from heaven to earth, and lay slumbering in the manger. A bow without an arrow!

> "No thunder clothes his brow,
> No bolts to drive our guilty souls
> To fiercer flames below."

Beloved, Christ *is* vengeance satisfied. Those wounds, those bright and burnished jewels of his hands, betoken that God demands no more of man.

The rainbow, yet again, is a token that vengeance itself has become *on our side*. You see, it is an unbroken "bow." He did not snap it across his knee. It is a bow still. Vengeance is there, justice is there; but which way is it pointed? It is turned upward; not to shoot arrows down on us, but for us, if we have faith enough to string it, and to make it our glorious bow—to draw it with all our might, to send our prayers, our praises, our desires, up to the bright throne of

112

God. Mighty is that man, omnipotent is his faith, who has power to bend that bow and draw it, and shoot his prayers to heaven.

Nay, more, inasmuch as it is a bow not black, nor blood-red, but a bow painted with the colours of holiday and delight, it seems to me as if heaven hangs out its streamers of joy, while angels sing, ''Glory to God in the highest, and on earth peace, goodwill towards men.'' *They* pull the banners from the standards of glory, and they hang them out across the sky, as *we* do on our ships upon marriage days. Heaven hangs out its glorious banners, to show that God is so completely satisfied with Christ, and so at peace with man, that He joys in man's joy, rejoices in man's rejoicing, ''rests in his love, and rejoices in us with singing.'' Look up, believer, to the person of Christ, behold the *joy* of God, ''the pleasure of the Lord'' prospering ''in his hands,'' and your soul will be full of ecstacy and delight.

Once again. In the rainbow we see the one colour of light, which appeareth to us to be but white, broken up, refracted, distributed, blended, harmonised, brought out in all its distinct elements. There is no doubt that there are more colours in light than our eyes have ever seen. The spectrum of eye can only compass a certain quantity of the colours; but beneath the lowest, and above the highest, there are others. There is infinitely more in God than you and I will ever be able to see. One of the best sights of light, as dissolved and analysed, is to be had in the rainbow. There you see the colours arranged in their proper order, and you are able to mark the red melting into the orange, and the orange into the yellow, and the yellow yet again into the green, and the green into the blue, and the blue into the indigo and the violet. They are all there—not one put out of place, not one left out. The character of God is one, like his essence; yet to us, that we may read it, it must be, as it were, broken up, but not thrown out of harmony. He that hath seen Christ ''hath seen the Father.'' He that sees the rainbow sees ''Light.'' He that sees Christ sees the Father: God's justice meeting and blending into his truth, God's truth melting into his mercy, that mercy melting into his love, that love in contact with his faithfulness; and so every attribute standing side by side with its next of kin; the whole of them absolutely necessary to complete the glory of that arch, and every one of them necessarily to be put in its proper place also, to make the arch a harmony and a very music of colours.

Beloved, such is Jesus Christ. If we could but understand Jesus

113

Christ, we could not make mistakes about *God*. In Jesus how I see blood-red justice, justice as fierce as if there were no mercy; but what love I see also! What boundless love! As Watts puts it, we cannot tell

> "Which of the letters best is writ,
> The power, the wisdom, or the grace."

They are all so clearly there. The *whole* of God written out in Christ! And yet, I warn you, we can never *see* the whole of God — in this life never. I do not know whether it is quite correct, but two or three of the older commentators, in glossing upon that passage, "there was a rainbow round about the throne," say that it means entirely round it, and that therefore there is a complete circle — that we only see one half of it, but that in fact the covenant rainbow is a circle. Now, whatever you may think of that gloss, there certainly is one circular rainbow in the Bible, for that angel, in the tenth of Revelation had "a rainbow round his head," he wore it as a crown round his head. We may, without straining a point, say, the most we can ever see even in Christ, as revealed to us, while we are here, is just a glorious semi-circle of truth — an arch, like a divine ladder, by which we may mount to the very loftiness of God himself. But there is another half which you and I have not seen, and we shall not see it till we get to the throne of God. Moreover, that rainbow that is in heaven differs from ours; for there it is "like unto an emerald." The green preponderates. The mild lustre of the mercy of God, and his love, will seem to triumph over the fiery sardus and jacinth of his justice.

3. How ought we to act, dear friends, with regard to this rainbow, and Jesus Christ as the symbol of the covenant?

First, let us act *like little children*. Little children run in clapping their hands with glee: "Father, there's a rainbow!" Out they run to look at it; and they wonder whether they could find the end of it; they wish you would let them run till they could catch it; they look, and look, and look, and look, and when the shower begins to abate and it dies out, they are so sorrowful because they have lost the splendid vision. Beloved, let us be children. Whenever we think of Christ let us be little children, and look, and look, and look again; and let us long to get at him, for, unlike the rainbow, we *can* get at *him*. Pliny, who by the way talks a deal of nonsense, declares that wherever the rainbow's foot rests the flowers are made much sweeter; and Aristotle says, the rainbow is a great breeder of honey-dew. I do not know how that is, but I know that wherever Jesus Christ is he makes the perfume of his people very sweet. "His name is as ointment poured forth," and I know *He* is "a great breeder of honey-dew." There is sure to be much more lovingkindness in that man's heart who has seen much of Jesus. I recommend you to follow that divine rainbow till you reach the foot of it, and till you embrace it, and say with Simeon, "Now let thou thy servant depart in peace, for mine eyes have seen thy salvation." Play the child then.

While we *gaze*, ought we not *praise and admire?* One or two of the nations of antiquity had it as a part of their religion always to sing hymns when they saw the rainbow. Should not we whenever we see Christ? Should it not be a red-letter day marked in our diary? "This day let us praise his name." And as we ought *always* to see him, I may improve upon this, and bid you say, —

"I will praise thee every day;
   now thine anger's passed away,
Comfortable thoughts arise from the bleeding sacrifice."

And again, when we see Christ, we ought to *confess our sin with humiliation*. An old writer says, that the Jews confess their sins when they see the rainbow. I am sure, whenever we see Christ, we ought to remember the deluge of wrath from which he has delivered us, the flames of hell from which he has saved us; and so, humbly bowing ourselves in the dust, let us love, and praise, and bless his name.

To some of you there is nothing in this sermon, because you have never laid hold on the covenant. You have never believed in Jesus. Remember, that a simple faith in Christ is the evidence of your being in the covenant. If thou believest in the Lord Jesus Christ with all thine heart, then thy name is written in the roll of the blessed; but if thou wilt not believe in him, however excellent thy character, however goodly thy works, thou shalt perish in thy sins; for "he that believeth and is baptized shall be saved; he that believeth not," be he who he may or what he may, "shall be damned." Believe, and believing, thou puttest thyself under the divine arch of the blessed

115

covenant; thou shalt see its glorious colours with exultation and delight, and thou shalt be secure, whatever catastrophies shall shake the earth, whatever calamities shall trouble the race of man.

"The Message of the Rainbow"

"I do set my bow in the cloud" — Genesis 9:13.

Whether now for the first time the bow appeared upon the cloud, or whether it had been always there since God created mist and sunshine, is a quite secondary matter. The stress of the narrative is not on the creation of the rainbow, it is on the message that the rainbow speaks. There are some books that have stood upon my shelves for years, and all these years I have seen nothing in them. But a great sorrow comes to me, or a great trial, and my eye falls on the forgotten volume, and I take it down, and every page of it is bright with new meaning now. My new experience makes a new book of it. And out of the familiar rainbow the new experience of man made a new bow. It takes a flood sometimes to open the eyes. It takes the cries and terrors of the storm to waken us to the symbols of God's covenant. Because they have no changes, therefore they fear not God. But when a man has passed through the deep waters as Noah passed, there is a new depth in the familiar Bible, there is a new meaning in the familiar bow.

Now, I want this evening to reach some of that meaning. I want you to carry home something of the rainbow's prophecy and poetry. And first this comes: what we most dread, God can illuminate.

If there was one thing full of terror to Noah, it was the cloud. You cannot realise what awful memories spoke to him out of these black and thunderous banks. He saw the horrors of the Flood again, he heard the cries of infuriated beasts, he lived through all that wreckage of death, whenever the great clouds came rolling up. How a man dreads the lightning when it has struck his child! How the poor women of Galveston will wake with a cry when the wind howls at night, and think of the storm that ruined life for them! How Noah, with the fearful memories of the flood, would tremble at the raincloud in the sky! Yet it was *there* that the Almighty set his bow. It

116

was that very terror He illuminated. He touched with the radiance of His master-hand the very object that was the dread of Noah.

And a kind God is always doing that. What we most dread, He can illuminate. We thought it would be dark, almost unbearable, and there has been the bow upon the cloud. How often have we said, Ah, if that fell on us, we could not stand it. And it has fallen on us, that very thing, the thing we dreaded, that haunted us in dreams, and God has set His rainbow on the cloud. Was there ever anything more dreaded than the cross, that symbol of disgrace in an old world, that foulest punishment, that last indignity that could be cast upon a slave? And Christ has so illumined that thing of terror, that the one hope today for sinful men, and the one type and model of the holiest life, is nothing else than that. Was there ever anything more dreaded than the cross? Yes, perhaps one thing—death. But, 'O death, where is thy sting? O grave, where is thy victory?' We are begotten into an everlasting hope, and the rainbow of immortality is on the cloud. It is a fine aphorism in that fine book, *Guesses at Truth,* that while the ancients dreaded death, the Christian only fears dying. For a risen Christ has set His bow upon the cloud, and what men dreaded, God illuminates.

But now another lesson, and it is this: there is unchanging purpose in the most changeful things. All things are changeful, even the very hills. But in the whole of nature there is scarce anything so changeful as the clouds. Did you ever mark them when the wind was whistling? Did you ever follow the cloud race under the stars? We see the clouds, and there is one artist in a thousand who can paint the clouds; but not for two seconds on end, so we are taught, are the form and outline of any cloud the same. What a strange tablet for the pen of God! What a strange parchment for the symbol of that covenant that is to be unchanging and for ever! Engrave it upon brass, and it will stand. Write it on marble, and it will breast the ages. But God says, No, but My unchanging covenant with man is to be painted on the ever-changing cloud! Is not that strange? When poor John Keats was dying, you remember the sentence that he would have them write upon his tombstone in the little churchyard at Rome: "Here lies one whose name was writ in water." But God, living and full of power, would have His name and covenant upon the cloud.

And if that means anything, surely it is this: that through all

117

change, and movement, and recasting, run the eternal purposes of God. Happy the nation that has risen to that! Happy the woman who cherishes that faith! It is through the infinite changes of the universe that creation is moving to its far-off purpose. It is through the endless resettings of its life that every nation struggles to its ideal. It is through the lights and shadows of your little day, and the varying duty, and the shifting mood, and the tears, and the smiles, and the crosses, and the graves, — it is through these, swift, changeable as any cloud, that the unchangeable purposes of love and mercy, which far in eternity were willed for you in Christ, are moving, and growing to their triumph.

But I lift my eyes up to that bow again, and I am taught another lesson now: there is meaning in the mystery of life. I think it would be hard to find a literature in which that cloudland has not stood for mystery. I think it would be hard to find a child that has not built its palaces, and seen its marching armies, and caught a glimpse of ships upon the sea, all in that cloudy kingdom of the sky. The oldest poem and the youngest child feel something of the mystery of clouds. I could understand a southerner being light-hearted, for he has lived and sung under that open blue. But if I want a man on whom has fallen the mystery of things, I go to one who has been crooned and cradled where the grey mists come creeping up the glen, and the heavy clouds come down over the hills. It is no chance that the sense and feeling of mystery should be so strong among these Highland dwellings, where the chasms are shrouded and the summits are hid. Clouds are the symbol, clouds are the spring of mystery.

And so, when God sets his bow upon the cloud, I believe that there is meaning in life's mystery. I am like a man travelling among the hills, and *there* is a precipice and I know it not, and yonder is a chasm where many a man has perished, and I cannot see it. But on the clouds that hide, God lights His rainbow; and the ends of it are here on earth, and the crown of it is lifted up to heaven. And I feel that God is with me in the gloom, and there is meaning in life's mystery for me. O heart, bowed with the inscrutable mysteries of things, have you felt that?

> I trace the rainbow thro' the rain,
> And feel the promise is not vain,
> That morn shall tearless be!

118

But there is another message of the bow. It tells me that the background of joy is sorrow. I remember reading in the life of Frederic Robertson of Brighton some memorable words. If ever there was a brave man, it was Frederic Robertson. He was the last to take a pessimistic view of anything. Yet he said this: "The deep undertone of the world is sadness. A solemn bass recurring at measured intervals, and heard through all other tones. Ultimately all the strains of this world's music resolve themselves into that tone, and I believe," he says, "that only the cross interprets the mournful mystery of life."

And one has only to walk with open eyes to feel that Frederic Robertson is right. Laughter is real, thank God. And joys innumerable flash like the swallows under the eaves of the most humble life. But God has painted His rainbow on the cloud, and back of its glories yonder is the mist. And underneath life's gladness is an unrest, and a pain that we cannot well interpret, and a sorrow that is born we know not how. Will the cross of Calvary interpret life if the deepest secret of all life is merriment? Shall the Man of Sorrows be the ideal of man if laughter is the undertone of all? Impossible! I cannot look at the rainbow on the cloud, I cannot see the Saviour on the cross, but I feel that back of gladness there is agony, and that the richest joy is born of sorrow.

And this last not least. This to take with you to your homes. This to lie down to sleep with and waken with when tomorrow morning breaks. This message of the bow never forget: there is mercy over the portal of God's dwelling. For what are the clouds in Scripture? They are God's pavilion. What were the clouds to this old Hebrew prophet? They were the Almighty's tent, His tabernacle. "He cometh in a cloud." "Clouds and thick darkness are about His throne." "Out of the cloud there came a voice." And there God set His bow, and His bow is the token of mercy to the world. And I feel that in this early dawn the poet-prophet had got the mind of Christ, and had seen mercy written on God's dwelling-place.

Have you seen that, my brother? Have you seen that, my sister? It is the sweetest syllable that ever fell from heaven into the bosom of a guilty world. O sinful heart, prayerless and God-forgetting, there is mercy, mercy, mercy for you tonight. The dwelling-place of God is bright with it. And the heart of God is full of it. And the entreaties of Jesus Christ are throbbing with it. Who will go out into the crowded streets under the stars tonight crying for the first time for years, "God be merciful to me a sinner"?

Will you?

Something to Do

1. Why do you think Spurgeon spent so much time on the *fact* of the covenant before dealing with the *symbol* of the rainbow? (Note that he also closes with a reference to the covenant.) Is there a principle here for us to follow?

2. How do Spurgeon and Morrison each deal with the clouds and the rain? Do you think their treatment is satisfactory?

3. Generally speaking, Spurgeon approaches the theme doctrinally while Morrison treats it more devotionally. Spurgeon's is the longer sermon; but apart from that, do both preachers accomplish their purpose and deal with the passage satisfactorily?

4. Are the two approaches affected by the fact that Spurgeon preached to a Sunday morning congregation but Morrison to a Sunday evening congregation? Or are the sermons only reflecting the personal styles of the preachers? What might Morrison have changed if he were preaching to a Sunday morning congregation? Should the nature of the meeting help determine the approach of the message?

5. Is this a good choice for a text or should preachers avoid building whole sermons on a biblical symbol? How can the preacher avoid extreme allegorizing of the symbol?

6. It was said of Spurgeon that no matter what text he chose, he headed as rapidly as possible to Christ and the cross; and he does this in the first paragraph of the message. Do both men preach the Gospel clearly?

10

"As an Eagle...
the Lord...Did Lead"
G. Campbell Morgan

"The Divine Discipline"
Charles Haddon Spurgeon

"The Eagle and Its Brood"
Alexander Maclaren

GEORGE CAMPBELL MORGAN (1863–1945) lacked formal training for the ministry but so applied himself to disciplined Bible study that he became known in England and America as "the prince of expositors." He began as an itinerant evangelist, was rejected by the Methodists (they said he couldn't preach) but ordained by the Congregationalists, and during his long life published more than sixty books and booklets. Twice he pastored Westminster Chapel, London (1904–

121

1917; 1933–1943), and during his second term there, his associate was Dr. D. Martyn Lloyd-Jones who became his successor.

A "nomad" by nature, Morgan seemed to prefer itinerant ministry to the settled work of the pastorate. Even while pastor of Westminster Chapel, he often preached elsewhere between Sundays. His famous Friday night Bible class at Westminster regularly drew 2,000 people. Many of his sermons are found in *The Westminster Pulpit,* originally published in ten volumes by Hodder and Stoughton, London. The official biography is *Campbell Morgan: A Man of the Word,* by his daughter-in-law Jill Morgan.

This sermon is from volume 10 of *The Westminster Pulpit,* pages 263–74.

Spurgeon preached "The Divine Discipline" on Thursday evening, May 9, 1867, at the Metropolitan Tabernacle in London. However, it was not published as part of the Tabernacle's weekly series until January 2, 1913; and therefore it is found in volume 59 of *The Metropolitan Tabernacle Pulpit* (p. 1). Note that the word "discipline" in the title refers to training and maturing and not to punishment.

Alexander Maclaren (1826–1910) pastored the Union Chapel, Manchester, England, from 1858 to 1903 and was widely known as a gifted expositor of the Word. His monumental *Expositions of Holy Scripture* is a set that should be in every preacher's library. However, read Maclaren *after* you have prepared your own message, because you will be tempted to preach Maclaren's message! Many times I have read Maclaren and said, "Now, why didn't I see that?"

Maclaren did not participate in denominational activities or spend time attending committee meetings or conferences. His life focus was preaching the Word of God, which, by the way, he always studied in the original languages. Many of his sermons have three divisions, and he claimed that he "fed [his] people with a three-pronged fork."

"The Eagle and Its Brood" is taken from *Triumphant Certainties and Other Sermons,* by Alexander Maclaren, published in 1902 by Funk and Wagnalls.

"As an Eagle . . . the Lord . . . Did Lead."

As an eagle that stirreth up her nest,
That fluttereth over her young,
He spread abroad his wings, he took them,
He bare them on his pinions:
The Lord alone did lead him.
Deuteronomy 32:11-12a.

These words are taken from the swan song of Moses. In that song there is a remarkable alternation between praise and blame. It celebrates the goodness and faithfulness of God; it chronicles the wickedness and unfaithfulness of His people.

Calling to mind how God had found the people in a desert land, in the waste howling wilderness, and given them among the nations the place of prosperity and privilege, the singer employed this pictorial method of setting forth the way of the Divine government. It is peculiarly a figure of the wilderness, where for forty years Moses had kept his flocks. Probably he had often watched the eagles with their brood on some rocky height or sweeping over the broad and silent expanses. It was a daring figure, but he was warranted in using it, for forty years before he sang this song God Himself had employed it in speaking to him: "I bare you on eagles' wings, and brought you unto Myself."

The Bible is full of fine figures of speech and parabolic illustrations of the various aspects of the Divine government; but in all that it is intended to teach, none is more simple and sublime than this. It thrills with tenderness and with strength. It makes us conscious of the passion and power and purpose of God in all His dealings with those whom He loves.

First, let us observe the comparison broadly. In the eleventh verse we have a picture of the eagles in their activities, the mother stirring up her young, fluttering over them, the father spreading abroad his wings, taking the young and bearing them on his pinions. These words reveal to us the activities of the eagles, but they do not suggest their purpose. In the first phrase of the next verse we have a revelation of God's purpose — "The Lord . . . did lead him" — but there is no suggestion as to His activities, as to His methods. In the figure we discover the activities of the eagles: in the declaration we find the purpose of God. When we allow the first part of the text to be illuminated by the second, and the second by the first, we have the figure in its completeness. The purpose of the eagles is revealed by what is said concerning the purpose of the Lord. Why is this eagle stirring up her nest, fluttering over her young? Why is this eagle spreading abroad his wings, taking them, bearing them on his pinions? In order that they may lead the eaglets, in order that they may guide them. The activities of the Lord are revealed by what is said concerning the activities of the eagles. How does He lead His people? He stirs up their nests, He broods over them, He spreads His wings before them, He catches them on His wings, and carries them.

In the text, then, in its entirety, we have a revelation of God, a revelation of His activities in government, and a revelation of His purpose through those activities.

First, let us consider the revelation of God. There is a touch of genuine Eastern color about this. In the Bible, the eagle is more than once employed as the symbol of Deity. When Ezekiel was in captivity on the banks of the river Chebar he had a vision of God, and in the midst of the flashing glory of the light, and amid the turning of the mystic wheels, he saw faces: the face of the lion, the face of the ox, the face of a man, and the face of an eagle, all being manifestations of life proceeding from God, having its origin in God. Authority was suggested by the face of the lion; service, by that of the ox; the highest form of creation, by that of the man; while the eagle, with unflinching eyes, and wings spread for flight into the abysmal depths of mysteries that are beyond human ken, was the symbol of Deity. When, long after, the seer of the Galilean lake was imprisoned in Patmos, washed by the waters of the sea, he saw a door open in heaven, and round about the throne four living ones having the same faces that Ezekiel saw, the faces of the lion, the ox, the man, and the eagle. The Fathers of the Church interpreted the Gospel narratives by this symbolism, not always agreeing in their placing of the signs, but all making the eagle the symbol of John. For myself, I find in Matthew the face of the lion of the tribe of Judah, the King; in Mark, the face of the ox, pointing to service, priesthood, sacrifice; in Luke, the face of a man, the highest glory in God's creation; and in John, the face of the eagle, the symbol of Deity.

In our text, all the mystic wonder of the symbolism is brought down to simplest terms. Let us watch the scene as therein described. First, the mother eagle is seen doing a strange thing, stirring up the nest, the nest in which the eaglets, having been fed, are sleeping, and will sleep on until they are hungry again. The word "stirreth" is, undoubtedly, an accurate one here, but its root meaning is suggestive: the mother is awakening the birds, disturbing them in their slumber. Next, she is seen fluttering over her young, and the word "fluttering" means—and I prefer to use it—brooding. She is brooding over the birds she has disturbed. Then the father bird is seen spreading his wings in the air. The mother has wakened the eaglets, she has made them conscious of her mother heart as she brooded over them; and now the father spreads his wings, and the eaglets try to do the same thing—they flutter and stumble, and fall. Now the last phase is seen, the father is beneath them, has caught them on his wings, and is bearing them back.

That is God, said the singer of the olden time, and that is how God deals with His people. What, then, does this figure reveal to us of God? It is, first of all, a revelation of His Parenthood, that is, of the Motherhood of God and of the Fatherhood of God. The personal pronoun "He" is capitalized at the beginning of the third and fourth lines of this eleventh verse simply to conform to the rules of poetry, and not to suggest that the figure merges into a direct description of the activity of God at that point. The masculine pronoun is undoubtedly accurate, and thus we see the mother and father, the mother bird disturbing the eaglets and brooding over them, while the father bird spreads his wings, and presently bears them on his pinions. As an eagle stirreth up her nest, the feminine; fluttereth over her young, the feminine; he, the masculine, spread abroad his wings, and he, the masculine, bare them on his pinions. Thus we have a revelation of that supreme and glorious fact, that in God fatherhood and motherhood merge. We have never grasped the fullest fact concerning God until we have recognized the double truth.

Look at the eagles again as they are seen with their young, and mark them well. The eaglets are of the very being and nature of the

125

eagles, and therefore are the supreme objects of the love of the mother bird as she broods over them, and of the father bird as he spreads his great wings before them. Here also the figure holds good. Man is of the very being and nature of God, and therefore he is the supreme object of God's love. This is the poetic and beautiful suggestion of this picture of the eagles with the eaglets. As the eagles love the eaglets because they are of their very nature and being, so God loves man because he is of God's very nature, of His very Being. This is fundamental. It is only in proportion as we grasp this underlying truth that all the beauty of that which follows will be apprehended. All that we see in the picture, the disturbing of the young birds, the brooding over them, the spreading of the wings, and the carrying on the pinions, all must be interpreted by motherhood and fatherhood.

But, again, as I watch the eagles at their work I am impressed with their strength and the consequent security of the eaglets. Watch the eagles' wings in the storm. They seem to beat back the rushing of the wind and master it, or travel with it in excellency of strength. Watch the eagles' wings in the hour of conflict, and see with what skill they beat down the foe that would harm the eaglets. Watch the wings as they brood over the eaglets, and mark their gentleness. Gentleness is not weakness; gentleness is strength held in restraint. We talk, said George Matheson, of the gentleness of the brook. The brook has no gentleness. It rushes and roars down its way over the pebbles. If we would speak of gentleness let us stand on the beach and see the mighty ocean with silver foam kiss the feet of the little child that plays on the shore. That is gentleness.

That is the true picture of God. Listen to some of the ancient singers:

Hide me under the shadow of Thy wings.
The children of men take refuge under the shadow of Thy wings.
I will take refuge under the covert of Thy wings.
Under the shadow of Thy wings will I rejoice.

Or listen to another, who employs the same figure, but in another way. Singing of God, he said:

He flew swiftly upon the wings of the wind.

The wings of the eagle seem stronger than the wind, but when this singer used the figure he magnificently modified it, and made the wind itself the wings of God:

He flew swiftly upon the wings of the wind.

When, then, did He fly swiftly on the wings of the wind? This is what the singer said:

In my distress I called upon the Lord.

That was when "He flew swiftly upon the wings of the wind."

The glorious strength of God is such that the figure breaks down, and the metaphor fails, and we are left face to face with the naked fact, and of the consequent security of all those who are underneath His wings as they brood, or over His wings as He carries them.

In the figure there is, at least, a suggestion of the nature of God. What is the nature of the eagle? It dwells on high, and it takes its flight sunward, with eyes that never flinch as they are fixed on the light. But here supremely the figure suggests, and then breaks down; and whenever a figure thus breaks down it is fulfilling its highest function, for it is leading us beyond itself to the fact which it is intended to suggest. The eagle is the mystic sign of Deity because of its flight to the heights; but there the figure halts, for God is the ultimate height. The eagle is the symbol of Deity, because with unflinching gaze it beholds the light of the sun and soars into it, until human eyes can no longer follow it; but there the figure breaks down, for God is the light.

But now let us consider the activities of the eagles as representing the activities of God in His government. The first activity is suggested by the words: "As an eagle that stirreth up her nest"; that is disturbance. The next, by the words: "That broodeth over her young"; that is love assuring the disturbed ones that it is still active. The next, by the words: "He spread abroad his wings"; that is inspiration and illustration in order that those disturbed should be taught to fly. The last, by the words: "He took them, he bare them on his pinions"; that is protection that comes when, essaying to obey inspiration and illustration, the eaglets flutter and fall.

These are the elements of the Divine government of human lives.

The first is ever that of disturbance. The life that is never disturbed by God is dying and withering and falling. God is forever more stirring up the nest, rousing us from our lethargy, lest, perchance, we also should become like Jeshurun, who waxed fat and kicked in his sleekness, forgetting not God only, but his own manhood. God disturbs the place of our abode; the home is stricken, and we are flung out. Our plans, so carefully and so prayerfully made, are broken down. Our very conceptions, the highest and the best, have to be reconsidered, and we discover that somewhere in our highest thinking we were wrong. God plunges us into a maelstrom in order that we may know how wrong we were. Our very service, the highest service we can render, service which He has appointed, is suddenly interfered with by the changing of our strength to weakness, or by a command that we relinquish it for another that seems less important. God is always disturbing us.

There is nothing more perilous than forming a false estimate of the meaning of disturbed life, that we should say of some soul who, through long years has always been tempest-tossed, buffeted, hurled hither and thither by storms, that there must be something wrong with him. It may be that God is preparing that soul for larger vision, clearer seeing of the light, and upward movement toward heights to which we have never mounted. As the eagle stirs up the nest, and will not allow the eaglets to settle into the lethargy of a sleep that follows feeding, so God stirs up the nest, takes away the loved one, brings into the midst of life the pain and shadow of suffering, contradicts our highest plans, hurls us out from the place where we love to be, makes us feel the sweeping of the storm, and so prevents the fatal lethargies that destroy.

But that is not all. The eagle also "broodeth over her young." The figure is the more striking in that it so closely follows the other. Probably, if I had been writing this, I should have put it the other way: first, the brooding, and then the disturbing, and this because I know neither the eagle nor God as perfectly as did Moses. He knew both. He had watched the eagle, and he knew God. The first thing is disturbance, and then the brooding over the young. Here we cannot be too realistic in our imagination. Look carefully at that eyrie on the rocky height. There are the eaglets and the mother bird, and she disturbs them who fain would sleep in the quietness that follows feeding; she will not have it so, she wakes them, she pushes them with her wings to the very edge of the nest, and presently will push them out. Then, as they are puzzled and fearful, she flutters over them, she broods over them, she says to them, in effect: Yes, I have disturbed you, but I am your mother! She broodeth over her young. That, also, is a picture of God. He disturbs, but He gives to the soul an immediate qualification of the disturbance, not by explaining its meaning, but by assuring the heart concerning Himself. Nothing is more wonderful than this. Souls that are struggling, but who, nevertheless, believe in God, are constantly made conscious of this brooding love of God. Again and again, during these months of desolation and disturbance, when some loved one has been taken away, plans have been broken up, and all that looked so fair has become desolate, have we heard it said: "I cannot understand it; but I am perfectly sure of His love. It is the Lord, let Him do what seemeth to Him good!" What has inspired the word? God—God brooding over the heart, giving the heart that knowledge of Himself, offering no explanation of the meaning of the disturbance, but assuring the troubled soul that there is a meaning in it, that there is wisdom in it. "The Lord gave, and the Lord hath taken away." Why has He taken away? I do not know, I cannot tell, I cannot see the meaning of it; it seems to have no meaning! But "blessed be the name of the Lord." When the soul says that, it is because God, like a mother, broods over the heart, and whispers the sweet secret into the soul: "As one whom his mother comforteth, so will I comfort you."

But the figure moves on in its revelation of the Divine activity. The mother eagle who has disturbed, and who has fluttered broodingly over the young, now watches; and the father spreads abroad his wings. By this act he is insisting on the fulfilment of the purpose of the disturbance and the brooding of the mother. He spreads his wings in front of them, they being now fully awake, and fully comforted. She waked them when she disturbed them, comforted them when she brooded over them. Now, in effect, he says: This is what we mean. He spreads his wings, and by inherent instinct, the eaglets begin to spread their wings. As in imagination, we watch them, we cannot help laughing at them, their movements are so grotesque. I am sure the mother and the father laugh at them with that tender sympathetic laughter that is always in the heart of parents for the follies of child life.

All that also is a true picture of God, Who is always going before us, and yet is ever near enough to show us how to do the things He demands if we are but looking at Him. Too often the trouble with us is that we are not watching our God. If we were doing so we should find that when He has disturbed us, comforted us, He will show us what He means, and so help us to spread our wings.

I watch the eaglets doing it, fearful as they find themselves flung out of the nest; in the element of the air, so strange to them, they begin to beat with their wings, but they are going down, they are falling. Now comes the last phase of the revelation. The father swoops beneath them, catches them on his broad pinions. They try and fail, but they never fall! In their trying and their failing he is nigh, and when they fail and would fall, he is beneath them, bearing them on his pinions. That process is repeated until the day comes when the eaglets will not want the father underneath; their own wings will find their strength, and they will fly. So with us. We shall fail, but we shall not fall. Our attempts will seem grotesque to us, and to others who watch us, but our Father will always catch us on His wings, and bear us up.

Finally, let us consider the purpose revealed by the figure. What are the eagles doing with the eaglets? The eagles are developing the eaglets' natural powers. They are eagles too. What is God doing in His government of our lives? He is developing our natural powers. Man is made for God; he is in the Divine image and likeness. By all God's government, by His disturbing of us, by His brooding over us, by His guidance of us, when on His wings He is catching us when we fail and flutter and fall; by all these things He is bringing us to the fulfilment of our own destiny, to the realization of our own manhood. The supreme tragedy of human life is that man thinks so much less of himself than God thinks of him.

> Man is not flesh, man is not flesh, but fire!
> His senses cheat him, and his vision lies.
> Swifter and keener than his soul's desire,
> The flame that mothers him eludes his eyes.

That is why God disturbs him. God wakes man from the lethargy which oftentimes comes from overfeeding, from the attempt to satisfy the life with the things of dust. The purpose of the Divine government is to end weakness. Only by flight can eagles fly, only by struggle can strength be gained. That is an illuminative story of the boy who came to his mother with the chrysalis of a glorious butterfly. He knew something of the beauty that was hidden there; he had been told about it. He watched the chrysalis until he saw it beginning to burst; he observed the struggle, and a mistaken pity in his heart said, Oh, let me help it! Then with scissors he snipped the chrysalis, and made it easy! With what result? Those gorgeous wings were never spread! You cannot help the butterfly; from the chrysalis it must struggle to the glory of its final beauty.

So also man can come to the final dignity of his own being and the fulness of the meaning of his own life only as God disturbs him, rouses him from the lethargy which means death. By all the processes of stain and stress and disturbance, by His brooding love, by the inspiration of His outspread wings as He lures us toward flight, by the great strength with which He swoops beneath us and catches us on His pinions, by all this He is perfecting our strength and leading us to the heights as He develops within us His own thought for us.

In its first application, the word of the singer is national. It was to a nation that this thing was said. Oh the peril, the ghastly peril of failing to fulfil national destiny by reason of prosperity! No nation ever failed to fulfil its destiny because of adversity. It is prosperity that blasts a nation. Jeshurun waxed fat and kicked. He became sleek and forgot God. That was the trouble threatening our own nation, and therefore I say it with great solemnity, we thank God when He disturbs us. He is waking us from our lethargy that we may find our wings and reach the heights.

But if the first application is to the nation, the application of the song is also personal. Let it sing to us the sacred story of our own dignity. Let it argue His meaning as He disturbs us, and broods over us. Let us trust and obey, knowing that if we fail and fall, His pinions will be underneath; and if we wake with the horror of the disturbance His wings will be over us. The day will come when we shall spread our wings and find the meaning of God and the meaning of our own lives.

Developing a Christian Imagination

"The Divine Discipline"

"As an eagle stirreth up her nest, fluttereth over her young, spreadeth abroad her wings, taketh them, beareth them on her wings: so the Lord alone did lead him, and there was no strange god with him."—Deuteronomy 32:11-12.

Moses in this chapter is speaking concerning Israel in the wilderness. When the great host came out of Egypt, they were, through the debasing influences of slavery—which are not easily or quickly shaken off—not much better than a mere mob. They were not at all fitted to march at once to take possession of Canaan, nor to take part in the compacts of organised social life. Therefore God, instead of taking them by the short way along which they might have passed in a very few days, ordained it so in his providence that they should wander about for forty years in the wilderness—partly, it is true, as a punishment for their unbelief, but also in order that the nation might be trained and educated for its future destiny; made as fit as it could be, to be the custodian of the oracles of truth, and to be the receiver of the revelation which God intended to give to men.

If you will read carefully over the history of the children of Israel in the wilderness, I think you will see that the practical training which God adopted was, if they had been right-minded men, splendidly adapted to bring them to the very highest state of spiritual life. In some respects it was weak through their flesh, but the method itself was superlatively excellent. Here was a people taken away from the multitude of gods which they had been wont to see on every hand in Egypt, and they were taught to reverence an unseen God for whom they had no symbol whatsoever for some time; and afterwards, when symbolical worship in some form was ordained, yet there was still so little of symbol that Moses could say, "They saw no similitude." They were trained to worship a spiritual God—in spirit and in truth. They never saw him, but every morning they had the best testimonies of his existence, for round about the camp lay the manna like hoar-frost, or dew, upon the ground. Their feet waxed not weary, neither did their garments become old all those years, and thus about their very clothes on their bodies, and before them on their tables, they had constant proofs of the great God existing and caring for the sons of men. The whole of their training,

132

whilst it educated and developed their patience and their faith, had also the high purpose of teaching them gratitude, and to bind them by the cords of love and the bands of a man to the service of God. It was not because the training was not wise in the highest degree, but because they were children that were corrupters, and, like ourselves, an evil and stiff-necked generation, that they did not learn, even when God himself became their Teacher.

Now in drawing a parallel between the children of Israel and ourselves, we shall invite you to notice, first, in the text: *the Divine Instructor,* "the Lord alone did lead them;" and then *the method of instruction illustrated:* they were trained as an eagle trains the eaglet for their flight. First, then, we have —

I. A DIVINE INSTRUCTOR.

The Israelites had for their guide, instructor, and tutor, in order to prepare them for Canaan, none other than Jehovah himself. He might employ Moses and Aaron, and he did also make use of those marvellous picture-books, if I may so call them, of sacrifice, and type, and metaphor, but still God himself was their guide and their instructor. And it is so with us. The Holy Spirit is the teacher of the Christian Church. Although he useth this Book, of which we can never speak too highly, although he useth still the ministry of the Word, for which we are thankful as for a candlestick which we trust may never be taken out of its place, still our true teacher is God the Holy Ghost. He instructeth us in the truth, and, meanwhile it is also God who in the rulings and guidings of providence, is our Instructor if we will but learn; teaching us sometimes by sweet mercies, and at other times by bitter afflictions, instructing us from our cradles to our graves, if we will but open our eyes to see and our ears to hear the lessons which he writes and speaks. We, alas! are often as the horse and as the mule which have no understanding; and will not be taught by the providential teachings, but still we have God to be our teacher, and it is none other than our heavenly Father who is daily training us for the skies. If we be indeed his children, and can say, "Our Father, which art in heaven," we may also go to him as our Teacher, believing he will yet, notwithstanding all our folly, make us "meet to be partakers of the inheritance of the saints in light."

The text speaks of "the Lord alone." Brethren, it is well for us that in providence we are led by "the Lord alone." There is an overruling hand after all, notwithstanding our follies and our wilfulness, so that God's purposes are ultimately fulfilled. But I wish this were more true to our consciousness, that we are led by "the Lord alone;" I mean that we waited upon him at every step of life. I am persuaded that the holiest of characters take more matters to God than you and I are accustomed to do: I mean they not only consult him, as we do, upon certain great and critical occasions; but those saints who live nearest to Christ, go to him about little matters, thinking nothing to be too trifling to tell into the ear of Christ.

Some things about which they will not even consult their kindest and wisest human friends will be matters of consultation between them and their Saviour. Oh, what mistakes we should escape, what disasters we should avoid, if "the Lord alone" did guide us: and if we watched the signs of his hands in guiding us, if our eyes were to him as the eyes of the handmaidens are to their mistress, anxious to know the Lord's will, and saying ever to our own self-love, "Down, down, busy will; down thou proud spirit! What wouldest *thou* have me to do, my Master, for thy will shall be my will, and my heart shall ever give up its fondest wish, when once I understand what thy will is concerning me." Beloved, I am afraid that some strange god is often with us, even with us who are the people of God. We are united to God, and he will gladly teach us, and from him alone should we learn; but oftentimes we harbour in our heart idolatrous thoughts. All selfishness is idolatry; all repining against the providence of God hath in it the element of rebellion against the Most High. If I love my own will, and if I desire my own way in preference to God's way, I have made a god of my own wisdom, or my own affection, and I have not been true in my loyalty to the only living and true God, even Jehovah. Let us search, and look, and see if there be not some strange god with us. It may be hidden away, perhaps, and we may scarce know it; it may be hidden, too, in that very part of us where our dearest affections dwell. Some Rachel may be sitting in the tent on the camel furniture under which the false gods are concealed. Let us, therefore, make a thorough search, and then invite the Great King himself to aid us. "Search me, O God, try me, and know my ways, and see if there be any wicked way in me, and lead me in the way everlasting."

The great truth which I want to bring forward, if I can, is this: that God in his providence and in grace, as far as we have been made

134

willing to learn of him, is educating us for something higher than this world. This world is the nature in which we dwell. Sometimes we who love the Lord, mount up from it with wings as eagles, but we do not keep on the wing. We drop again: we cleave to earth. 'Tis our mother, and it seems as though we can never rise permanently above our kinship to it. Very powerful is it in its attraction over us. Down we come again. We have not yet learned to keep up yonder, where the atmosphere is clear, and where the smoke of the world's cares will not reach us. But God is educating us for the skies. The meaning of these trials of yours, the interpretation of your sorrows, is this: God is preparing you for another state, making you fit to dwell with angels and archangels, and the spirits of the just made perfect. If this earth were all, then, your teachers at school, or your tutors when you passed through college, might have sufficed; but this world is but the vestibule to the next, and if you know, as well as man can teach you, how to play your part here with a view only to secular advancement, yet are you not educated at all in the highest sense. God himself must teach and train you, that you may be fit to sit among the princes of the blood-royal before his throne, and to have communion with those celestial spirits who—

> With songs and choral symphonies
> Day without night circle his throne rejoicing.

God is teaching you. God alone can do it, and he will do it, but take care that you put away all strange gods, and give yourselves up wholly to his guidance, submitting your will and your affections, and all parts of your spirit and nature to his teaching; that so you may be found fully ready when he shall say, "Come up hither to dwell with me forever." Now, passing from that, we shall notice very briefly indeed—

II. THE METHODS OF THE DIVINE INSTRUCTION.

These methods of divine instruction are given to us under the very poetical picture of the eagle training its young ones for flight. God, to accommodate himself to our poor understandings, sometimes compares himself to a father with children, at other times to a mother with her little ones; sometimes even to an animal. In this case, even to a bird of prey, so that we may but learn no depths of condescension are too great for the Great Teacher. He compares

135

himself here, then, to the eagle. I suppose that Moses was well acquainted with the eagle's natural habits. He describes it, first of all, *as stirring up its nest,* as though the young birds were loth to stir from their pleasant home. Having from the time of their birth been quiet and happy there, they had no anxiety whatever to try the blue unfathomable oceans of the air. They had no wish to leave the rocky refuge where they had been reared. They feared, perhaps, lest they might fall over the precipices and be dashed in pieces. Therefore is it said, "The eagle stirreth up her nest." She makes it uncomfortable for the little ones, so that they may be willing to quit it, and that which would have been obnoxious and burdensome to them, they may come even to desire, namely, to be out of the nest. Someone has quaintly said, that the eagle puts thorns into the nest, which prick the fledgelings, so that they are anxious to get away.

Certain it is that God does thus with those he would train for the skies. He stirs up their nest. Cannot some of you recollect times when your nests were stirred *by providential dealings* while you were in sin? All things went well with you for a season, but you forgot God, and his son Jesus had no attractions for you. But suddenly the child sickened or the wife was smitten with death, or trade separated from you, or you yourselves were ill, or there was a famine in the land. Then it was, when you were in want, your nest being thoroughly stirred up, that you said, "I will arise and go unto my Father." The land of Goshen was like a nest to the Israelites. They had no desire to come out of it, but God stirred them up by means of Pharaoh, who kept them in heavy bondage, put them to brickmaking, and then to make bricks without straw, and then slew their male children. In all sorts of ways they were made to cry out under the bitter yoke. We know that they loved that nest, for they often longed to be back in it. They talked of the leeks, and the garlic, and the onions, and the cucumbers which they did eat when they were in Egypt, so that the nest seems to have been a tolerably downy one to them at one time. But God so stirred it up, that they longed to be away, and even the howling wilderness seemed a paradise compared with the house of bondage. So was it with you. You found that the world was not what it seemed to be. Troubles increased, providential afflictions trod on each other's heels, and then you turned unto your God, and bethought yourselves of your sins. And so he stirred up your nest, *by inward trouble under conviction of sin.* I know my soul's nest was very soft once. I thought I had done no great evil, that I had kept God's commandments from my youth up. But when conviction of sin came, then I discovered my heart to be deceitful above all things, and desperately wicked. Then my sins, like so many daggers, were at my heart, My soul was rent: I could say with gracious George Herbert—

> My thoughts are all a case of knives,
> Wounding my heart.

There was no rest, no peace, no joy, no comfort to be found. Well, that was God stirring up the nest. If there are any of you in that condition now—uneasy and troubled about sin, I am glad of it. Your nest is being stirred, and God grant that you may fly from it and never come back to that nest again!

If all had gone smoothly with you, if sin had always been a sweet morsel to your tongue, we might despair of your ever being saved; but now you feel the smart of it, I trust it is, in order that you may be delivered from the guilt of it, and led to find a Saviour. Well, since that, dear friends, how many times we have had our nests stirred up! I do not know your history, but you do, and I ask you now to look it over. Oh, you planned, and planned, and planned, and said, "Now I shall live in this house for the next twenty or thirty years; I shall live here, certainly, as long as I live anywhere," and now you find yourselves, perhaps, fifty or a hundred miles from it. You were in the service of a certain kind man, and you felt very happy in it, but the firm has broken up, and where are you now? There is that dear child you have set your heart upon; you have said, "What a mercy it will be to see him growing up! What a comfort he will be to me!" He is not a comfort to you, but just the very reverse, for he is your greatest sorrow. It is God stirring up your nest. Whereas a few years ago you were in good, sound health, now the eyes begin to fail, or the ears are giving way, or there is some internal complaint, or some constant pain. Whereas years ago you were a master, you are now a servant; whereas years ago everybody looked up to you, now everybody looks down upon you. It is all the stirring up of the nest, because you have no abiding city here; because you were too prone to say, "My mountain standeth firm; I shall never be moved," therefore God has stirred up your nest, and he will do it yet again and again. Between now and heaven how many times will the nest of ours be stirred? Oh, blessed be God for it! "Moab is settled upon his lees: he hath not been emptied from vessel to vessel"; and then comes a curse upon him. Sometimes these long periods of prosperity, and rest, and ease are very unhealthy for us poor unworthy and sinful beings. If we were more like Jesus, if we were more pure and heavenly, we could bear prosperity; but because we are so sinful, I question if any of us can bear it long. If the Master shall give some of us outward prosperity, he will have to whip us behind the door in private, to keep us right. We must have some thorn in the flesh, some secret grief: there must be some skeleton in the cupboard, some spectre in some chamber of the house, or else we shall say, "Soul, take thine ease, thou hast much goods laid up for many years," and when we do this we shall be modern fools, like the great fool of old. But the gracious Lord will not let his people get into that state. Again and again, and yet again, against their wishes, and contrary to their expectations, he will stir their nest, and they shall cry out against it, but if they did but only know the meaning of it, or could read the whole of it in the light of eternity, they would bless the hand which tears away their comforts, seeing divine wisdom and infinite affection in it all. That, then, is the first thing: God instructs his people to mount aloft by stirring up their nests.

The next picture is *the eagle fluttering over her young*. What is that for? She wants them to mount, my brethren. Well, then, in order to teach them to mount she first mounts herself, "she fluttereth over her young." She moves her wings to teach them that thus they must move their wings, that thus they must mount. There is no teaching like teaching by example. We always learn a great deal more through our eyes and ears than we do merely through our ears, and those of us who cannot preach with our mouths would do well to preach with our lives, which is the very best kind of preaching. So God preaches to us. If he would have us holy, how holy he is himself! "Be ye holy for I am holy." Would he have us generous? How generous is he! "He spared not his own Son, but freely delivered him up for us all." Would he have us forgive our enemies? How he delights in mercy himself! If we want a picture of perfection, where can we get it but in God? "Be ye perfect even as your Father which is in heaven is perfect." God shows us his law in his holy actions, he being himself the very mirror and paragon of everything that is absolutely pure and right. Above all, the Lord has been pleased to set us an example of mounting above the world, in the person and life of his own dear Son. Oh, how the eagle flutters when I look upon the Saviour!

> Such was thy truth and such thy zeal,
> Such deference to thy Father's will,
> Such love and meekness so divine
> I would transcribe and make them mine.

> "Cold mountains and the midnight air
> Witnessed the fervour of thy prayer:
> The desert thy temptations knew,
> Thy conflict and thy victory too.

> "Be thou my pattern: make me bear
> More of thy gracious image here,
> Then God the Judge shall own my name
> Amongst the followers of the Lamb.

Beloved, see how our Lord Jesus this day mounts to heaven. There is he: he has gone there that our hearts may follow him. He fluttered to the skies that we might also follow, and might rise above the world, setting our affections no longer upon the things of earth, but upon things above, where Christ sitteth at the right hand of God. What way could there be of teaching us tenderness like the tenderness of the Saviour? What method of teaching us love, like the display of the love of God in Christ Jesus? Would you learn? If you will not learn with Christ for your pattern, in what school shall you be trained? Brethren and sisters, I commend you to the picture of the eagle fluttering and thus setting an example to its little ones. You also may see before your eyes the great incarnate God teaching you how to mount above the trials and temptations of this mortal life, and living even on earth a celestial life.

This, however, is not all the eagle does. We read in our text that she then *spreadeth abroad her wings, taketh them, beareth them on her wings.* I suppose this means just this, that spreading her wings she entices her young ones to get between her wings upon her back, and then she mounts and flies towards the sun. It may be fable or not, I do not know, that she flies towards the sun to teach her eaglets to bear its blaze. Then, when she has mounted to a good height, she suddenly shifts her wings and throws the young eaglets off, and there they are on their wings. They begin to descend to earth, not able to keep themselves up, but compelled to fly, but before they fall on the rock she makes a swoop and comes under them, and catches them on her wings again, gives them a little rest; bears them up once more, and then throws them off again, so that they must fly. But she takes care that these early trials, for which they are scarcely able, shall not end in their destruction, for again she makes another swoop and catches them between her wings once again.

This is the picture of what God does to us again. We must speak of him after the metaphor which he himself uses—he takes us up between those mighty wings, and bears us as high as we dare go, and only pauses because he knows we cannot bear more now. Then, when we have had full fellowship, and looked the sun in the face, and have had bright enjoyment of heaven, as far as we could bear them, he throws us off suddenly and makes us try our own wings, and alas! they are very feeble and weak indeed. We discover then our own impotence, and we think we shall fall like stars, and be dashed in pieces, but lo! he comes, and underneath us are the everlasting wings, and just when we thought we should surely come to destruction, we find ourselves safely sheltered between the mighty pinions of the Eternal God. Up, again, we mount, and before long we are thrown off again—cast away, as it were, for a time; his face is hidden from us, or else by some outward trial of providence we are made to try our wings again to see whether our faith will keep us up, and by degrees it comes to pass that we learn to fly till we love flying, and are not satisfied to come back to earth any more, loving to fly, and often sighing and longing for the day when we shall be permitted to—

> Stretch our wings and fly
> Straight to yonder worlds of joy.

Do you not feel sometimes as if your wing-feathers were come, my brethren? Surely you must sometimes feel as though your faith were growing stronger, and your communion with Christ getting clearer;

140

as though you anticipated and felt that the time must be drawing near when you could mount to dwell where Jesus is. I am thankful if such be your experience, but I should not wonder if you find that all the wing-feathers which you have got will be all too few for you, for you may yet be made to have another descent from between the almighty wings, and be made once again to see how great your weakness is. One other thought, however, occurs to us. There is no doubt that the idea of *security* as well as of teaching is here, because when the eagle bears her young ones on her wings, if the archer, or in these modern days the hunter with his rifle, should seek to destroy the eaglets, it is plain there is no reaching them without first killing the mother-bird. So there is no destroying possible to the true people of God. "Greater is he that is for us, than all that can be against us." God puts himself between his people and the danger which threatens them, and unless the foe should be mightier than God himself—which is inconceivable—there is no soul that trusts in him which shall know eternal hurt.

Oh, how glorious a thing it is to feel, when the light air is all around me, and I know that if I fall I should perish, that yet I cannot fall, for God's wings bear me up, and to feel that though there are hosts of enemies able to destroy me if they can get at me, yet they cannot, for they must first get through God himself before they can get to the weak soul who hangs upon Jesus and rests alone in him. Well did David say, "In the time of trouble he will hide me in his pavilion: in the secret of his tabernacle shall he hide me: he shall set me up upon a rock." You know the three-fold figure. The "pavilion" stood in the middle of the camp, and all the armed men kept watch around the royal tent. There was no slaying the man who was hidden in the royal pavilion unless the king himself were destroyed. And unless divine sovereignty be overthrown not one of the elect can perish. Then, again, there was "the secret of the tabernacle." That was the most holy place, into which no one entered but the high priest once a year, and there God said he would put his child, so that they must first break through and dare the very Shekinah, and come before the brightness, the destroying brightness, of Jehovah's face, before they can reach the soul that trusts in the mercy-seat on which the blood was sprinkled. Then there is the third figure—"he shall set me up upon a rock"—so that the rock itself must shake; the immutability of God itself must cease to be, and

God's everlastingness must die before it shall be possible for a soul to perish that rests in him. The eagle taketh up the eaglets on her wings, and beareth them, so in this way does God lead, and train, and guide us for the skies.

Dear brethren and sisters, I shall not detain you longer, except to say that if God is training you for the skies—oh, *let your hearts go up.* Grovel not below.

> Go up, go up, my heart,
>   Dwell with thy God above;
> For here thou canst not rest,
>   Nor here give out thy love.
>
> Go up, go up, my heart,
>   Be not a trifler here:
> Ascend above these clouds,
>   Dwell in a higher sphere.
>
> Let not thy love flow out
>   To things so soil'd and dim;
> Go up to heaven and God,
>   Take up thy love to him.
>
> Waste not thy precious stores
>   On creature-love below;
> To God that wealth belongs,
>   On him that wealth bestow.

Thou art a stranger here. If thou be God's child, then, thou art a citizen of another country. Are there any bands to bind thee here? I thought he had broken them. Hast thou never said—

> The bands that bind my soul to earth
>   Are broken by his hand:
> Before his cross I find myself
>   A stranger in the land.

Are there loved ones to bind thee here?

142

Thy best-beloved keeps his throne
On hills of light in worlds unknown.

All the love thou dost dare to give, if thou be true to Christ, to all below, can be as nothing compared with the love which thou givest to him. Dost thou not feel thy soul now drawn towards him? At least, if thou canst not fly on the wings of confidence, fly on the wings of desire. A sigh will mount to him, or he will come down to it. Only be not fond of this world. Do not let this thick clay cleave to thee. Thou art not earth-born now; thou art born from above. This corruptible world must not claim thee, for thou art born again of incorruptible seed. Thou art not this world's property; thou art bought with a price by him who prays for thee that thou mayest be with him where he is and behold his glory. I am ashamed of myself that I who talk thus with you should so often grovel here; but this one thing I must say—I am never happy except when my soul is up with my Lord. I know enough of this to own that it is my misery to feed upon the ashes of this world, to lie among the pots, to serve the brick-kilns of this Egypt. There can be no peace between my soul and this world. Oh, I know this, for this painted Jezebel has mocked me too often, and she has become so ugly in my esteem that I cannot endure her. But yet—what shall we say of our nature!—we go back again to the Marah, which was bitter for us to drink, and try to drink from it again, and the broken cisterns which held no water aforetime we fly to, again and again. Oh, for more wisdom! The Master has taught us, but he has been so long a time with us, and we have not known him. Yet may he have patience with us, until he has taught us to mount above the world and dwell where he is!

Ah, dear friends, there are some of you to whom I cannot talk in this fashion because you cannot mount. You have nowhere to mount to. Oh, may the Master stir up your nests! I pray that he may put the thorns of conscience into your pillows tonight. May you recollect those sins which God hateth and which God will punish, and if you do remember them and feel bowed down under their weight, then remember that there is one who can help you and who will help you, even the Lord Jesus Christ. Look to him in the hour of trouble, and he will be your deliverer. May the Lord bless these thoughts to all our souls for Jesu's sake.

"The Eagle and Its Brood"

"As an eagle stirreth up her nest, fluttereth over her young, spreadeth abroad her wings, taketh them, beareth them on her wings."—Deuteronomy 32:11.

This is an incomplete sentence in the Authorised Version, but really it should be rendered as a complete one; the description of the eagle's action including only the two first clauses, and (the figure being still retained) the person spoken of in the last clauses being God Himself. That is to say, it should read thus, "As an eagle stirreth up his nest, fluttereth over his young, *He* spreads abroad His wings, takes them, bears them on His pinions." That is far grander, as well as more compact, than the somewhat dragging comparison which, according to the Authorised Version, is spread over the whole verse and tardily explained, in the following, by a clause introduced by an unwarranted "So"—"the Lord alone did lead him, and there was no strange god with him."

Now, of course, we all know that the original reference of these words is to the deliverance of the Israelites from Egypt, and their training in the desert. In the solemn address by Jehovah at the giving of the law (Ex. 14:4), the same metaphor is employed, and, no doubt, that passage was the source of the extended imagery here. There we read, "Ye know what I did to the Egyptians, and how I bore you on eagles' wings, and brought you unto Myself." The meaning of the glowing metaphor, with its vivid details, is just that Jehovah brought Israel out of its fixed abode in Goshen, and trained it for mature national life by its varied desert experiences. As one of the prophets puts the same idea, "I taught Ephraim to go," where the figure of the parent bird training its callow fledglings for flight is exchanged for that of the nurse teaching a child to walk. While, then, the text primarily refers to the experience of the infant nation in the forty years' wanderings, it carries large truths about us all; and sets forth the true meaning and importance of life. There seem to me to be three thoughts here, which I desire to touch on briefly; first, a great thought about God; then an illuminating thought about the true meaning and aspect of life; and lastly a calming thought about the variety of the methods by which God carries out our training.

"The Eagle and Its Brood"

I. Here is a grand thought about God.

Now, it may come as something of a shock if I say that the bird that is selected for the comparison is not really the eagle, but one which, in our estimation, is of a very much lower order—viz., the carnivorous vulture. But a poetical emblem is not the less fitting, though, besides the points of resemblance, the thing which is so used has others less noble. Our modern repugnance to the vulture as feeding on carcasses was probably not felt by the singer of this song. What he brings into view are the characteristics common to the eagle and the vulture; superb strength in beak and claw, keenness of vision almost incredible, magnificent sweep of pinion and power of rapid, unwearied flight. And these characteristics, we may say, have their analogues in the Divine nature, and the emblem not unfitly shadows forth one aspect of the God of Israel, who is "fearful in praises," who is strong to destroy as well as to save, whose all-seeing eye marks every foul thing, and who often pounces on it swiftly to rend it to pieces, though the sky seemed empty a moment before.

But the action described in the text is not destructive, terrible, or fierce. The monarch of the sky busies itself with tender cares for its brood. Then, there is gentleness along with the terribleness. The strong beak and claw, the gaze that can see so far, and the mighty spread of wings that can lift it till it is an invisible speck in the blue vault, go along with the instinct of paternity: and the fledglings in the nest look up at the fierce beak and bright eyes, and know no terror. The impression of this blending of power and gentleness is greatly deepened, as it seems to me, if we notice that it is the male bird that is spoken about in the text, which should be rendered: "As the eagle stirreth up *his* nest and fluttereth over *his* young."

So we just come to the thought that we must keep the true balance between these two aspects of that great Divine nature—the majesty, the terror, the awfulness, the soaring elevation, the all-penetrating vision, the power of the mighty pinion, one stroke of which could crush a universe into nothing; and, on the other side, the yearning instinct of Fatherhood, the love and gentleness, and all the tender ministries for us, His children, to which these lead. Brethren! unless we keep hold of both of these in due equipoise, and inseparably intertwining, we damage the one which we retain almost as much as the one which we dismiss. For there is no love

like the love that is strong, and can be fierce, and there is no condescension like the condescension of Him who is the Highest, in order
that He may be, and because He is ready to be, the lowest. Modern
tendencies, legitimately recoiling from the one-sidedness of a past
generation, are now turning away far too much from the Old Testament conceptions of Jehovah which are concentrated in that metaphor of the vulture in the sky. And thereby we destroy the love in
the name of which we scout the wrath. "Infinite mercy, but I wis as
infinite a justice, too." As the vulture stirreth up his nest—that is the
Old Testament revelation of the terribleness and gentleness of Jehovah. "How often would I have gathered thy children together, even
as a hen gathereth her chickens under her wing"—that is the New
Testament modification of the image. But you never could have had
the New unless you first had the Old. And you are a foolish man if,
in the name of the sanctity of the New, you cast away the teaching of
the Old. Keep both the metaphors, and they will explain and confirm each other.

II. Here we have an illuminating thought of the meaning of life.
   What is it all for? To teach us to fly, to exercise our half-fledged
wings in short flights, that may prepare us for, and make it possible
to take, longer ones. Every event that befalls us has a meaning
beyond itself; and every task that we have to do reacts upon us, the
doers, and either fits or hinders us for larger work. Life as a whole,
and in its minutest detail, is worthy of God to give, and worthy of us
to possess, only if we recognise the teaching that is put into picturesque form in this text—that the meaning of all which God does to
us is to train us for something greater yonder. Life as a whole is "full
of sound and fury, signifying nothing" unless it is an apprenticeship
training. What are we here for? To make character. That is the aim
and end of all—to make character; to get experience; to learn the
use of our tools. I declare it seems to me that the world had better
be wiped out altogether, incontinently, unless there is a world beyond, where a man shall use the force which here he made his own.
"Thou hast been faithful in a few things; behold I make thee ruler
over many things." No man gets to the heart of the mystery of life or
has in his hand the key which will enable him to unlock all the doors
and difficulties of human experience, unless he gets to this—that it
is all meant as training.

If we could only carry that clear conviction with us day by day into the little things of life, what different things these, which we call the monotonous trifles of our daily duties, would become! The things may be small and unimportant, but the way we do them is not unimportant. The same fidelity may be exercised, and must be brought to bear, in order to do the veriest trifle of our daily lives rightly, that needs to be invoked, in order to get us safely through the crises and great times of life. There are no great principles for great duties, and little ones for little duties. We have to regulate all our conduct by the same laws, life is built up of trifles, as the mica-flakes, if there be enough of them, make the Alpine summits towering thousands of feet into the blue. Character may be manifested in the great moments, but it is made in the small ones. So, life is meant for discipline, and unless we use it for that, however much enjoyment we get out of it, we misuse it.

III. Lastly, there is here a calming thought as to the variety of God's methods with us.

"As the eagle stirreth up his nest." No doubt the callow brood are much warmer and more comfortable in the nest than when they are turned out of it. The Israelites were by no means enamoured with the prospect of leaving the flesh-pots and the onions and the farm-houses that they had got for themselves in Goshen, to tramp with their cattle through the wilderness. They went after Moses with considerable disinclination. Here we have, then, as the first thing needed, God's loving compulsion to effort. To "stir up the nest" means to make a man uncomfortable where he is—sometimes by the prickings of his conscience, which are often the voices of God's Spirit; sometimes by changes of circumstances, either for the better or for the worse; and oftentimes by sorrows. The straw is pulled out of the nest, and it is not so comfortable to lie in; or a bit of it develops a sharp point that runs into the half-feathered skin, and makes the fledgling glad to come forth into the air. We all shrink from change. What should we do if we had it not? We should stiffen into habits that would dwarf and weaken us. We all recoil from storms. What should we do if we had not them? Sea and air would stagnate, and become heavy and putrid and pestilential, if it was not for the wild west wind and the hurtling storms. So all our changes, instead of being whimpered over; and all our sorrows, instead of being taken reluctantly, should be recognised as being what they are, loving summonses to effort. Then their pressure would be modified, and their blessing would be secured when their purpose was served.

But the training of the father-eagle is not confined to stirring up the nest. What is to become of the young ones when they get out of it, and have never been accustomed to bear themselves up in the invisible ether about them? So "he fluttereth over his young." It is a very beautiful word that is employed here, which "flutter" scarcely gives us. It is the same word that is used in the first chapter of Genesis, about the Spirit of God "*brooding* on the face of the waters"; and it suggests how near, how all-protecting, with expanded wings the Divine Father comes to the child whose restfulness He has disturbed.

And is not that true? Had you ever trouble that you took as from Him, which did not bring that hovering presence nearer you, until you could almost feel the motion of the wing, and be brushed by it as it passed protectingly above your head? Ah, yes! Stirring the nest is meant to be the precursor of closer approach of the Father to us; and if we take our changes and our sorrows as loving summonses from Him to effort, be sure that we shall realise Him as near to us, in a fashion that we never did before.

That is not all. There is sustaining power. "He spreadeth abroad His wings; He taketh them; beareth them on His wings." On those broad pinions we are lifted and by them we are guarded. It matters little whether the belief that the parent bird thus carries the young, when wearied with their short flights, is correct or not. The truth which underlies the representation is what concerns us. The beautiful metaphor is a picturesque way of saying, "In all their afflictions He was afflicted; and the Angel of His presence saved them." It is a picturesque way of saying, "Thou canst do all things through Christ which strengtheneth thee." And we may be very sure that if we let Him stir up our nests and obey His loving summons to effort, He will come very near to strengthen us for our attempts, and to bear us up when our own weak wings fail. The psalmist sang that angels' hands should bear up God's servant. That is little compared with this promise of being carried heavenwards on Jehovah's own pinions. A vile piece of Greek mythology tells how Jove once, in the guise of an eagle, bore away a boy between his great wings. It is foul where it stands, but it is blessedly true about Christian experience. If only we lay ourselves on God's wings — and that not in idleness, but having ourselves tried our poor little flight — He will see that no harm comes to us.

During life this training will go on; and after life, what then? Then, in the deepest sense, the old word will be true, "Ye know how I bore you on eagle's wings and brought you *to Myself*"; and the great promise shall be fulfilled, when the half-fledged young brood are matured and full grown, "They shall mount up with wings as eagles; they shall run and not be weary; they shall walk and not faint."

Something to Do

1. The ways of eagles would be familiar to Israel, but what would urban Christians today know about these rare birds? How did each of these preachers instruct the congregation about these matters so the people could better understand the analogy? How would you have done it?

2. In your opinion, which outline was the easiest to follow? Why? What similarities do you see among the three messages?

3. When dealing with symbolism, it is important that we stick to the main truth being illustrated, in this case, the maturing of the young and the developing of latent powers. Do any of the preachers carry the analogy too far?

4. Both Morgan and Maclaren felt it was important to "defend" the eagle image of God. Which is the better defense?

5. To what extent did the preachers remain in the Old Testament context? What New Testament truths or quotations might have been introduced? How can the text be related to Jesus Christ and His Gospel?

6. What other biblical images of "maturing" can you recall?

11

"The Principle of the Spiritual Harvest"
Frederick W. Robertson

HE WAS MINISTER for only six years at Trinity Chapel, Brighton, but the messages of Frederick W. Robertson (1816–1853) have gone around the English-speaking world and are known wherever good preaching is appreciated. He penetrated to the heart of a text and, often using a two-point dialectical approach, caused the truth of the Word to search the inner recesses of the human heart.

This sermon is taken from *Sermons, First Series,* published in London in 1898 by Kegan Paul, Trench, Trubner and Company. Robertson preached it at Brighton on December 5, 1849.

"The Principle of the Spiritual Harvest"

"Be not deceived; God is not mocked; for whatsoever a man soweth, that shall he also reap. For he that soweth to his flesh shall of the flesh reap corruption; but he that soweth to the Spirit shall of the Spirit reap life everlasting" — Galatians 6:7-8.

There is a close analogy between the world of nature and the world of spirit. They bear the impress of the same hand; and hence the principles of nature and its laws are the types and shadows of the Invisible. Just as two books, though on different subjects, proceeding from the same pen, manifest indications of the thought of one mind, so the worlds visible and invisible are two books written by the same finger, and governed by the same Idea. Or rather, they are but one book, separated into two only by the narrow range of our ken. For it is impossible to study the universe at all without perceiving that it is one system. Begin with what science you will, as soon as you get beyond the rudiments, you are constrained to associate it with another.

You cannot study agriculture long without finding that it absorbs into itself meteorology and chemistry: sciences run into one another till you get the "connection of the sciences;" and you begin to learn that one Divine Idea connects the whole in one system of perfect Order.

It was upon this principle that Christ taught. Truths come forth from His lips not stated simply on authority, but based on the analogy of the universe. His human mind, in perfect harmony with the Divine Mind with which it is mixed, discerned the connection of things, and read the Eternal Will in the simplest laws of Nature. For instance, if it were a question whether God would give His Spirit to them that asked, it was not replied to by a truth revealed on His *authority;* the answer was derived from facts lying open to all men's observation. "Behold the fowls of the air," — "behold the lilies of the field," — learn from them the answer to your question. A principle was there. God supplies the wants which He has created. He feeds the ravens — He clothes the lilies — He will feed with His Spirit the craving spirits of His children.

It was on this principle of analogy that St. Paul taught in this text. He tells us that there is a law in nature according to which success is

152

proportioned to the labour spent upon the work. In kind and in degree—success is attained in kind; for example, he who has sown his field with beechmast does not receive a plantation of oaks: a literary education is not the road to distinction in arms, but to success in letters: years spent on agriculture do not qualify a man to be an orator, but they make him a skilful farmer. Success again, is proportioned to labour in degree: because, ordinarily, as is the amount of seed sown, so is the harvest: he who studies much will know more than he who studies little. In almost all departments it is "the diligent hand which maketh rich."

The keen eye of Paul discerned this principle reaching far beyond what is seen, into the spiritual realm which is unseen. As tare-seed comes up tares, and wheat-seed wheat, and as the crop in both cases is in proportion to two conditions, the labour and the quantity committed to the ground—so in things spiritual, too, whatsoever a man soweth, that shall he also reap. Not something else, but "*that*." The proportion holds in kind—it holds too in degree, in spiritual things as in natural. "He which soweth sparingly shall reap also sparingly; and he which soweth bountifully shall reap also bountifully." If we could understand and rightly expound that principle, we should be saved from much of the disappointment and surprise which come from extravagant and unreasonable expectations. I shall try first to elucidate the principle which these verses contain, and then examine the two branches of the principle.

I. The principle is this, "God is not mocked: for whatsoever a man soweth, that shall he also reap."

There are two kinds of good possible to men: one enjoyed by our animal being, the other felt and appreciated by our spirits. Every man understands more or less the difference between these two; between prosperity and well-doing: between indulgence and nobleness: between comfort and inward peace: between pleasure and striving after perfection: between happiness and blessedness. These are two kinds of harvest; and the labour necessary for them respectively is of very different kinds. The labour which procures the harvest of the one has no tendency to secure the other.

We will not depreciate the advantages of this world. It is foolish and unreal to do so. Comfort, affluence, success, freedom from care, rank, station—these are in their real way goods; only, the labour

153

bestowed upon them does not procure one single blessing that is spiritual.

On the other hand, the seed which is sown for a spiritual harvest has no tendency whatever to procure temporal well-being. Let us see what are the laws of the sowing and reaping in this department. Christ has declared them: "Blessed are the pure in heart; for they shall see God." "Blessed are they that hunger and thirst after righteousness: for they shall be filled (with righteousness.)" "Blessed are they that mourn: for they shall be comforted." You observe, the beatific vision of the Almighty—fulness of righteousness—divine comfort. There is nothing earthly here,—it is, spiritual results for spiritual labour. It is not said that the pure in heart shall be made rich; nor that they who hunger after goodness shall be filled with bread; nor that they who mourn shall rise in life and obtain distinction. Each department has its own appropriate harvest—reserved exclusively to its own method of sowing.

Everything in this world has its price, and the price buys *that*, not something else. Every harvest demands its own preparation, and that preparation will not produce another sort of harvest. Thus for example, you cannot have at once the soldier's renown and the quiet of a recluse's life. The soldier pays his price for his glory—sows and reaps. His price is risk of life and limb, nights spent on the hard ground, a weather-beaten constitution. If you will not pay that price, you cannot have what he has—military reputation. You cannot enjoy the statesman's influence together with freedom from public notoriety. If you sensitively shrink from that, you must give up influence; or else pay his price, the price of a thorny pillow, unrest, the chance of being to-day a nation's idol, to-morrow the people's execration. You cannot have the store of information possessed by the student, and enjoy robust health: pay his price, and you have his reward. His price is an emaciated frame, a debilitated constitution, a transparent hand, and the rose taken out of the sunken cheek. To expect these opposite things: a soldier's glory and quiet—a statesman's renown and peace—the student's prize and rude health, would be to mock God, to reap what has not been sowed.

Now the mistakes men make, and the extravagant expectations in which they indulge, are these:—they sow for earth, and expect to win spiritual blessings; or they sow to the Spirit, and then wonder that they have not a harvest of the good things of earth. In each case they complain, What have I done to be treated so?

The unreasonableness of all this appears the moment we have understood the conditions contained in this principle, "Whatsoever a man soweth, *that* shall he also reap."

It is a common thing to hear sentimental wonderings about the unfairness of the distribution of things here. The unprincipled get on in life: the saints are kept back. The riches and rewards of life fall to the lot of the undeserving. The rich man has his good things, and Lazarus his evil things. Whereupon it is taken for granted that there must be a future life to make this fair: that if there were none, the constitution of this world would be unjust. That is, that because a man who has sown to the Spirit does not reap to the flesh here, he will hereafter; that the meed of well-doing must be somewhere in the universe the same kind of recompense which the rewards of the unprincipled were here, comfort, abundance, physical enjoyment, or else all is wrong.

But if you look into it, the balance is perfectly adjusted even here. God has made his world much better than you and I could make it. Everything reaps its own harvest, every act has its own reward. And before you covet the enjoyment which another possesses, you must first calculate the cost at which it was procured.

For instance, the religious tradesman complains that his honesty is a hindrance to his success: that the tide of custom pours into the doors of his less scrupulous neighbours in the same street, while he himself waits for hours idle. My brother! do you think that God is going to reward honour, integrity, high-mindedness, with this world's coin? Do you fancy that He will pay spiritual excellence with plenty of custom? Now, consider the price that man has paid for his success. Perhaps mental degradation and inward dishonour. His advertisements are all deceptive. His treatment of his workmen tyrannical: his cheap prices made possible by inferior articles. Sow that man's seed, and you will reap that man's harvest. Cheat, lie, advertise, be unscrupulous in your assertions, custom will come to you. But if the price is too dear, let him have his harvest, and take yours; yours is a clear conscience, a pure mind, rectitude within and without—Will you part with that for his? Then why do you complain? He has paid his price, you do not choose to pay it.

Again, it is not an uncommon thing to see a man rise from insignificance to sudden wealth by speculation. Within the last ten or twenty years, England has gazed on many such a phenomenon. In this case, as in spiritual things, the law seems to hold: He that hath, to him shall be given. Tens of thousands soon increase and multiply to hundreds of thousands. His doors are besieged by the rich and great. Royalty banquets at his table, and nobles court his alliance. Whereupon some simple Christian is inclined to complain: "How strange that so much prosperity should be the lot of mere cleverness!"

Well, are these really God's chief blessings? Is it for such as these you serve Him? And would these indeed satisfy your soul? Would you have God reward his saintliest with these gauds and gewgaws — all this trash, — rank, and wealth, and equipages, and plate, and courtship from the needy great? Call you *that* the heaven of the holy? Compute now what was paid for that. The price that merchant prince paid, perhaps with the blood of his own soul, was shame and guilt. The price he is paying now, is perpetual dread of detection: or worse still, the hardness which can laugh at detection: or one deep lower yet, the low and grovelling soul which can be satisfied with these things as a Paradise, and ask no higher. He has reaped enjoyment — yes, and he has sown too, the seed of infamy.

It is all fair. Count the cost. "He that saveth his life shall lose it." Save your life if you like: but do not complain if you lose your nobler life — yourself: win the whole world: but remember you do it by losing your own soul. Every sin must be paid for: every sensual indulgence is a harvest, the price for which is so much ruin for the soul. *"God is not mocked."*

Once more, religious men in every profession are surprised to find that many of its avenues are closed to them. The conscientious churchman complains that his delicate scruples, or his bold truthfulness, stand in the way of his preferment: while another man, who conquers his scruples, or softens the eye of truth, rises, and sits down a mitred peer in Parliament. The honourable lawyer feels that his practice is limited, while the unprincipled practitioner receives all he loses; and the Christian physician feels sore and sad at perceiving that charlatanism succeeds in winning employment; or, if not charlatanism, at least that affability and courtly manners take the place that is due to superior knowledge.

Let such men take comfort, and judge fairly. Popularity is one of the things of an earthly harvest, for which quite earthly qualifications are required. I say not always dishonourable qualifications: but a certain flexibility of disposition—a certain courtly willingness to sink obnoxious truths, and adapt ourselves to the prejudices of the minds of others: a certain adroitness at catching the tone of those with whom we are. Without some of these things no man can be popular in any profession.

But you have resolved to be a liver—a doer—a champion of the truth. Your ambition is to be pure in the last recesses of the mind. You have your reward: a soul upright and manly—a fearless bearing, that dreads to look no man in the face—a willingness to let men search you through and through, and defy them to see any difference between what you seem and what you are. Now, your price— your price is dislike. The price of being true is the Cross. The warrior of the truth must not expect success. What have you to do with popularity? Sow for it, and you will have it. But if you wish for it, or wish for peace, you have mistaken your calling—you must not be a teacher of the Truth—you must not cut prejudice against the grain—you must leave medical, legal, theological truth, to harder and nobler men, who are willing to take the martyr's cross, and win the martyr's crown.

This is the mistake men make. They expect both harvests, paying only one price. They would be blessed with goodness and prosperity at once. They would have that on which they bestowed no labour. They take sinful pleasure, and think it very hard that they must pay for it in agony, and worse than agony, souls deteriorated. They would monopolize heaven in their souls, and the world's prizes at the same time. This is to expect to come back, like Joseph's brethren from the land of plenty, with the corn in their sacks, and the money returned too, in their sacks' mouths. No, no! it will not do. "Be not deceived; God is not mocked." Reap *what* you have sown. If you sow the wind, do not complain if your harvest is the whirlwind. If you sow to the Spirit, be content with a spiritual reward—invisible— within—"more life and higher life."

II. Next, the two branches of the application of this principle.

First: He that soweth to the flesh, shall of the flesh reap corruption. There are two kinds of life: one of the flesh—another of the spirit. Amidst the animal and selfish desires of our nature, there is a Voice which clearly speaks of Duty: Right: Perfection. This is the

157

Spirit of Deity in Man—it is the life of God in the soul. This is the evidence of our divine parentage.

But there is a double temptation to live the other life instead of this. First, the desires of our animal nature are *keener* than those of our spiritual. The cry of Passion is louder than the calm voice of Duty. Next, the reward in the case of our sensitive nature is given *sooner*. It takes less time to amass a fortune than to become heavenly-minded. It costs less to indulge an appetite than it does to gain the peace of lulled passion. And hence, when men feel that for the spiritual blessing, the bread must be cast upon the waters which shall not be found until after many days (scepticism whispers "never!"), it is quite intelligible why they choose the visible and palpable, instead of the invisible advantage, and plan for an immediate harvest rather than a distant one.

The other life is that of the flesh. The "flesh" includes all the desires of our unrenewed nature—the harmless as well as sinful. Any labour therefore, which is bounded by present wellbeing is *sowing* to the flesh: whether it be the gratification of an immediate impulse, or the long-contrived plan reaching forward over many years. Sowing to the flesh includes therefore,

1. Those who live in open riot. He sows to the flesh who pampers its unruly animal appetites. Do not think that I speak contemptuously of our animal nature, as if it were not human and sacred. The lowest feelings of our nature become sublime by being made the instruments of our nobler emotions. Love, self-command, will elevate them all: and to ennoble and purify, not to crush them, is the long, slow work of Christian life. Christ, says St. Paul, is the Saviour of the Body. But if, instead of subduing these to the life of the spirit, a man gives to them the rein and even the spur, the result is not difficult to foresee. There are men who do this. They "make provision for the flesh, to fulfil the lusts thereof." They whet the appetites by indulgence. They whip the jaded senses to their work. Whatever the constitutional bias may be, anger, intemperance, epicurism, indolence, desires, there are societies, conversations, scenes, which supply fuel for the flame, as well as opposite ones which cut off the nutriment. To indulge in these, knowing the result, is to foster the desire which brings forth the sin that ends in death. This is "sowing to the flesh."

If there be one to whom these words which I have used, veiled in the proprieties due to delicate reserve, are not without meaning, from this sentence of God's word let him learn his doom. He is looking forward to a harvest wherein he may reap the fruit of his present anticipations. And he *shall* reap it. He shall have his indulgence—he shall enjoy his guilty rapture—he shall have his unhallowed triumph: and the boon companions of his pleasures shall award him the meed of their applause. He has sown the seed: and in fair requital he shall have his harvest. It is all fair. He *shall* enjoy. But tarry awhile: the law hath yet another hold upon him. This deep law of the whole universe goes further. He has sown to the flesh, and of the flesh he has reaped pleasure: he has sown to the flesh, and of the flesh he shall reap corruption. That is in his case, the ruin of the soul. It is an awful thing to see a soul in ruins: like a temple which once was fair and noble, but now lies overthrown, matted with ivy, weeds, and tangled briers, among which things noisome crawl and live. He shall reap the harvest of disappointment—the harvest of bitter, useless remorse. The crime of sense is avenged by sense, which wears by time. He shall have the worm that gnaws, and the fire that is not quenched. He shall reap the fruit of long indulged desires, which have become tyrannous at last, and constitute him his own tormentor. His harvest is a soul in flames, and the tongue that no drop can cool. Passions that burn, and appetites that crave, when the power of enjoyment is gone. He has sowed to the flesh. "God is not mocked." The man reaps.

2. There is a less gross way of sowing to the flesh. There are men of sagacity and judgment in the affairs of this life, whose penetration is almost intuitive in all things where the step in question involves success or failure here. They are those who are called in the parable the children of this world, wise in their generation. They moralize and speculate about eternity: but do not plan for it. There is no seed sown for an invisible harvest. If they think they have sown for such a harvest, they might test themselves by the question, What would they lose if there were to be no eternity? For the children of God, so far as earth is concerned, "If in this life only they have hope in Christ, then are they of all men most miserable." But *they*—these sagacious, prudent men of this world—they have their reward. What have they ventured, given up, sacrificed, which is all lost for ever, if this world be all? What have they buried like seed in the ground, lost for ever, if there be no eternity?

Now we do not say these men are absolutely wicked. We distinguish between their sowing to the flesh, and the sowing of those profligates last spoken of. All we say is, there is "corruption" written on their harvest. It was for earth: and with earth it perishes. It may be the labour of the statesman, planning, like the Roman of old, the government and order of the kingdoms of the earth: or that of the astronomer, weighing suns, prescribing rules of return to comets, and dealing with things above earth in space, but unspiritual still: or that of the son of a humbler laboriousness, whose work is merely to provide for a family: or, lastly, the narrower range of the man of pleasure, whose chief care is where he shall spend the next season, in what metropolis, or which watering-place, or how best enjoy the next entertainment.

All these are objects more or less harmless. But they end. The pyramid crumbles into dust at last. The mighty empire of the eternal city breaks into fragments which disappear. The sowers for earth *have* their harvest here. Success in their schemes — quiet intellectual enjoyment — exemption from pain and loss — the fruits of worldly-wise sagacity. And that is all. "When the breath goeth forth, they return to their dust, and all their thoughts perish." The grave is not to them the gate of paradise, but simply the impressive mockery which the hand of death writes upon that body for which they lived, and with which all is gone. They reap corruption, for all they have toiled for decays!

Ye that lead the life of respectable worldliness! let these considerations arrest your indifference to the gospel. You have sown for earth — Well. And then — what? Hear the gospel, which tells of a Saviour whose Sacrifice is the world's life — whose death is the law of life: from whose resurrection streams a Spirit which can change carnal into spiritual men — whose whole existence, reflecting God, was the utterance of the Divine truth and rule of heavenly life, the blessedness of giving — To live so, and to believe so, is to sow to the Spirit.

Lastly — Sowing to the Spirit. "He that soweth to the Spirit, shall of the Spirit reap life everlasting."

What is meant by sowing to the Spirit here is plain. "Let us not be weary in well-doing," says the apostle directly after: "for in due season we shall reap if we faint not." *Well-doing:* not faith, but works of goodness, were the sowing that he spoke of.

160

There is proclaimed here the rewardableness of works. So in many other passages: "Abounding in the work of the Lord, forasmuch as ye know that your labour is not in vain in the Lord." "Laying up a good foundation for the time to come," was the reason alleged for charging rich men to be willing to give — and so all through. There is an irreversible principle. The amount of harvest is proportioned to the seed sown exactly. There are degrees of glory. The man who gives out of his abundance has one blessing. She who gives the mite, all she had, even all her living, has another, quite different. The rectitude of this principle, and what it is, will be plainer from the following considerations.

1. The harvest is Life Eternal. But Eternal Life here does not simply mean a life that lasts for ever. That is the destiny of the *Soul:* all souls, bad as well as good. But the bad do not enter into this "Eternal life." It is not simply the duration, but the quality of the life which constitutes its character of Eternal. A spirit may live for ever, yet not enter into this. And a man may live but for five minutes the life of Divine benevolence, or desire for perfectness: in those five minutes he has entered into the life which is Eternal, never fluctuates, but is the same unalterably, for ever in the life of God. *This* is the Reward.

2. The reward is not arbitrary, but natural. God's rewards and God's punishments are all natural. Distinguish between arbitrary and natural. Death is an arbitrary punishment for forgery: it might be changed for transportation. It is not naturally connected. It depends upon the will of the law-maker. But trembling nerves are the direct and natural results of intemperance. They are in the order of nature the results of wrong-doing. The man reaps *what* he has sown. Similarly in rewards. If God gave riches in return for humbleness, that would be an arbitrary connection. He did give such a reward to Solomon. But when He gives Life Eternal, meaning by Life Eternal not duration of existence but heavenly quality of existence, as explained already, it is all natural. The seed sown in the ground contains in itself the future harvest. The harvest is but the development of the germ of life in the seed. A holy act strengthens the inward holiness. It is a seed of life growing into more life. "Whatsoever a man soweth, *that* shall he reap." He that sows much, thereby becomes more conformed to God than he was before — in heart and spirit. That is his reward and harvest. And just as among the apos-

161

tles, there was one whose spirit, attuned to love, made him emphatically the disciple whom Jesus loved, so shall there be some who, by previous discipline of the Holy Ghost, shall have more of His mind, and understand more of His love, and drink deeper of His joy than others—They that have sowed bountifully.

Every act done in Christ receives its exact and appropriate reward. They that are meek shall inherit the earth. They that are pure shall see God. They that suffer shall reign with Him. They that turn many to righteousness shall shine as the stars for ever. They that receive a righteous man in the name of a righteous man—that is, because he is a righteous man—shall receive a righteous man's reward. Even the cup of cold water, given in the name of Christ, shall not lose its reward.

It will be therefore seen at once, Reward is not the result of merit. It is in the order of grace, the natural consequence of well-doing. It is life becoming more life. It is the soul developing itself. It is the Holy Spirit of God in man, making itself more felt, and mingling more and more with his soul, felt more consciously with an ever-increasing heaven. You reap what you sow—not something else—but that. An act of love makes the soul more loving. A deed of humbleness deepens humbleness. The thing reaped is the very thing sown, multiplied a hundredfold. You have sown a seed of life—you reap Life everlasting.

Something to Do

1. Did you note how the first three paragraphs of the sermon expressed convictions that agree with the thoughts of Emerson, Spurgeon, and Bunyan? Why do you think Robertson began his sermon this way?

2. How does Robertson contrast "flesh" and "spirit"?

3. A popular American adage says, "There are no free lunches." How would Robertson respond to that maxim? How does he use the harvest image to apply its truth to everyday life?

4. Does Robertson believe it's possible to expect *both* harvests? How does he express this truth?

5. What images does Robertson use to help us see the folly of sowing to the flesh?

6. How does the preacher sustain interest in the "harvest" image so that it doesn't become boring?

12

"Christ the Day-Dawn and the Rain"
John Ker

JOHN KER ("care," 1819–1886) was
an esteemed preacher and professor
of preaching and pastoral work at
the United Free Church seminary in
Glasgow. He was one of George H.
Morrison's favorite preachers. Unfortunately, we have only two volumes
of his sermons, one of them published posthumously. This one is
from *Sermons, First Series,* published in Edinburgh in 1870 by
Edmonston and Douglas.

Developing a Christian Imagination

"Christ the Day-Dawn and the Rain"

"His going forth is prepared as the morning; and He shall come unto us as the rain" — Hosea 6:3.

These ancient Jews must have been very much like ourselves, neither better nor worse, and as we read about them we can read our own hearts. The preceding chapter contains an account of their sins and backslidings, and of their vain attempts, under the miserable consequences, to find help in man. At last, it concludes with a declaration on the part of God that He will return to his place, till they seek him, and with a promise that this shall not be in vain, "In their affliction they shall seek me early."

The present chapter begins with a fulfilment of this promise. The children of Israel take with them words and say, "Come and let us return unto the Lord." It is not in the power of any creature to assuage the wounds of the heart when they have been felt in all their depth. It is only in Him who made the heart, then to heal it, and He can and will. The God who has established great laws around us for the preservation of his world, for giving man life and light and sustenance, has made his arrangements also for the cure of our hearts' maladies, and the salvation of our souls. He has gathered all these arrangements closely around his own person. Our body's life may lie in knowing his laws, but our soul's life consists in knowing *Himself*: "Then shall we know, if we follow on to know the Lord: His going forth is prepared as the morning; and He shall come unto us as the rain."

These words were, no doubt, fulfilled in many a deliverance of the Jewish people; but their own most ancient commentators find their last fulfilment in the great promised Messiah, to whom all the prophets gave witness. The promises of the Old Testament are waves which urge each other on, to rise and fall in many a deliverance, until at length they break on the great shore of all safety — the salvation which is in Christ, with eternal glory. And it would, surely, be a shame for us Christians to do less than ancient Jewish doctors did, to fail in finding here a prophecy of the world's Redeemer. It is Christ, then, whom our faith must grasp under these two figures, the *Day-dawn* and the *Rain*.

The world is a great book of symbols for the soul of man to read

166

God by, and they are never so interesting and beautiful as when, with the warrant of Scripture, the name of Christ is put within them, not for mutual obscuration, but that they may shine forth illuminated and illuminating.

The *Day-dawn* and the *Rain*, — there must be something of common likeness in them, for they both apply to the same great Person, and yet there must be something distinctive meant to be conveyed, for the Word of God uses no vain repetitions, no mere figures of rhetoric. When we come to the New Testament we find clearly revealed what the ancient prophets dimly suggested. There is a twofold coming of the Son of God, the first in his own Person to establish and confirm the gospel, the second in his Holy Spirit to apply it to the heart. The one of these may very fitly be compared to the morning, the other to the rain. Indeed, these are the two figures most frequently used in this connexion all through the Bible. Christ himself is the light of the world, the Sun of righteousness; his Spirit is poured forth as floods on the thirsty; and when on the great day of the feast (John 7:39) He invited men to come unto him and drink, "He spake of the Spirit which they that believe on him should receive." We shall seek to apply these figures, then, to Christ, — to look upon his personal coming as represented by the *morning,* his coming in his Holy Spirit as symbolized by the *rain,* and to present them, first, in *the common resemblances which they have;* and second, in *some of their points of distinction.*

I. The Day-dawn and the Rain represent some resemblances between the coming of Christ in his Gospel and in his Spirit.

They have this resemblance, first, that they have *the same manifest origin.* The day-dawn comes from heaven, and so also does the rain. They are not of man's ordering and making, but of God's. They are of the good and perfect gifts which come from above, from the Father of lights. And they bear the imprint of God's hand upon them — the morning, when it walks forth from the opening clouds of the east, tinges the mountain-tops with gold and floods the earth with glory, — and the rain, when it shakes its bountiful treasures far and wide over waiting lands till the little hills rejoice on every side. Their height, their power, their breadth of range, mark them out from all man's works.

And it is not less so with the Gospel and Spirit of Christ. Man neither invented them nor discovered them. It is that God "who commanded the light to shine out of darkness that shines into men's hearts the light of the knowledge of his glory in the face of Jesus Christ." And to a man who can look aright they have the same impress of divinity. They carry their evidence with them, like heaven's sun and heaven's rain. They are above man's finding out, naturally above his conception. As the heavens are high above the earth, so are the great thoughts of God in them above man's thoughts. The Son of God coming from heaven to die for man, the Spirit of God coming from heaven to live in man—to change man, the enemy of God, into his friend, his son, his heir, and to do this for all who are but willing to make God's Son and Spirit welcome— these are thoughts which have a majesty and range so great and godlike, that they show their origin. "This is not the manner of men, O Lord God!"

Men may discuss these things hardly and coldly when they are outside of them, and may admit or deny them, as a nation of the blind might the sunlight, or the tribes of a waterless desert the rain; but let them know and feel their power, and there is but one re- source—to say, "It is of God." It is the sunlight within which lets men see the sun without. When a man is brought to say, "One thing I know, that whereas I was blind now I see," he becomes witness to a spiritual world opening around him in all its brightness and bless- edness, with "its eyes like unto the eyelids of the morning," and he can challenge all who would impugn its Divine reality, "Hast thou commanded the morning since thy days, or made this dayspring to know its place?"

If he come to feel the gracious showers of the Spirit of God upon his soul, in refreshment, in comfort, in strength for hard duty, in patience under sore trial; if he feel the weary heart revived as a flower after a sultry noon-day lifts its head amid the rain-drops; if he should learn that this experience belongs to many beside and around him, he can answer the scorner of a Divine Spirit—"Canst thou lift up thy voice to the clouds that abundance of waters may cover thee?"

Here, then, let us seek to learn the origin of our faith in a study of the grandeur and comprehensiveness of its plan and in a feeling of its power in our souls. The same God who makes morning to the world by the sun, gives the dawn of a new creation to the spirits of men through the Saviour.

The next point of resemblance we mention is that they have *the same mode of operation on the part of God.* That mode of operation is soft and silent. The greatest powers of nature work most calmly and noiselessly. What so gentle as the day-dawn rising mutely in the brightening east, and pouring its light upon the eye so softly that swift as are those rays, the tenderest texture of the eye endures no wrong? And what more soft than the spring's falling rain? It may come preceded by the thunder, but it is gentle itself, and when most efficacious descends almost as a spiritual presence, "as the small rain on the tender herb, and as showers that water the earth."

And like to these in their operations are the Gospel and Spirit of Christ. When our Saviour came into the world it was silently and alone. All heaven was moved, and followed Him down to the threshold, but few on earth were aware. One solitary star pointed to the humble birthplace, and hymns sang of it, heard only at night by the watching shepherds. He walked our world through years softly in the bitterness of his soul; He left where the common eye beheld but an ignominious sufferer, one of three, and men became conscious that the Son of God had come and gone only when the clear light began to break in the eastern sky from that great work of his, and when the open gate of mercy was thrown back, with a cross before it to call the lost and wandering home.

And as it was with his descent into the world, so is it, in the general, with his entrance by his Spirit into the heart. There may be the thunder and the mighty rushing wind before it, the providences may be loud and violent, but the Spirit itself is like the rain. It moves from soul to soul among the rising generations, and there is no outward crisis to tell of the birth of souls. It is like the dew that falls at night, and in the morning it is there, and man cannot tell when it formed itself, like a celestial guest, within the flower-cup. The kingdom of heaven cometh not with observation. And, even in times of revival more marked, for such times are promised and should be expected, — yet even in such times, the Spirit's great work is not in the earthquake or the mighty rushing wind, but in the still small voice. Unless it meet us there, in the secrecy of the soul, in the privacy of the closet, in the rising to seek Christ at his grave in the quiet resurrection morn when the busy world and all the guards are fast asleep, unless it bring the soul into close and secret communion

169

with Christ himself, it meets us not at all. In his Gospel and his Spirit, Christ is moving through the great inner world which men too much neglect, the world of souls, and there in the solitude of the heart, alone with Him, it must be ours to seek and find.

There is a further point of resemblance in this, that they have the *same form of approach to us* — in perfect freeness and fulness. The morning light comes unfettered by any condition, and so, also, descends the rain. They are, like God's greatest gifts, without money and without price; and they come with an overflowing plenty, for freeness and fulness go hand in hand. The morning sun shines with light for the eyes of all, however many; and were there millions more, there is enough for each one. So it is with the rain. Every field and flower may have its full share, and none need envy or rob another. "Thou visitest the earth and waterest it, thou greatly enrichest it with the river of God, which is full of water."

And in this they are fit and blessed emblems of the way in which Christ approaches us, both with his Gospel and his Spirit. That Gospel opens on the world priceless and free as the light which waits but for the eye to be unclosed to see and share it all. And there it stands, as full as it is free. It is one thing, like the sun, for all, and it is all for each one. However many have come to Christ, there is enough for us in the Sun of Righteousness to-day, as if He had risen but for the first time, and there will be to the world's close. How plain and simple this is, and yet it needs an effort on our part to appreciate it in its simplicity, to appropriate it in its perfect freeness, to feel that we can do no more to earn Christ's grace than to earn the daylight, and that it is just as freely offered to us. Fellow-sinners and fellow-Christians, let us ask Himself to teach it to us, to teach it by appearing in his own person and work, as the Light of life. "Behold me, behold me! Look unto me, and be ye saved, all ye ends of the earth!" and then, blessed revelation, by that opening of the eyes to Him, it shall be all our own! "They looked unto Him and were lightened; and their faces were not ashamed."

So free is the Gospel, and so free, also, is the Spirit of Christ. He is that "free Spirit," that "*liberal Spirit,*" of whom the Psalmist speaks, who waits but for our request to come down and fill our hearts with his refreshing rain. Nay, the petition we raise is of his prompting. He comes unasked, and when we think not of Him, like the "dew of the Lord that waiteth not for man, nor tarrieth for the sons of men." The

170

Spirit and the bride both say "Come!" Let us be firmly persuaded that Christ is offering his Spirit as freely to us as his Gospel. Nor has the Spirit less fulness. He is ready to pour water on the thirsty, and floods on the dry ground. It is his special work to exhibit the abundant freeness and riches of the gospel of Christ, to unfold and analyse it, that we may see it in its manifold beauty, as the sunlight is analysed by the glittering dew-drops or held up before the world in the emerald rainbow. So Christ himself has said of the Spirit, "He shall glorify Me, for He shall receive of mine, and shall show it unto you" (John 16:14). Therefore, let us be assured that the Spirit of Christ draws near to us without any fettering condition and without any restraining measure, even as the gospel does. "Behold, I will pour out my Spirit unto you, I will make known my words unto you." And let us carry this faith into our prayers. The promise of the Spirit by Christ is followed by this command, "Ask, and ye shall receive, that your joy may be full."

The last point of resemblance we mention is, *that they have the same object and end*. It is the transformation of death into life, and the raising of that which lives into higher and fairer form. The morning sun and the morning rain-cloud may seem wide apart in their purpose, may appear at times to obstruct each other, but they have one great aim. The sun and the rain come to the dying seed, and both together draw it from darkness to light, and build it up into the blade, the ear, and the full corn in the ear, that God's world may live and praise his name. Both are rich in times of refreshment: the sun after the dark night, the rain after the parched day; and, after both, the flower raises its head, and the birds sing, and men are glad.

Here, too, they are emblems of the Gospel and Spirit of Christ. These, in like manner, have the same aim—life and revival. The gospel of Christ is the word of life. Its aim is to bring dead souls into contact with Him who has said, "I am come that they might have life." The Holy Ghost is the Spirit of life. It is for this that He urges, entreats, and strives with the soul in secret,—that He is so patient in waiting, and so loath to leave. Christ is no less earnest for our eternal life in the one than in the other. We are too ready to forget this, to think less of the love of the Spirit sinking down into the communings of the heart and conscience, and working there in silence and in secret, than of that transparent love which is written on the Word with a beam of light; but they unite in the same merci-

171

ful purpose; and it will never be well with us until we meet Christ as willingly when He comes to strive with us in solitude, as when He openly proclaims his gracious call.

And as both work together for life, so both must cooperate for revival. If God's heritage is to be refreshed when it is weary, it must be with the outpouring of the Spirit, equally with the presentation of a clear, full gospel. The ancient Church was aware of this, as well as we who look back to the day of Pentecost. They knew that upon "the land of God's people shall come up thorns and briers, until the Spirit is poured upon us from on high," and when the individual believer prayed for return of life to his soul, he bent his knees with these words, "Restore unto me the joy of thy salvation; and uphold me with thy free Spirit."

II. We come now to some of the points of distinction between them.

The first we mention is, that Christ's approach to men has *a general and yet a special aspect.* The sun comes every morning with a broad unbroken look, shining for all, and singling out none. There is a universality of kindness about him which men, with all their powers of limitation, have never been able to abridge. The poorest man and the richest, all classes and all things, have the same access to his undivided effulgence. But the rain as it descends breaks into drops, and hangs with its globules on every blade. "God maketh small the drops of water." There is a wonderful individualizing power in the rain. It comes to the minutest part of God's world with its separate message, trickles from joint to joint of every grass stem, creeps into the smallest crevice that is opening its parched lips, pierces to the blind roots of things, and, where it cannot carry God's light into darkness, seeks to allure from darkness up into the light of God.

There is this twofold aspect in the coming of Christ. The Gospel of his grace enters the world with the broad universal look of daylight. It is as wide and open to all with its "Behold the Lamb of God!" It singles out none, that it may exclude none, — that it may be ready to bless a whole guilty world with the same impartiality as the sun, as God himself when "He looketh abroad and seeth under the whole heaven." And this lies not only in the words of the gospel offer, but in the real provision of it. The arms of God are as wide as his call, and the power of Christ's atonement is as unlimited as the invitation to it. Each one of us knows here, not merely what God is doing for ourselves, but for every other man of the race, and can say with confidence, "Come with me into this broad and blessed sunlight; it is for thee as for me; nay, I could not know that it is for me unless I were sure that it is for thee also, and for every man, in as entire sincerity."

But Christ comes after another manner with his Spirit. Here no man can tell how God is dealing with another. He approaches the door of the single heart, and says, when there is no ear to listen, "Behold, I stand at the door and knock." In the hour of thought, in the depth of night, in the shadow of trial, in the agony of remorse, He makes the soul feel that it is alone with Himself. With every one of us, surely, Christ has been thus dealing; taking us apart, and speaking to us of things that none knew but the soul and He; making our heart thrill and tremble as He touched it, till we have cried out, "Lord, what wilt *Thou* have *me* to do?" If we have felt this, if we are feeling it, there is a terrible responsibility in it, where none can help but Himself. He wrestles with us in the dark, that we may cling to, and cast ourselves on Him who wrestles with us: "Lord, I believe; help *Thou mine* unbelief," — until, bearing the soul's burden, He helps us from the dark into the daylight, and gives us the assurance of a love there that is also special and personal, "Christ loved *me*, and gave Himself for *me*."

Our next remark is, that Christ's coming is *constant, and yet variable.* The sunrise is of all things the most sure and settled. What consternation would seize the world if it delayed one hour, if God had not commanded the dayspring to know its place! But for the rain man knows no fixed rule. It may come soon or late, in scanty showers or plentiful floods. This is dependent on arrangements which are no doubt certain, but which we have not ascertained, and never may. The sovereign hand of God, giving and withholding, appears distinctly in the rain, as if He wished that we should always have before our eyes, in his working, the two great features of law and freedom.

And it is thus, too, with the coming of Christ. He visits men in his Gospel, steady and unchanging as the sun. Wheresoever we open the pages of his Book, his promises shine out sweet as the light and pleasant to the eyes. They come with a constant clearness and freshness which ought to make us feel that at every moment God is waiting to be gracious to us, — "I bring near my righteousness: it shall not be far off, and my salvation shall not tarry." Whatever changes may take place in us, whatever sins and backslidings, and fearful imaginings of unpardonable guilt, there, written in the Rock of Ages for ever, stand the words, "Him that cometh unto Me, I will in no wise cast out." The sun of Christ's gospel remains moveless in the midst of heaven till the world's day is closed, and makes it to every sinner a day of salvation and an acceptable time.

But with the Holy Spirit it is otherwise. His coming may vary in time and place — like the wind, which bloweth where it listeth, or the rain, whose arrival depends on causes we have not fathomed. The gift of God's Spirit is no doubt regulated also by laws, but these laws are hidden from us in their final grounds. God has linked these more directly with his own absolute sovereignty, and reserved the ultimate moving powers of the universe in the hollow of his hand. The clouds of revival which pass from land to land, — who can predict their course, or trace their laws, and say why they pass on, and why they fall in blessing? This one thing we do know, and it is the most practical, that prayer is closely connected with the outpouring of the Spirit. He who has bidden us ask our daily bread from our heavenly Father, and the rain that is to give it, has bidden us ask also from Him this good gift of his Holy Spirit, and has assured us that He will not deny it. The spirit of prayer is itself, indeed, the spiritual rain begun, but we may detain it, and increase the refreshing showers. We can lift up our voice to the clouds, that abundance of waters may cover us. And, if there be intermission in the coming of Christ by his Spirit, while there is constancy in his Gospel, it is that we may be kept from the presumption of spiritual delay. He who says to us, all through life, "Now is the day of salvation," says also, "To-day, if ye will hear his voice, harden not your hearts." If it be in the early rain, or the latter, in the tender feelings of youth or the solemn thoughts of darkening years, let us beseech life from the quickening Spirit while He is near, lest the gracious influences pass by, and our souls be left parched for ever.

We observe, further, that Christ's coming may be *with gladness, and yet also with trouble*. What in the world can be more joyful than the returning sun! Every creature feels it, and wakes up in cries and songs, and the dead, dumb earth puts off its dark and on its bright and many-coloured robes, when God covers it with light as with a garment. It is the emblem of God's sunrise in Christ, to the world, and to every individual soul. "I have blotted out as a thick cloud thy transgressions, and as a cloud thy sins. Sing, O ye heavens, for the Lord hath done it: shout, ye lower parts of the earth; break forth into singing, ye mountains, O forest, and every tree therein; for the LORD hath redeemed Jacob, and glorified Himself in Israel!"

But God comes also in the cloud, and there is a shade over the face of nature, — sometimes in the thunder-cloud, dark and threatening, and bird and beast shrink into their coverts, silent and awed. This represents the manner in which Christ sometimes comes, through his Spirit, in the conviction of sin. The conscience is shaken by the threatening thunder of his law, and his eye looks into the heart like lightning, while his voice declares, "Thou art the man." It was this coming that so shook the Jews, at the preaching of Peter, and that made an earthquake in the soul of the Philippian jailer, more terrible than that around him, till he cried, "What must I do to be saved?"

These operations may seem at times to conflict with each other, but as the God of nature is consistent in all his works, so also is the great God our Saviour Jesus Christ. The same wisdom and wonderful power of combination which are seen in external creation, appear also in the spiritual universe, of which Jesus Christ is Lord and God. The things that are around us, in the world of matter and sense, are patterns of things in the heavens. We are not only destined for an eternal life, but we are in the midst of it, in so far as we realize a spiritual existence, and the symbols and shadows of it are pressing in upon us every day, in these works of God, which are not dead works, but, to a true eye, spirit and life. And as God's sun and cloud in the world around us are not at variance, neither are the gladness that lies in the light of his Gospel, and the trouble that may come from the convictions of his Spirit.

We remark, last of all, that Christ's coming in his Gospel and Spirit may be separate for a while, *but they tend to a final and perfect union.* They are indispensable to each other. The sun may come and beat upon the earth, but it will make it only parched and dead without the rain. No more can the clearest shining of the Gospel save the soul or comfort it, without the Holy Spirit. Or again, the rain might come without the sunlight. The dew might lie all night

175

long on the branches, but there will be no life nor gladness till the morning comes to change sorrow into joy, to brighten dew-drops into sparks of sunlight, and scatter them over all the boughs, till they break out into the green of leaves and the hues of blossoms. No more could the sorrows of a broken heart and the convictions of the conscience give the Christian life, and its flower and fruit, without the presence of Christ in the gospel of his grace. The Gospel, without the Spirit, would be the sun shining on a waterless waste. The Spirit, without the Gospel, would be the rain falling in a starless night. Blessed be the Lord God, who hath showed us light, who hath sent us also rain from heaven, and fruitful seasons, filling our hearts with food and gladness!

There are some Christians to whom Christ is present more in the cloud. His Spirit works in them by conviction of sin, and depressing views of themselves, but they have only a small portion of the sunlight and the joy. What they need is, to keep before them the clear, simple view of Christ in the gospel, doing all, suffering all, and leaving us only to receive with thankful hearts—becoming all our salvation, that He may be all our desire. There are others who have a very distinct perception of the gospel in its freeness and fulness, but they have ceased to derive from it the comfort they once enjoyed. They need the rain. They have been too neglectful of the secret life of religion, which is its soul. They have been, if not falling into habitual sin, yet treading only the hard round of some outward duties, and avoiding communion of soul with God. This is to grieve the Holy Spirit, and so to lose his seal. What these need is, more earnest prayer for his refreshing influences, and a heart open to welcome them and use them: "I will be as the dew unto Israel; and they shall revive as the corn, and grow as the vine." Our souls can only live and grow when the sun and the showers intermingle; when the Spirit's dew comes by night, and the Gospel brings in the day. Then it shall be with us as "the light of the morning when the sun ariseth, even a morning without clouds; as the tender grass springing out of the earth, by the clear shining after rain."

It must not be forgotten, with all this, that there are those who know Christ neither as the morning nor the rain, who have been resisting alike invitation and conviction. It is possible to be in the midst of light and remain blind, to have the dews of God falling thick and free, and to continue in the centre of them parched and dry. It is well to think of another appearance which is as sure as this. He who visits us now as the morning, shall come as the consuming fire, and who may abide that day of his coming? He who makes his descent now like the rain, shall cause it to be as "the storm that shall sweep away the refuges of lies, and as the waters that shall overflow the hiding-place." This coming is also prepared, as sure as sunrise, fixed as the great ordinances of heaven, which approach us with incessant and silent steps when we think not of them. How dreadful to have the brightness of his coming flash upon our sins till we cry to mountains and rocks to hide us! Prepare to meet thy God! and may He himself prepare us by inclining our souls now to open to that Saviour who has long been visiting us, morning by morning, that we may be ready to welcome his final appearance as the end of all our sorrows, the sum of all our hopes, and the dawn of an everlasting and ever blessed day.

Something to Do

1. How did the preacher prepare the congregation for this sermon dealing with symbolism and analogy? Did he perhaps suspect resistance? Is there resistance to such preaching today or is the climate better?

2. Is he correct in referring to the sun as Christ and the rain as the Spirit? Do both the sun and the rain symbolize other spiritual entities in Scripture?

3. How does he preach the Gospel in this sermon?

4. Perhaps he anticipated listeners saying to themselves, "Well, that's pretty plain to see! So what?" How, then, did he make "obvious" comparisons and contrasts interesting and special?

5. Is it wise to deal with *both* comparisons and contrasts in one message, or was this the unique message of the text? Did the preacher succeed in keeping your thinking clear, or was there confusion at any point?

6. How does the preacher use New Testament texts to illuminate and illustrate the Old Testament pictures in his sermon text?

13

"Where Is Zebedee?"
William A. Quayle

WILLIAM A. QUAYLE (1860–1925) pastored churches in Kansas City, Indianapolis, and Chicago before being ordained a bishop of the Methodist Church in 1908. A popular preacher, he had a "homespun" approach not unlike that of Will Rogers or the late Vance Havner. This sermon is taken from his book *The Healing Shadow*, published in 1923 by Abingdon Press.

"Where Is Zebedee?"

"And they left their father Zebedee in the ship" — Mark 1:20.

This is the first and last we hear of Zebedee; and my inquiry this hour shall be, Where is Zebedee? As you notice, his sons went with Christ — left their father, left the ship, left the hired servants, left all and followed Christ. And the Gospels have much to say about these Zebedee boys, who, fishermen by birth, then fishermen in their own right of vocation, went away with Christ. James Zebedee was the first apostle martyr, and John Zebedee was a writer, and wrote what is in some regards the most clinging book in literature, namely, the Gospel of John. The Zebedee boys went with Him on the Mountain of Transfiguration, they were at the cross on which Christ died. John Zebedee was the man to whom the dying Christ bequeathed his mother, and John Zebedee was the fast runner, who when Mary Magdalene came and said, "The grave is empty," outran logy Peter, and came to the grave and looked in and saw not Christ entombed, but Christ arisen, and believed. And these Zebedee boys were together that great morning on Galilee's shore when Christ stood on the beach and called, "Children, have ye any meat?" And John Zebedee looked, when the voice came and thrilled him like a shock of lightning from the clouds, and said, "It is the Lord."

They were there. But where was Zebedee? That seems a sad question, does it? Yes, it is a sad question. I am not propounding it because I think it a joyous question. You shall hear no clanging of happy cymbals this morning. Where is Zebedee? His sons are with the Christ; but did I read you, "They left their father in the ship with the hired servants"? And Zebedee is busy fixing the nets, and says, "Good-by, boys."

"Father, come and go."

"Lads, I am too busy."

Fixing the nets.

And Christ says, "Come over!"

"Too busy, fixing the nets."

Where is Zebedee?

Where is Zebedee's wife? She was with Christ. She is called the mother of Zebedee's children; and she is with Jesus. And sometimes she was impertinent and sometimes she was a little foolish; but I

180

wonder if there was ever a woman born who was not foolish about her boys. I wonder if there was, I say. I haven't chanced to see her, and I won't look her up. And so she wanted her boys to have a place highest in the kingdom of God, and said so. She didn't keep anything back. There was a touch of femininity about her and she told her mind to Christ. But, but, at the cross when the Christ died there was the mother of Zebedee's children. And the boys were with Christ? Yes, truly. And the wife was with Christ? Yes, truly. But where is Zebedee? Didn't I tell you? He is mending the nets in the boat— staying with the servants; and the boat drifts out over the sea. What is Zebedee doing? Mending the nets. Never looks up, never looks up. Busy with the nets, and hears not. And Zebedee's fluttering ship's sail waning on the horizon, and the last rag of it melts out of the sky; and the last we see of Zebedee is as the first we saw of him—busy mending the nets. Never looks up. Where is Zebedee? Now, you remark that Zebedee had some commendable points in his character. He let his wife go to Christ. He didn't fuss and sulk. Some men who are mean and don't go to church will sulk and fuss and say, "I am not at home much and I think you could stay with me when I am home." I should hate to be that mean. If I let on to be a man, I wouldn't be that mean. But Zebedee didn't find fault with his wife for going with Christ and didn't find fault with his sons for going with Christ. O "Zebedee! Where are you, Zebedee?" But he does not hear; he is so busy mending the nets.

But did you think how much Zebedee missed? Is there anything wrong with mending the nets? Nothing. The nets must be mended lest the fishes escape. Is there anything wrong with fishing? Nothing. Fishing must be done or people would go hungry. Is there anything wrong with owning a boat? Not in the least. The best prevention against anarchy is the owning of something. What is the wrong? The wrong is that he never was with Christ—in the boat with the nets and the servants. And his wife, she is hearing Christ, and his boys, they are hearing Christ, and the father, Zebedee—don't speak of it lest we weep. Now, what was it Zebedee missed?

Well, he missed seeing Jesus. Friends, if you were to raise this interrogatory with your heart, "What man in history would I care most to see?" (Will you take this in your heart? It will take but a moment.) "What man in history would I love most to see—Homer, Abraham, Moses, or Elijah, or Pericles, or Themistocles, or Epaminondas, or Julius Caesar, or Mark Antony, or Cato, or Cicero, or Plato, or Plutinus, or Socrates, or Cromwell, or Lincoln, or Milton, or Shakespeare—whom would I most wish to see?" And I think I may not trespass upon the honest purlieus of your thinking when I say there is not a woman or a man in this company who, if he wandered through the universe of history, would not rather see the face of Christ. Oh, folks, pretty soon we shall. To-morrow, to-morrow, when the mists have wiped their veils from the face, and the blue sky will not hedge us in, and the stars of the skies made to roof us are no more, we shall see him. But Zebedee missed seeing Christ; missed ever seeing him. Why didn't he see him? I told you, didn't I? He was busy mending the nets. Busy with the boats and with the servants. Busy and never saw him; never saw the smiling come over his lips; never saw the wonder of revelation and redemption; never saw him. Why, Zebedee, why, Zebedee, didn't you ever go and look at Christ? Busy—nets broken—busy? Not a bad face; no. Nor a hard face; no. Just a visionless face. Didn't see Christ? Why, I would run through the universe a million, million years to see him just once. Wouldn't you? Just once. Oh, folks! Oh, folks! In heaven it is always sunup, because they always see the face of Christ.

"Oh, Zebedee, wouldn't you quit toying with the nets to see the Christ?"

"Busy," he said; "busy. Bread and butter got to be made."

Zebedee missed seeing Christ.

Then Zebedee missed hearing Christ. I have been much interested in Justin McCarthy's *Reminiscences.* Because he talks about so many people we would have liked to have seen and talked to, and nothing in his book impresses me so much as the folks he saw and heard. He heard Gladstone and Disraeli, and heard Wendell Phillips and Beecher, and Thomas Huxley and Charles Dickens, and Robert Browning and William Makepeace Thackeray, and heard Garibaldi and Kossuth, and Prince Napoleon and our poet, Russell Lowell. Wouldn't you have liked to have heard Charles Dickens read *The Child's Dream of a Star*? Wouldn't you? And wouldn't you have liked to have heard "The Death of Sydney Carton"? Wouldn't you? Wouldn't you have liked to have heard Thackeray read the four Georges lectures? Ah, well, let us not waste breath or time. What is that compared with hearing Christ talk? Wouldn't you have liked to have heard him say grace? I would hate to be a Christian parent and leave

182

in the memory of my children this, that they never heard their father say grace before meat. Wouldn't you have liked to have heard Jesus say grace? Wouldn't you have liked to have heard Jesus at his prayer. Wouldn't you have liked to have heard Jesus preach the Sermon on the Mount? Oh, that was a big sermon, but I would (you would not think unkindly of me, would you?) trade off a dozen times a day this sermon if I could only hear the Sermon at the Well. These sermons, preached to lonely or wicked or broken-hearted people — just one at a time — they make my heart itch to hear more about. John Zebedee heard it. Don't think that it says all the disciples were gone away to the city to buy meat. All the disciples were not. John could not have felt all that gust of passion and thrill of wonder, and those wide winds of God blowing if he had not heard the sermon. Why, where was Zebedee? His boy heard it. Where was Zebedee? Why didn't Zebedee hear it? One of these mornings — it will be morning when he talks, even if it is midnight — one of these mornings the voice of Christ will speak, not with the voice of reverberant thunders to shake the heavens, only a voice, but I tell you it will go to the tangled universe of death, and the grave will hear it. Whose voice is it? Oh, it is Christ's voice. "Everybody, get up!"

And the dead shall hear his voice and answer, "Here!"

And Zebedee didn't hear the Christ. Never heard him.

"O Zebedee, what are you doing?"

"Mending the nets, mending the nets. Bread and butter. Somebody's got to earn the bread and butter. Mending the nets."

Then Zebedee never saw Christ do miracles of mercy. Now, some of these times we will see Christ lift up his left hand and the universe will grow black as ink and there shall be no lights scattered through the heavens, and all the whereabouts throughout created things shall be as black marl. But I won't wonder at that. That will be Christ doing away with things he brought into being. But the wonder to me would be to see Christ take a sick woman by the hand and say: "Daughter, you are so sick and I am so sorry. You are well now. Go home and do your own housework; go on home." Wouldn't you have liked to have heard that? Upon my heart I'd go while life lasted to see that. Wouldn't you have liked to have seen Jesus when he walked along the road by the fringe of the desert and the leper came and looked in upon the world from which he was an outcast; and when Christ came toward him he thought that because he was busy he didn't see him, and so cried, "Leper, unclean; leper, unclean," and tried to cover up his face, and thought that Christ would stop and flee; but Christ walked straight toward him and never stopped, but rather hastened his springing step. And the leper called, "Leper, unclean! Leper, leper, unclean!"

And Christ said, "I will cure you, I will cure you!"

And the hand of God touched him on the cheek. Wouldn't you have liked to have seen that? You could have. Wouldn't you have liked to have seen Christ when he came to where two women had heartbreak? They had no father, they had no mother, and they just had their two selves and their brother; Lazarus was his name. Women have got to have a man to love somehow, if they have to borrow him; and so these women had no husband and they poured all that amazing wealth of womanhood love on their brother; and then he sickened; and the sickness grew tragical, and death came with breakneck haste and broke their house door wide open. Wouldn't you have liked to have been there when Christ said: "You are so lonesome. Lazarus, boy, come out. Your sisters want you; come out in a hurry."

"Zebedee, where are you?"

He says, "Busy fixing the nets broken by the fish haul."

And Zebedee missed seeing the cross. I think I would go farther to see the Sphinx than any other thing man has made on this planet. I think I would. Never had money enough to go there to see it yet. Maybe I won't. I would walk there if the ocean were good walking, but it is too wet, I am told. But I would go a long way to see the Sphinx. It is to me the most fascinating thing man ever shaped with his hands. You would rather see the Coliseum, would you? Very well. You would rather see the Cathedral at Rheims, would you? Very well. You would rather see the mosque of Saint Sophia, would you? Very well. I tell you what you would rather see. The cross on the hill and the Christ on the cross.

"But, Zebedee, what are you doing?"

"Mending the nets. Mending the nets."

"What is on the hill?"

"I do not know. Busy mending the nets."

On the hill is the cross, and on the cross the Christ, and the earth shakes and Galilee's waters tumble, and for a moment Zebedee looks up and says: "Storm brewing, servants; set the sails. I am busy mending the nets."

And Zebedee doesn't know it was Christ that shook the lake. Mending the nets. Missed the Christ. "O Zebedee, where are you?"

"Busy mending the nets."

Then Zebedee missed seeing an empty grave. I will not talk about that now. Why? Well, I think my heart would stop preaching and start singing to see a grave where a Man slept and a grave that couldn't grip a Man and hold him. O Death, your hands are so white with the frosts of death, and your might is so mighty, and so mighty those sinews on thumb and fingers that have choked the throat of the world — and Death, what ails you now? And Christ got up and left death snarling. And Zebedee, you might have seen that. What is he doing? He doesn't know there is a grave empty at all. He is busy mending the nets.

Don't you feel like going and weeping for Zebedee? What he did was not wrong; but he missed in his sense of proportion. Life is not making a living; life is making a life; and we are not to work for our board. We are here to make an immortal soul that is worth God's keeping alive forever. That's what life's for. What's life for Zebedee? He answers, "Fishing." I could weep for Zebedee, but I tell you honestly I haven't time to weep for him. There are so many Zebedees around. There are so many Zebedees around *now* that it takes my time to weep for them.

"Zebedee, what are you doing? Your children are in the church and your wife is in the church. Zebedee! Zebedee! Where are you?"

"Oh," he says. "Busy, busy!"

Some Zebedees on the Sabbath morning go down town and get their mail and read it. Now, that amazes me, that a man wouldn't know enough to know that six days are enough work days. There are enough days for business, and for the vigor of business. You ought to leave your mail alone for one day. Don't you businessmen know you can go at your six days' job with more prehensile fingers and with more sagacious intelligence if you leave your job alone for the Sabbath day. Oh, where is Zebedee now? He is sitting around home, smoking and lounging and taking it easy. His wife and his children go to church, perchance, and when they go home he says:

"Well, the preacher got through, did he? Preacher got through. He

185

quit at the expiration of ideas, did he?"

"O Zebedee! What ails you, Zebedee?"

Now, I will say that Zebedee ought to belong to the Church of Jesus Christ. I do not say the Methodist Church. Don't you think it. Lots of people ought to belong to the Methodist Church. It would be good for them. But I am talking about the God Church. Why ought Zebedee to be here in the church? Why? Well, because he is the head of the household. It makes a man stuck up to think that a woman will trade her name off for his. I never think of that but that I walk big. And it is funny what kind of a name a woman will trade off for, what other kind of a name, because the man is thrown in with the name. By the laws of this country a woman is not required to take a man's name, but you would need to work hard to have a nice woman marry a man and have him take her name. She would say, "My husband is too nice a man to be humiliated that way." You are pretty nice women. You are funny, but you're pretty nice. And I notice that woman will not only trade off her last name, but her first name. Her woman's name is often Susan Miranda, but she trades off that name and has her cards printed, "Mrs. James G. Thus-and-So." She traded off her name for a man's name. And I am saying this, Zebedee, when you give a name you ought to give Christ's name to the family. When your name is worn by your children you ought to see that your children have a Christian name. What are you doing? Mending the nets? And what happens? Why, we don't remember that John's name is John Zebedee, and that James' name is James Zebedee. And we say, "What gospel is this?"

"John's."

"John what?"

"John nothing."

And so Zebedee lost his chance. Zebedee, Zebedee! Why don't you, when you give your name to the household, give your household Christ's likeness. O Zebedee, quit fooling with the nets for a minute.

And then Zebedee ought to be with Christ, because a man has some influence with his own family. I didn't say much, did I? I said some. And it is a poor stick of a man that doesn't find himself consequential at home. There were some children of a preacher in Chicago some time ago going down by a structure in the city yclept Chicago, going down the street with their mother and they looked at a church — it was just before Conference, and it was a Methodist church, and these were a Methodist preacher's children, and they said, "Mama, let's go here." And she laughed — her husband wasn't there — and she laughed. And they said, "Why mama, why can't papa go there? He is as big a preacher as there is. He is as big a preacher as there is." O children, that is right. If the preacher doesn't cut much figure anywhere else he is somebody at home. And if a man is much a vagabond and torn and tattered, his children look up and say: "My papa said so. My papa said!" And I think fathers and mothers ought to have the sense to talk religiously before their children when they know their children take their cue from them. If a man cuts figure in his family I tell you this, that Zebedee is the father of the Zebedee boys, and he is the husband of the Zebedee woman, and he ought — and I am not one to absolve him from his duty — to give those children and that wife a specimen of his being with the Christ. "O Zebedee, what are you doing?"

"Mending the nets."

Then Zebedee ought to be with Christ because the religious function is the highest function of the soul; and in the old, patriarchal days, the old men of the tribe were the priests of the tribe. Mark you this, the highest function is the Christian priestly function, standing for God. Where is Zebedee? And my heart has ached so for Zebedee, and my lips and my heart have conspired to pray for Zebedee.

"Zebedee, where are you? Why aren't you at church, Zebedee? Why don't you pray, Zebedee? You want your wife to be a Christian. I think ninety-nine men out of the one hundred would marry a Christian woman in preference to an unChristian woman. Where is your logic, Zebedee? Zebedee! Zebedee! Some one calling you? Oh, Zebedee!"

"I am Zebedee!"

"What are you doing, Zebedee?"

"Busy making ends meet."

"Where is your wife, Zebedee?"

"She has gone to church to hear Christ preach, I reckon. She does often."

And he catches up the torn thread of the torn net and ties it with deft fingers.

"Say, Zebedee, where are your boys — where's Jim and where's John?"

187

"Oh, they have gone to church to hear Christ preach."
"Zebedee, Brother Zebedee, why aren't you at church."
"Oh, I am busy mending the nets."
"O Zebedee, Zebedee, Zebedee! Where are you, Zebedee?"

Prayer: O God, call Zebedee this morning—call him not away from his nets, but call him away with his nets—call him, O Christ. Then let Zebedee come to the Christ with his wife on his arm and with his children by him. Let Zebedee and the mother of Zebedee's children and the children of Zebedee all sit in the house of the Lord together, for Christ's sake. Amen.

Something to Do

1. Is the preacher using his imagination, indulging in fantasy, or both?

2. How can we distinguish fantasy from imagination? Do you think his approach is permissible? Explain.

3. When we don't have a clear biblical basis for a sermon, how do we approach the subject honestly? Can there be strength in supposition? What pitfalls must we avoid?

4. How much of the power of this message would depend on the preacher's delivery and his relationship to the congregation?

5. Why does the preacher keep repeating the phrase about "mending the nets"?

6. Did reading the sermon make an impact on your own heart?

14

"Kings As Servants"
John Henry Jowett

IN HIS PRIME, John Henry Jowett (1864–1923) was known as "the greatest preacher in the English-speaking world." A master of the English language, Jowett said that he used words the way a jeweler handled precious gems. He pastored some famous churches, including Carr's Lane Church, Birmingham, where he succeeded R.W. Dale, Fifth Avenue Presbyterian in New York City, and Westminster Chapel, London, where he followed G. Campbell Morgan.

This sermon is taken from *God— Our Contemporary,* published in 1922 by Fleming H. Revell Company.

"Kings As Servants"

"And kings shall be thy nursing fathers, and their queens thy nursing mothers; they shall bow down to thee" — Isaiah 49:23.

What a startling figure of speech this is! It is steeped in Oriental brilliancy of light and colour. And it is like a thousand other figures in the Old Testament, very aggressive in their strength, full-blooded things, discharging their mission in almost boisterous strength. What a power of brain and imagination belonged to these Old Testament prophets, and with what decision they married it to equally robust expression! They were poets as well as prophets. They had imagination as well as reason. They had vision as well as sight. And they gave their thoughts and dreams verbal bodies of amazing life and virility.

Look, for an example of all this, at the figure in my text. "And kings shall be thy nursing fathers, and their queens thy nursing mothers." Let us disregard its historical application for the moment. Let us examine it merely as a product of the imagination. What, then, is the imagery? Kings are to put off their imperial purple and to put on the apron of the slave. They are to lay aside their regality and clothe themselves in humility. The sceptre, which is the symbol of rule, is to be exchanged for the towel, which is the symbol of service. Kings are to translate their sovereignty into simple tasks, and they are to humbly minister to people over whom they are supposed to reign. This is something other than kings in mufti. It is power converted into gentleness; it is tyranny transformed. Such is the figure of the text.

And now let us grasp the prophet's application of it. He is speaking to a people who are in exile. They are like the deported captives of Belgium, under the indifferent heel of the Kaiser, and spurned by the imperial militarism of Germany. And what have kings meant to these Jewish exiles? Kings have been the symbols of an alien tyranny. Kings have been the slave-drivers in the bleak fields of their desolation. Kings have been the despots before whom they have marched in degrading bondage. To this disheartened little people kings have meant invasion, captivity, homelessness, exile.

But now a prophet arises among them with power to pierce the immediate gloom of brutal circumstance. He is a prophet of hope.

He is endowed with sight and insight. He sees the alluring light of a wonderful dawn. In glowing imagery he foretells their return to their native land. Tyranny shall be ended, and liberty shall be reborn. With an almost gorgeous wealth of pictorial setting he portrays the blessedness of their restoration. The parched ground is to become a pool. The dry land is to become musical with rivers of water. The wilderness is to become alive with the sound of joy and laughter. The desert is to rejoice and blossom like the rose. The old, heavy roads of affliction are to be highways of revelry. The crooked is to become straight, and the rough places plain. And as for kings, those grim symbols of tyranny and oppression, this is to be their fate: "kings shall be thy nursing fathers," nourishing and cherishing the people they had spurned, "and queens shall be thy nursing mothers; they shall bow down to thee." Such is the prophet's imagery, and such is the interpretation of his quickening vision. Kings are to become servants: ancient tyranny is to wear the apron of the slave.

Well now, I am going to suggest that, although we are a long, long way from any circumstances which have any sort of likeness to the condition of these captive Jews, it is not altogether a remote land of legend and dream. I am going to suggest that, as far as we are concerned, something analogous happens on our road whenever our life is governed and ordained by God. There are kingly and despotic things on our road, grim presences which hold us in paralysing servitude, but their alien power is transformed into an ally whenever our life passes into surrendered fellowship with the Lord. The tyrannical kings on the road become our servants, and in vital religion we discover our own sovereignty and freedom. "And kings shall be thy nursing fathers, and their queens thy nursing mothers; they shall bow down to thee."

Let us begin on the outermost circle. Science has laid a firm hand on some despotic kings and she has set them to work as our slaves. For instance, she has harnessed the tyranny of the lightning to the gentle ministries of the garden, and on the plains of Evesham the lightning is the nursing father and the nursing mother of all the fruits in their season. Yes, that grim agent of destruction and death is now quickening the life of delicate growths, and adding stores of vigour to their resources. And what about that imperial presence called Niagara—so awe-inspiring in its eternal flow, so overwhelming in its weight and power? Science has transformed that mighty king into a servant, and he is made to visit distant towns and to light up the homes of Buffalo and Toronto. Niagara's energy is sent on knightly errands to kindle a gentle radiance in the chambers of the sick and the pain-ridden. "And Niagara shall be thy nursing father; it shall bow down to thee." Science has hitched our wagons to stars. She has yoked the tempest to our service. She has captured mighty giants in the material world, and she has ordained them as hewers of wood and drawers of water in the ministry of man.

But there are kings much more overbearing than these. There are other tyrants on the road, and they drive us about, and knock us about; they oppress us with their ceaseless assaults, and they crush the very life out of us. And it is the marrow of the gospel of Christ that when we enter into the intimate fellowship of God these grim kings become our servants; they bring their strength to our necessities, and so far from pinching us into penury they are made to enlarge and enrich the circuit of our lives. That is what happens when we are in the benign friendship of the Lord. We drive vigorous ministries from age-long tyrannies. Ancient royalties are made to serve us. Their power is transmuted, and we gather our honey from the carcase of the lion.

Let me ask you to let your eyes rest upon one or two of these kings as they pass before us in sombre procession. Here is one of them. What is his name? His name is Pain, and he is a king with an almost endless domination. Every hospital is one of his palaces. Every sick chamber is a room in one of the residences of this imperial monarch. Do you know any home where he has never crossed the threshold, and over the lintel of whose door you could write the amazing words, "Pain is unknown here"? He seems to brook no exception. We are all dragged within his sovereignty, and we are all stamped with the impress of his iron rule. Every wail on the planet is a weird sign of his presence, whether it be the sudden cry of agony, or the moan of a sufferer whom he never leaves . . . I think you will agree with me that, amid all the crumbling thrones and trembling monarchies of our day, King Pain maintains his sway.

Well, what can we say about him? What can we say? We can say this, that King Pain can be so controlled that his tyranny becomes a ministry, that his oppression is leagued with service, and that he is compelled to leave infinitely more than he takes. In the fellowship of

God, Pain becomes our nursing father, and his directed and appointed business is to cherish and nourish the precious life of the soul. I do not say that when we become the friends of God King Pain loses his sharp implements; perhaps he does not lose any of them; but I do say that they are not allowed to hack and slash away with brutal destructiveness. The sharp tool is made to carve some exquisite bit of tracery in the essential character of the soul. I cannot say that Pain loses his harrow, and that he ceases to do harrowing things, but I can say that in the communion of God the harrow is not dragged to and fro over the field of our life with absolutely aimless ravage. The harrow is wedded to the ministry of a coming harvest, and it is made to serve the call and needs of the far-off ripening grain. I cannot say that King Pain is deprived of the power of giving pain. He is not bereft of his sword, but it is changed into a ploughshare. He is not robbed of his spear, but it is transformed into a pruning hook. In the wonderful appointments of God's Will Pain becomes a servant and ambassador of grace, and all he does is connected with a higher purpose which he is unable to defeat.

King Pain is transformed into a nursing mother for the nourishing of virtues and graces. King Pain is made to serve the virtue of endurance until our fortitude has all the splendid strength of an oak. And what else? King Pain is made to serve the virtue of sympathy, and the sympathy subtly widens our discernments until we can take things in which are far away. And what else? King Pain is made to serve the virtue of tenderness, and we acquire that gentleness of touch whose tapping opens anybody's door. . . . And how is all this to be brought about? It is to be brought about in the friendship and companionship of God. There was a man of the name of Paul, who was greatly troubled by King Pain, for he had afflicted him with a thorn in the flesh. "And I besought the Lord thrice that it might depart from me." And did it go? No, it did not go, but it remained in the guarding alliance of the divine grace. "And the Lord said unto him, My grace is sufficient for thee, for My strength is made perfect in weakness." And so the thorn remained. King Pain retained his sway, but it was all directed to the enlargement and enrichment of the apostle's spiritual treasures, and in the fulness of his wealth you and I are privileged to share to-day. . . . Well, then, this is one of the kings on life's road, King Pain. And King Pain shall be thy nursing father and thy nursing mother; it shall bow down to thee.

Developing a Christian Imagination

There is another king on the road. What is his name? His name is Mammon. He has a number of aliases, such as Gold, Money, Property, Possessions, but it is the same despotic power beneath them all. I do not know that any one of us has special prerogative, and is therefore able to complete the journey of life without ever meeting this king upon the way. It is not a question as to whether we are rich or poor. Our relationship to the tyrant Mammon is not determined by our account at the bank. It is not a matter of more or less. One man may have an income of a thousand pounds a week, and he may be gloriously resisting the despotism of King Mammon, while another man may have an income of five pounds a week, and yet be piteously and completely under his sway. If we had the requisite powers of discernment, and if we wished to estimate how far anyone had become a victim of the tyranny of money, we should have to apply a sort of level-test to their life. We should have to bring the soul and the money into the same plane of vision, and then compare their different levels in relation to each other. Which is on the higher level, the soul or the money? Which is upper, and which is under? Which is superior, and which is inferior? What is the attitude of the soul when it looks out upon gold? Does it look up, or does it look down? Is the posture one of homage, or is it one of command? It is in this way that the crucial question resolves itself into a test of levels, and attitudes, and points of view, and angles of vision. Where is Mammon in relation to our souls? Is he on the throne, or is he kneeling at our feet? Are we his victims, or is he our servant? Is he our master, or is he the menial of our aspiring and consecrated will? It is all a question of comparative levels; it is not in any way a matter of amounts.

But now the peril in the tyranny of Mammon is this—he never displays his tyranny, and he snares us into bondage on the plea that he is leading us into freedom. In a certain very subtle way he hypnotizes his victims, and in their unnatural sleep he marches them into his thraldom. Mammon does not coerce, he allures. He does not throw a cartrope around us, and violently drag us into captivity. He inveigles us with cords of vanity, delicate things, silken things, and in quite an air of festivity he leads us to our doom. We start out on a gay crusade, but the gay crusade is ere long changed into a prison. At the beginning money is our highway, along which we are marching to something else; in the feverish quest it becomes our goal. We begin by making money for finer ends, we end by making money. We make money, and that is all we make, and we are unmade in the making.

Such appears to be the tyranny of King Mammon. He hypnotizes his victims, and no Pied Piper of Hamelin has ever had such multitudes in his train. And how he mocks his retinue! Mammon creates desires which he never fulfils. He pleases us with a few flashy adornments while he robs us of our spiritual wealth. He gratifies us with the outer shows of things, but he is all the while consuming our virtue, just as the white ant eats out the inner pith and pulp of great trees, and leaves only the bark, the seeming forms of trees, which a single night's tempest can blow into dust. "Money," says Emerson, "often costs too much." And indeed it does! We gain it at the cost of our moral and spiritual freedom. "At a great price purchased I this bondage!"

Well, what about this King Mammon? All the young folk have got to meet him. I should not know what streets to suggest to you, or by what names they are called, if you want to dodge him. You cannot dodge him even if you would, and there is no reason why you should wish it. Begin all your reasonings about it with one clear word of the Master: "Ye cannot serve God and Mammon." How then? Why, make Mammon serve God! And that is the transformation which is effected when we are living in intimate friendship and communion with God. By God's good grace this despot can be changed into a servant, and he is made to minister to the soul which he aspires to rule. "And kings shall be thy nursing fathers; they shall bow down to thee," and King Mammon shall be among those who bend at thy feet.

Just think of Mammon as a nursing father, nourishing and cherishing all the fledgling graces and virtues of the soul! And that is surely what Jesus meant what He said: "Make to yourselves friends of the Mammon of unrighteousness." What the Saviour meant is this—take My way, and in My companionship, and so compel your tyrant to befriend your soul. So think of money, and so make money, and so use money, that all the while it shall be as a nursing mother with her young—it shall feed and vitalize every offspring of your spirit which makes you the kinsman of your God. There is no more wretched sight on earth than the slave of money. On the other hand, there is no more noble sight than its master. "And kings shall be thy nursing fathers, and their queens thy nursing mothers; they shall bow down to thee."

There are many other tyrannical kings on the road of life, and I must leave you to inspect and challenge them at your leisure. But in all your examination of the royal procession give a good look at one very imperious monarch whose name is Temptation. He is as despotic and cunning a villain as you will find on the road, but, like every other tyrant, he falls upon his knees when you confront him in the presence and authority of your Lord. Give, I say, a good look at him, and study the gospel secrets which tell how to set him to service in burnishing and refining the jewels of the soul.

But let me, as I close, just name another king whose gloomy approach darkens the road as with the fall and pall of night. I mean King Death. Among all the kings on the road there is none more imperious than he. Every movement about him is kingly, even when he comes with gentlest steps. In all the sublime pictures in which Watts portrays the presence of Death, however tender Death may appear, and however light his touch, there is an air of authority and command about him which seems to leave no right of appeal. King Death goes everywhere, and he knocks at everybody's door. "Death lays his icy hand on kings," so imperial is his sovereign sway! He is a mighty king. Is he a necessary tyrant of our souls?

Dare I bring in the word of my text, and look for some transforming light even on this gloomy, dreary part of the road? Dare I look at King Death, then utter this word to my comfort — "And kings shall be thy nursing fathers; they shall bow down to thee?" Will King Death bend his proud back and become the servant of my soul? Yes, that is the sweet music of the gospel of grace. There are some arresting songs of emancipation in the sacred book which suggest that the singers had looked into the eyes of the tyrant and found that his tyranny was broken. For example, here is one believer in the Lord, and his word seems to be filled with something like a taunt, as though he were now playing lightly with an ogre which he feared in early days: "O death, where is thy sting?" . . . What can the adder do without its sting? . . . I say there is almost a triumphant laugh in the taunt. "O death, where is thy sting?" . . . Here is a king who has lost his despotism. He has lost his power to despoil and destroy, and all that is now left to him is the power to befriend the pilgrims he once terrified, and lead them into the sweet intimacies of home, and into the all-comforting love of their Father in Heaven.

Jesus Christ has some strange things to say about King Death. He speaks of him as though, in some mysterious way, his tyranny is so buried in service that the dreadful thing is never seen. Where is King Death in this word of our Lord—"He that liveth and believeth in Me shall never die"? . . . And where is King Death in this word of our Lord—"He that believeth in Me shall never taste death?" . . . And where is King Death in this word of our Lord—"He that believeth in Me shall never see death?" . . . Where is King Death, I say? The secret is here—the tyrant is lost in the servant, and his terrors are swallowed up in the blaze of immortality.

And so it is with all these kings; there is one secret by which their tyranny is broken. There is one King on the road, "and on His thigh this name is written, 'King of kings and Lord of lords.' " He is the lawful King of the road, and every other king bows before Him. "Kings shall fall down before Him." It is in His strong, sweet friendship that we find the right of way, and every other king will bend to do us service. King Jesus is not stingy in His friendship, nor is He stiff and reluctant in His communion. The stinginess is all on our side; the reluctance is in our own wills. "Behold, I stand at the door and knock. If any man open the door I will come in." . . . "Lift up your heads, O ye gates, and be ye lift up, ye everlasting doors, and the King of Glory shall come in."

Something to Do

1. In the first two paragraphs, why did Jowett bring the symbolical and the historical together? What was he trying to accomplish in the minds and hearts of his listeners? How does his introduction compare with the introductions by the other preachers whose sermons you have read so far?

2. Does he use good hermeneutical principles in making his interpretation and application?

3. Is this the kind of approach George Morrison would have taken? Spurgeon? Defend your answer.

4. What is your personal response to his approach to the subject of pain and suffering in this world? Is his reference to 2 Corinthians 12 a valid one in light of his approach to the text?

5. What was your response to his closing declarations about Jesus Christ the King of kings? Was this a fitting climax to the message?

15

"Hudson Taylor's Text"
Frank W. Boreham

ON MAY 28, 1911, the minister of
the Hobart (Tasmania) Baptist Tabernacle began preaching a series of
sermons on "texts that made history," a series that eventually com-
prised more than 100 sermons! The
preacher was Frank W. Boreham
(1871–1959), and the series is found
in five of the more than sixty books
that he published: *A Bunch of
Everlastings, A Handful of Stars, A
Casket of Cameos, A Faggot of
Torches,* and *A Temple of Topaz.*
Each sermon deals with a text that
played an important part in the life
and work of some famous person,
and undoubtedly the series is one of
the most imaginative ever preached
from an evangelical pulpit.

Along with books of sermons,
Boreham also published many collections of his quaint homey essays
that, in spite of—or maybe because
of—their Victorian flavor, are still
worth reading today. His essays re-

veal his quick insight and strong imagination as much as do his printed sermons. With essay titles like "Sermons and Sandwiches," "A Lion in Pincurls," and "A Baby's Baggage," Boreham proved himself the master of seeing spiritual truths in the strangest places in everyday life. For that reason, I recommend you read Boreham and learn from him how to see and learn from the world around you.

This sermon is from *A Handful of Stars,* published in 1922 by Judson Press.

"Hudson Taylor's Text"

I

The day on which James Hudson Taylor—then a boy in his teens— found himself confronted by that tremendous text was, as he himself testified in old age, "a day that he could never forget." It is a day that China can never forget; a day that the world can never forget. It was a holiday; everybody was away from home; and the boy found time hanging heavily upon his hands. In an aimless way he wandered, during the afternoon, into his father's library, and poked about among the shelves. "I tried," he says, "to find some book with which to while away the leaden hours. Nothing attracting me, I turned over a basket of pamphlets and selected from among them a tract that looked interesting. I knew that it would have a story at the commencement and a moral at the close; but I promised myself that I would enjoy the story and leave the rest. It would be easy to put away the tract as soon as it should seem prosy." He scampers off to the stable-loft, throws himself on the hay, and plunges into the book. He is captivated by the narrative, and finds it impossible to drop the book when the story comes to an end. He reads on and on. He is rewarded by one great golden word whose significance he has never before discovered: *The Finished Work of Christ!* The theme entrances him; and at last he only rises from his bed in the soft hay that he may kneel on the hard floor of the loft and surrender his young life to the Saviour who had surrendered everything for him. If, he asked himself, as he lay upon the hay, if the whole work was finished, and the whole debt paid upon the Cross, what is there left for me to do? "And then," he tells us, "there dawned upon me the joyous conviction that there was nothing in the world to be done but to fall upon my knees, accept the Saviour and praise Him for evermore."

"It is finished!"

"When Jesus, therefore, had received the vinegar he said, 'It is finished!' and He bowed His head and gave up the ghost."

"Then there dawned upon me the joyous conviction that, since the whole work was finished and the whole debt paid upon the Cross, there was nothing for me to do but to fall upon my knees, accept the Saviour and praise Him for evermore!"

II

"It is finished!"

It is really only one word: the greatest word ever uttered; we must examine it for a moment as a lapidary examines under a powerful glass a rare and costly gem.

It was a *farmer's* word. When, into his herd, there was born an animal so beautiful and shapely that it seemed absolutely destitute of faults and defects, the farmer gazed upon the creature with proud, delighted eyes. *"Tetelestai!"* he said, *"tetelestai!"*

It was an *artist's* word. When the painter or the sculptor had put the last finishing touches to the vivid landscape or the marble bust, he would stand back a few feet to admire his masterpiece, and, seeing in it nothing that called for correction or improvement, would murmur fondly, *"Tetelestai! tetelestai!"*

It was a *priestly* word. When some devout worshiper, overflowing with gratitude for mercies shown him, brought to the temple a lamb without spot or blemish, the pride of the whole flock, the priest, more accustomed to seeing the blind and defective animals led to the altar, would look admiringly upon the pretty creature. *"Tetelestai!"* he would say, *"tetelestai!"*

And when, in the fullness of time, the Lamb of God offered Himself on the altar of the ages, He rejoiced with a joy so triumphant that it bore down all His anguish before it. The sacrifice was stainless, perfect, finished! *"He cried with a loud voice Tetelestai! and gave up the ghost."*

This divine self-satisfaction appears only twice, once in each Testament. When He completed the work of Creation, He looked upon it and said that it was very good; when He completed the work of Redemption He cried with a loud voice *Tetelestai!* It means exactly the same thing.

III

The joy of finishing and of finishing well! How passionately good men have coveted for themselves that ecstasy! I think of those pathetic entries in Livingstone's journal. "Oh, to finish my work!" he writes again and again. He is haunted by the vision of the unseen waters, the fountains of the Nile. Will he live to discover them? "Oh, to finish!" he cries; "if only I could finish my work!" I think of Henry Buckle, the author of the *History of Civilization*. He is overtaken by fever at Nazareth and dies at Damascus. In his delirium he raves continually about his book, his still unfinished book. "Oh, to finish my book!" And with the words "My book! my book!" upon his burning lips, his spirit slips away. I think of Henry Martyn sitting amidst the delicious and fragrant shades of a Persian garden, weeping at having to leave the work that he seemed to have only just begun. I think of Doré taking a sad farewell of his unfinished *Vale of Tears;* of Dickens tearing himself from the manuscript that he knew would never be completed; of Macaulay looking with wistful and longing eyes at the *History* and *The Armada* that must for ever stand as "fragments"; and of a host besides. Life is often represented by a broken column in the churchyard. Men long, but long in vain, for the priceless privilege of finishing their work.

IV

The joy of finishing and of finishing well! There is no joy on earth comparable to this. Who is there that has not read a dozen times the immortal postscript that Gibbon added to his *Decline and Fall?* He describes the tumult of emotion with which, after twenty years of closest application, he wrote the last line of the last chapter of the last volume of his masterpiece. It was a glorious summer's night at Lausanne. "After laying down my pen," he says, "I took several turns in a covered walk of acacias which commands a prospect of the country, the lake and the mountains. The air was temperate, the sky was serene, the silver orb of the moon was reflected from the waters, and all nature was silent." It was the greatest moment of his life. We recall, too, the similar experience of Sir Archibald Alison. "As I approached the closing sentence of my *History of the Empire*," he says, "I went up to Mrs. Alison to call her down to witness the conclusion, and she saw the last words of the work written, and signed her name on the margin. It would be affectation to conceal the deep emotion that I felt at this event." Or think of the last hours of Venerable Bede. Living away back in the early dawn of our English story—twelve centuries ago—the old man had set himself to translate the Gospel of John into our native speech. Cuthbert, one of his young disciples, has bequeathed to us the touching record. As the work approached completion, he says, death drew on apace. The aged scholar was racked with pain; sleep forsook him; he could scarcely breathe. The young man who wrote at his dictation implored him to desist. But he would not rest. They came at length to the final chapter; could he possibly live till it was done?

"And now, dear master," exclaimed the young scribe tremblingly, "only one sentence remains!" He read the words and the sinking man feebly recited the English equivalents.

"It is finished, dear master!" cried the youth excitedly.

"Ay, *it is finished!*" echoed the dying saint; "lift me up, place me at that window of my cell at which I have so often prayed to God. Now glory be to the Father and to the Son and to the Holy Ghost!" And, with these triumphant words, the beautiful spirit passed to its rest and its reward.

V

In his own narrative of his conversion, Hudson Taylor quotes James Proctor's well-known hymn—the hymn that, in one of his essays, Froude criticizes so severely:

> Nothing either great or small,
> Nothing, sinner, no;
> Jesus did it, did it all,
> Long, long ago.

> "*It is Finished!*" yes, indeed,
> Finished every jot;
> Sinner, this is all you need;
> Tell me, is it not?

> Cast your deadly doing down,
> Down at Jesus' feet;
> Stand in Him, in Him alone,
> Gloriously complete.

Froude maintains that these verses are immoral. It is only by "doing," he argues, that the work of the world can ever get done. And if you describe "doing" as "deadly" you set a premium upon indolence and lessen the probabilities of attainment. The best answer to Froude's plausible contention is the *Life of Hudson Taylor.* Hudson Taylor became convinced, as a boy, that "the whole work was finished and the whole debt paid." "There is nothing for me to do," he says, "but to fall down on my knees and accept the Saviour." The chapter in his biography that tells of this spiritual crisis is entitled *"The Finished Work of Christ,"* and it is headed by the quotation:

> Upon a life I did not live,
> Upon a death I did not die,
> Another's life, Another's death
> I stake my whole eternity.

And, as I have said, the very words that Froude so bitterly condemns are quoted by Hudson Taylor as a reflection of his own experience. And the result? The result is that Hudson Taylor became one of the most prodigious toilers of all time. So far from his trust in *"the Finished Work of Christ"* inclining him to indolence, he felt that he must toil most terribly to make so perfect a Saviour known to the whole wide world. There lies on my desk a Birthday Book which I very highly value. It was given me at the docks by Mr. Thomas Spurgeon as I was leaving England. If you open it at the twenty-first of May you will find these words: " *'Simply to Thy Cross I cling' is but half of the Gospel. No one is really clinging to the Cross who is not at the same time faithfully following Christ and doing whatsoever He commands"*; and against those words of Dr. J.R. Miller's in my Birthday Book, you may see the autograph of *J. Hudson Taylor.* He was our guest at the Mosgiel Manse when he set his signature to those striking and significant sentences.

VI

"We Build Like Giants; We Finish Like Jewelers!" — so the old Egyptians wrote over the portals of their palaces and temples. I like to think that the most gigantic task ever attempted on this planet — the work of the world's redemption — was finished with a precision and a nicety that no jeweler could rival.

"It is finished!" He cried from the Cross.

"Tetelestai! Tetelestai!"

When He looked upon His work in Creation and saw that it was good, He placed it beyond the power of man to improve upon it.

> To gild refined gold, to paint the lily,
> To throw a perfume on the violet,
> To smooth the ice, or add another hue
> Unto the rainbow, or with taper-light
> To seek the beauteous eye of heaven to garnish,
> Is wasteful and ridiculous excess.

And, similarly, when He looked upon His work in Redemption and cried triumphantly *"Tetelestai,"* He placed it beyond the power of any man to add to it.

There are times when any addition is a subtraction. Some years ago, the White House at Washington — the residence of the American Presidents — was in the hands of the painters and decorators. Two large entrance doors had been painted to represent black walnut. The contractor ordered his men to scrape and clean them in readiness for repainting, and they set to work. But when their knives penetrated to the solid timber, they discovered to their astonishment that it was heavy mahogany of a most exquisite natural grain! The work of that earlier decorator, so far from adding to the beauty of the timber, had only served to conceal its essential and inherent glory. It is easy enough to add to the wonders of Creation or of Redemption; but you can never add without subtracting. *"It is finished!"*

VII

Many years ago, Ebenezer Wooton, an earnest but eccentric evangelist, was conducting a series of summer evening services on the village green at Lidford Brook. The last meeting had been held; the crowd was melting slowly away; and the evangelist was engaged in taking down the marquee. All at once a young fellow approached him and asked, casually rather than earnestly, "Mr. Wooton, what must *I* do to be saved?" The preacher took the measure of his man.

"Too late!" he said, in a matter of fact kind of way, glancing up from a somewhat obstinate tentpeg with which he was struggling. "Too late, my friend, too late!" The young fellow was startled.

"Oh, don't say that, Mr. Wooton!" he pleaded, a new note coming into his voice. "Surely it isn't too late just because the meetings are over?"

"Yes, my friend," exclaimed the evangelist, dropping the cord in his hand, straightening himself up, and looking right into the face of his questioner, "it's too late! You want to know what you must *do* to be saved, and I tell you that you're hundreds of years too late! The work of salvation is done, complete, *finished!* It was finished on the Cross; Jesus said so with the last breath that He drew! What more do you want?"

And, then and there, it dawned upon the now earnest inquirer on the village green as, at about the same time, it dawned upon young Hudson Taylor in the hay-loft, that *"since the whole work was finished and the whole debt paid upon the Cross, there was nothing for him to do but to fall upon his knees and accept the Saviour."* And there, under the elms, the sentinel stars witnessing the great transaction, he kneeled in glad thanksgiving and rested his soul for time and for eternity on *"the Finished Work of Christ."*

VIII

"The Finished Work of Christ!"
   "Tetelestai! Tetelestai!"
   "It is finished!"

It is not a sigh of relief at having reached the end of things. It is the unutterable joy of the artist who, putting the last touches to the picture that has engrossed him for so long, sees in it the realization of all his dreams and can nowhere find room for improvement. Only once in the world's history did a finishing touch bring a work to absolute perfection; and on that day of days a single flaw would have shattered the hope of the ages.

Something to Do

1. If today you began a sermon with the name "James Hudson Taylor," would most of your congregation recognize it? What would a preacher have to do today to make that name interesting so the congregation would want to hear more about him?

2. What is your response to Boreham's way of introducing and explaining the Greek word *tetelestai?* What traps must we avoid when we bring biblical languages into the pulpit? Does Boreham successfully avoid these traps?

3. What more contemporary illustrations could you use about people who finished their work and did it well?

4. Where does Boreham get most of his illustrative material in this sermon? What sources do you use?

5. Is the evangelistic appeal a strong one?

6. Did you expect to hear more about Hudson Taylor before the sermon closed? Should Boreham have said more?

Part Three

Discussions and Insights

This miscellaneous collection has one purpose in mind: to introduce you to the practical aspects of creative teaching and preaching by the use of imagination.

A.W. Tozer deals with the theological and personal meaning of "a sanctified imagination" and summons us to free ourselves from an approach to Scripture that is so mechanical that it strangles the text and smothers the sermon. I often heard Tozer preach; he was true to the Word, and one marveled at his creativity.

Beecher and Dale are the oldest contributors, yet it's remarkable to see how contemporary their ideas are. Both were gifted preachers, although Dale's style was more academic; yet both emphasize the importance of the imagination.

Halford Luccock represents the "classic" approach to imagination in preaching, and this approach is expanded by Ryken and Wheeler.

Eugene H. Peterson is one of our gifted contemporary writers and specialists in pastoral theology. The two selections from him are not only examples of creative communication, but they contain valuable insights into imagination and its place in ministry.

16

"The Value of a Sanctified Imagination"
A.W. Tozer

AIDEN WILSON TOZER (1897–1963) may well have been the twentieth century's leading "evangelical mystic." Identified with the Christian and Missionary Alliance, he pastored churches in West Virginia, Ohio, and Pennsylvania before moving to the Southside Alliance Church in Chicago in 1928. In 1959, four years before his death, he resigned the Chicago pastorate to become "preaching pastor" of the Avenue Road Church in Toronto.

His ministry was often called "prophetic," for Tozer fearlessly exposed the sins of the saints and summoned a worldly complacent church back to humble worship and the fear of God. He was a master of the interior life, having saturated himself with the Bible and the teachings of the Christian mystics. His philosophy was simply that "everything is wrong until

God sets it right." While his preaching was insightful and incisive, Tozer will probably be remembered most for his editorials in *The Alliance Weekly* (now *The Alliance Witness*), many of which are reprinted in his numerous books.

This essay is from A.W. Tozer, *Born After Midnight* (Camp Hill, Pa.: Christian Publications, 1959), 92–95, Used with permission.

"The Value of a Sanctified Imagination"

Like every other power belonging to us, the imagination may be either a blessing or a curse, depending altogether upon how it is used and how well it is disciplined.

We all have to some degree the power to imagine. This gift enables us to see meanings in material objects, to observe similarities between things which at first appear wholly unlike each other. It permits us to know that which the senses can never tell us, for by it we are able to see through sense impressions to the reality that lies behind things.

Every advance made by mankind in any field began as an idea to which nothing for the time corresponded. The mind of the inventor simply took bits of familiar ideas and made out of them something which was not only wholly unfamiliar but which up to that time was altogether nonexistent. Thus we "create" things and by so doing prove ourselves to have been made in the image of the Creator. That fallen man has often used his creative powers in the service of evil does not invalidate our argument. Any talent may be used for evil as well as for good, but every talent comes from God nevertheless.

That the imagination is of great value in the service of God may be denied by some persons who have erroneously confused the word "imaginative" with the word "imaginary."

The gospel of Jesus Christ has no truck with things imaginary. The most realistic book in the world is the Bible. God is real, men are real and so is sin and so are death and hell, toward which sin inevitably leads. The presence of God is not imaginary, neither is prayer the indulgence of a delightful fancy. The objects that engage the praying man's attention, while not material, are nevertheless

212

completely real; more certainly real, it will at last be admitted, than any earthly object.

The value of the cleansed imagination in the sphere of religion lies in its power to perceive in natural things shadows of things spiritual. It enables the reverent man to

> See the world in a grain of sand
> And eternity in an hour.

The weakness of the Pharisee in days of old was his lack of imagination, or what amounted to the same thing, his refusal to let it enter the field of religion. He saw the text with its carefully guarded theological definition and he saw nothing beyond.

> A primrose by the river's brim
> A yellow primrose was to him,
> And it was nothing more.

When Christ came with His blazing spiritual penetration and His fine moral sensitivity He appeared to the Pharisee to be a devotee of another kind of religion, which indeed He was if the world had only understood. He could see the soul of the text while the Pharisee could see only the body, and he could always prove Christ wrong by an appeal to the letter of the law or to an interpretation hallowed by tradition. The breach between them was too great to permit them to coexist; so the Pharisee, who was in a position to do it, had the young Seer put to death. So it has always been, and so I suppose it will always be till the earth is filled with the knowledge of the Lord as the waters cover the sea.

The imagination, since it is a faculty of the natural mind, must necessarily suffer both from its intrinsic limitations and from an inherent bent toward evil. While the word as found in the King James Bible usually means not imagination at all, but merely the reasonings of sinful men, I yet do not write to excuse the unsanctified imagination. I well know that from such have flowed as from a polluted fountain streams of evil ideas which have throughout the years led to lawless and destructive conduct of the part of men.

A purified and Spirit-controlled imagination is, however, quite another thing, and it is this I have in mind here. I long to see the imagination released from its prison and given to its proper place among the sons of the new creation. What I am trying to describe here is the sacred gift of seeing, the ability to peer beyond the veil and gaze with astonished wonder upon the beauties and mysteries of things holy and eternal.

The stodgy pedestrian mind does no credit to Christianity. Let it dominate the church long enough and it will force her to take one of two directions: either toward liberalism, where she will find relief in a false freedom, or toward the world, where she will find an enjoyable but fatal pleasure.

But I wonder whether this is not all included in the words of our Lord as recorded in the Gospel of John: "Howbeit when he, the Spirit of truth, is come, he will guide you into all truth: for he shall not speak of himself; but whatsoever he shall hear, that shall he speak: and he will shew you things to come. He shall glorify me: for he shall receive of mine, and shall shew it unto you" (16:13-14).

To possess a Spirit-indwelt mind is the Christian's privilege under grace, and this embraces all I have been trying to say here.

Something to Do

1. Tozer considered himself to be "an evangelical mystic." How does he define this term?

2. How do we distinguish "the imaginative" from "the imaginary"? Is the distinction important?

3. What does it mean to "see the soul of a text"? (Tozer amplifies this truth in "Revelation Is Not Enough.")

4. In paragraph 10, what does he describe as the major functions of the imagination?

5. What must we do before the Holy Spirit can liberate our imagination and use it to the glory of God?

17

"The Power of Imagination"
Henry Ward Beecher

HENRY WARD BEECHER (1813–1887) gave the first three series of lectures under "The Lyman Beecher Lectureship on Preaching" at Yale University (1871–1874); and this was only right, since the lectureship was named after his father. A famous Congregational preacher from a famous family, Beecher pastored Plymouth Congregational Church in Brooklyn for forty years (1847–1887) and had a great impact on the religious and political life of the nation.

Beecher's first series dealt with "the personal elements which bear an important relation to preaching," and it is from chapter 5 of that series that this excerpt is taken—"The Psychological Working-Elements." All three series are found in *Yale Lectures on Preaching: First, Second and Third Series*, by Henry Ward Beecher, published in New York City in 1881 by Fords, Howard and Hulbert.

215

"The Power of Imagination"

Yet, despite all these necessary differences, there are certain important elements that enter into all ministries. And the first element on which your preaching will largely depend for power and success, you will perhaps be surprised to learn is *Imagination,* which I regard as the most important of all the elements that go to make the preacher. But you must not understand me to mean the imagination as the creator of fiction, and still less as the factor of embellishment. The imagination in its relations to art and beauty is one thing; and in its relations to moral truth it is another thing, of the most substantial character. Imagination of this kind is the true germ of faith; it is the power of conceiving as definite the things which are invisible to the senses,—of giving them distinct shape. And this, not merely in your own thoughts, but with the power of presenting the things which experience cannot primarily teach to other people's minds, so that they shall be just as obvious as though seen with the bodily eye.

Imagination of this kind is a most vital element in preaching. If we presented to people things we had seen, we should have all their bodily organism in our favor. My impression is, that the fountain of strength in every Christian ministry is the power of the minister himself to realize God present, and to present him to the people. No ministry can be long, various, rich, and fruitful, I think, except from that root. We hear a great deal about the breadth of the pulpit, and about the variety of the pulpit, and about carrying the truth home to men's hearts. I have said a great deal to you about it, and shall say more. I claim that the pulpit has a right and a duty to discuss social questions,—moral questions in politics, slavery, war, peace, and the intercourse of nations. It has a right to discuss commerce, industry, political economy; everything from the roof-tree to the foundation-stone of the household, and everything that is of interest in the State. You have a duty to speak of all these things. There is not so broad a platform in the world as the Christian pulpit, nor an air so free as the heavenly air that overhangs it. You have a right and a duty to preach on all these things; but if you make your ministry to stand on them, it will be barren. It will be rather a lectureship than a Christian ministry. It will be secular and will become secularized. The real root and secret of power, after all, in the pulpit, is the preaching of the invisible God to the people as an ever-present God. The preacher, then, must have the greatness of the God-power in his soul; and when he is himself inspired with it, — and filled with it so familiarly that always and everywhere it is the influence under which he looks out at man, at pleasure, at honor, and at all the vicissitudes of human life, — still standing under the shadow of God's presence, he has the power of God with man when he comes to speak of the truths of the gospel as affecting human procedure. This power of conceiving of invisible things does not only precede in point of time, but it underlies, and is dynamically superior to, anything else.

Now, imagination is indispensable to the formation of any clear and distinct ideas of God the Father, the Son, or the Holy Ghost. For myself, I am compelled to say that I must form an ideal of God through his Son, Jesus Christ. Christ is indispensable to me. My nature needs to fashion the thought of God, though I know him to be a Spirit, into something that shall nearly or remotely represent that which I know. I hold before my mind a glorified form, there-fore; but, after all the glory, whatever may be the nimbus and the effluence around about it, it is to me the form of a glorified man. And I therefore fashion to myself, out of the spirit, that which has to me, as it were, a Divine presence and a Divine being, namely, a Divine man.

But now come the attributal elements, the fashioning of the dis-position, and not only that, but a fashioning of the whole interior. I bring to you some day the face, in miniature, of one very beautiful. You look upon it, and say, "Who is that?" I describe the person and give you the name. You say, "It is a beautiful face." But you do not, after looking at it, feel that you are acquainted with the person. Now I will take you home with me and introduce you to the friend whose name belongs to this picture; but still you would not feel that you knew her. You salute her morning and evening, converse with her, and take part in the social festivities. You admire her tact, her delica-cy, and her beauty. You say the acquaintance opens well. She seems to you very lady-like and attractive. On the Sabbath day the Bible-class assembles, and you go there with your friend. In the recitations and the low-toned conversations she shows great knowledge and moral feeling, a bright intellect, and marvelous discrimination. But, still, you do not feel that you know her. Then you fall sick, and experience that delicious interval just after a severe illness, which one sometimes has, — the coming dawn after a long night, heralding the morning of returning health. In that time the hours are to be filled up, and she becomes a ministering angel unto you. She is full of resources for your comfort. You notice the wisdom of her management, the power she has to stimulate thought, to play with the imagination, and to cheer the heart. I am not now speaking of one to whom you are to be affianced. It is not for you; only you are making the *acquaintance* of one whose *portrait* you had seen, but nothing more. And by thus living in communion with you, she has affected you, little by little, in such a manner that it has been brought home to you; and you say, "I have found a friend!" Well, who was she? Did you *know* her when you first saw her portrait?

Do you know the Lord Jesus Christ when you merely see his portrait, as it were, in the Evangelists? Do you know the Lord Jesus Christ when you simply range through his words of wisdom, and take them, germ-words as they are, with all the fullness that you can? No, not until you have been intimate with him, and have had your hearts lifted up in their noblest elements into that serener air through which God only communicates. It is not until you have been in this atmosphere, not only on the Lord's day, but on the intervening days. It is not until, by the Holy Spirit, you have been made sensitive in every part, and the Lord Jesus Christ becomes chief among ten thousand and altogether lovely. It is not until you have the power to transfuse Jesus Christ into your whole life that you know him, — until there is something in the morning dawn that brings you the thought of him, in the hush of the evening, at noontime, in the budding and springing of the trees, in the singing of the birds, when you sit listless on the grass in the summer, in the retreats of man, in the cities and towns, with the fertile power of suggestion and association by which you feel that the earth is the Lord's and the fullness thereof. When you know him in all the boundless domain of nature, everything speaks to you of your Lord Jesus Christ. Just so, in your father's house, every room speaks to you of your mother who is gone, — every stair in the staircase, every sound of the bell, every tick of the clock, and everything under the roof, bring back to you her memory. It is not until Jesus Christ fills the soul full, and he is yours, born into you, made familiar, rich, and various, touching something in every part of your nature, and spreading out over all the things around about you, that you have

218

the imagination to conceive of the Lord Jesus Christ, and you ..
living conception of him, which you can teach and present to others.

But this imagination is required still more vividly in the second step, namely, the power to throw out your conceptions before others, and such a preaching of the Lord Jesus Christ as shall bring him home to your hearers. How will you undertake to do this? You will have little children to deal with. You will have persons of great practical sense, but of very little imagination, if any. You will have persons of a wayward, coarse temperament, and again others of a fine, sensitive nature. You will have those who take moral impressions with extreme facility, and who understand analogies and illustrations; and you will have others who understand nothing of this kind. These persons you must imbue with a sense of Christ's presence with them. This is the prime question in your ministerial life, — how to bring Jesus Christ home to men, so that he shall be to them what he is to you. You may present Christ to them historically, and far be it from me to say that you must not put great emphasis upon the historical study of Christ; but you must remember that Christ, as he was eighteen hundred years ago, interpreted by the letter, is not a living Christ. It is an historical picture, but it is not a live Christ. Thence must you get your materials, out of which to make the living faith. Many a minister believes that after he has been delivering a series of sermons on the life and times of Christ, he has been preaching Christ. He has been merely preaching about him, not preaching him. There is many a minister who has been preaching the philosophy of Christ; that is, a view of Christ in which, with infinite refinements and cultured arguments, he makes him one of the persons in the Trinity, — who is jealous for his service, jealous for his honor, exactly discriminating where the line of infinity comes down and touches the line of finity, and pugnacious all along that line, — and then thinks that he has been preaching Christ. Some ministers think that they have been preaching Christ when they have been discoursing about the relations of Christ to the law, the nature of his sufferings, how it was necessary that he should suffer, what the effect of his suffering was upon the universe, and what was the nature of the effect of his suffering upon Divine law, and on the Divine sense of justice. They work out of the life and times of Christ, and out of his sufferings and death, a theory of Atonement, or, as it is called, a "Plan of Salvation," and present that to men, and then

219

they think they have presented Christ.

Now I am not saying that you should not discuss such themes, but only that you should not suppose in so doing you have been preaching Christ. You cannot do it in that way. To preach Christ is to make such a presentation of him as shall fill those who hear you. They must be made to conceive it in themselves, and he must be to them a live Saviour, as he is to you. One of the noblest expressions of Paul is where he exclaims, "Christ who died, yea, rather, who *liveth*," as if he bounded back from the thought of speaking about Christ as dead. He is one who liveth again and reigneth in the heavens over all the earth.

There is danger of a mistake being made here. You might ask me if you ought not to preach atonement. Yes. Ought you not, also, to preach the nature, sufferings, and death of Christ? Yes, provided you will not suppose you understand more than you really do on these subjects. There is much in that direction that may contribute to instruction; but it seems to me that what you need, what I need, and what the community needs, is that, in a world full of penalty, where aches, pains, tears, sighs, and groans bear witness to Divine justice, — where, from the beginning, groanings and travailings have testified that God is an avenger, — there shall be brought out from this discouraging background the truth of the gospel, that God *loves* mankind, and would not that they die. He is the God that shall wipe away the tears from every eye. He is the God that shall put out with the brightness of his face the light of the sun and of the moon. He shall put his arm around about men, and comfort them as a mother her child. That is the love of God in Christ Jesus. With this we would stimulate men when they are sluggish, would develop their better natures, give them hope in a future life, cheer them onward in the path of duty, and give them confidence in immortality and eternity; for in God we live and move, and have our being.

The imagination, then, is that power of the mind by which it conceives of invisible things, and is able to present them as though they were visible to others. That is one of its most transcendent offices. It is the quality which of necessity must belong to the ministry. The functions of the preacher require it. In godly families it was, formerly, the habit to discourage the imagination, or to use it only occasionally. They misconceived its glorious functions. It is, I repeat, the very marrow of faith, or that power by which we see the invisible and make others see it. It is the power to bring from the depths the things that are hidden from the bodily eye. A ministry enriched by this noble faculty will not and cannot wear out, and the preacher's people will never be tired of listening to him. Did you ever hear anybody say that spring has been worn out? It has been coming for thousands of years, and it is just as sweet, just as welcome, and just as new, as if the birds sang for the first time; and so it will be for a thousand years to come. These great processes of nature that are continually recurring cannot weary us. But discussions of the systems of theology will. Men get accustomed to repetitions of the same thoughts; but there is something in the love of God and Jesus Christ, and in the application of these things to the human soul, that will give an ever-varying freshness to a ministry which occupies itself with the contemplation and teaching of this law of love, and applying the knowledge to all the varying wants and shifting phases of the congregation. Even though you are forty years in one parish, you will never have finished your preaching, and you will not tire your people.

Something to Do

1. What is Beecher's definition of imagination?

2. Do you agree with his assessment that imagination is "the most important of all the [psychological] elements that go to make the preacher"?

3. What two vital ministries must imagination perform if it is to help us preach well?

4. Is Beecher's description of the working of imagination much like what we would today call "visualization"? Is it a safe approach to take with reference to spiritual matters?

5. What is the connection between imagination and "staying power" in ministry?

18

"Imagination and Preaching"
Robert William Dale

CARRS' LANE CHAPEL, Birmingham, England, was one of the leading Congregational churches in Great Britain, thanks to the effective ministry of John Angell James who served there for over fifty years. Robert William Dale (1829–1895) became his associate in 1854 and his successor in 1859, and under his preaching and leadership, the church continued to prosper. In 1877, Dale delivered the Lyman Beecher Lectures on Preaching at Yale University, published in 1877 in London by Hodder and Stoughton as *Nine Lectures on Preaching*. This excerpt is from the second lecture, "The Intellect in Relation to Preaching."

As you read, keep in mind that Dale uses "fancy" and "imagination" almost as synonyms. To my way of thinking, imagination penetrates the real world and makes it more meaningful to us, while fancy escapes the real world and creates an alternate world. However, in spite of this disagreement, I believe that what Dale says in this lecture about fancy and imagination is worth studying.

Note that Thomas DeQuincey (1785–1859) was an English literary critic and essayist whose book *Confessions of an English Opium-eater* is still a minor classic. And Edmund Burke (1729–1797) was an Irish writer and statesman whose speeches in parliament were recognized for their eloquence. One biographer said that Burke "had a glowing imagination."

"Imagination and Preaching"

If you are to preach effectively you must also endeavour to keep your fancy fresh and your imagination active. Every lecturer on preaching, every writer on rhetoric, insists on the importance of "illustrations." They tell us that logic may lay the foundations and build the walls of the house, but that "illustrations" are the windows which let in the light. But I wish to remind you that if fancy is active and imagination vigorous, the walls will not merely be pierced with occasional windows—the walls themselves will be transparent, the light will come through everywhere.

I do not mean, of course, that it is a merit for a sermon to be overlaid with ornament. Mere ornament, instead of making our meaning clearer, is likely to conceal it, just as architectural decoration sometimes conceals the true lines of a building. It is not of ornament I am thinking, but of the firm and vigorous expression of our thought. All language representative of intellectual acts and moral qualities was created by the imagination, and every word that stands for a spiritual idea was at first a picture and a poem. The imaginative process, which in the earliest periods of human history transmuted the names of material things into the symbols of intellectual and spiritual attributes and activities, is going on perpetually. It is one of the distinctions of an original and powerful writer or speaker that his thoughts have sufficient life and vigour in them to form for themselves, out of the common air and the common earth, a visible organisation—"a spiritual body"—of their own.

DeQuincey has some very striking observations on Edmund Burke which illustrate my meaning. In reply to those critics who are accustomed to speak of the fancy of Burke, he says, with his customary scorn of opinions which he rejects: "Fancy in your throats, ye miserable twaddlers! As if Edmund Burke was the man to play with his fancy for the purpose of separable ornament. He was a man of fancy in no other sense than as Lord Bacon was so, and Jeremy Taylor, and as all large and discursive thinkers are and must be; that is to say, the fancy which he had in common with all mankind, and very probably in no eminent degree, in him was urged into unusual activity under the necessities of his capacious understanding. His great and peculiar distinction was that he viewed all objects of the understanding under more relations than other men, and under more complex relations. . . . Now to apprehend and detect more relations, or to pursue them steadily, is a process absolutely impossible without the intervention of physical analogies. To say, therefore, that a man is a great thinker, or a *fine* thinker [by which DeQuincey has explained he means a *subtle* thinker], is but another expression for saying that he has a *schematising* (or, to use a plainer, but less accurate expression, a figurative) understanding. In that sense, and for that purpose, Burke is figurative; but understood, as he *has* been understood by the long-eared race of his critics, not as thinking in and by his figures, but as deliberately laying them on by way of enamel or after-ornament—not as *incarnating,* but simply as *dressing* his thoughts in imagery—so understood, he is not the Burke of reality, but a poor, fictitious Burke, modelled after the poverty of conception which belongs to his critics."

You will observe that DeQuincey says that Burke thought "in and by his figures." Imagination furnished him—not with mere jewellery for beauty and ornament—but with the very tools and instruments necessary to the process of thinking. In his case, according to DeQuincey, the sublety and originality of his thought imposed upon the imagination this service. The concrete symbols had to be created which were necessary to make definite and visible to himself the movements of his intellectual activity, and to fix their results. In our case it is probable that the symbols already formed to our hand by the creative genius of other men will be found sufficient for the purposes of our private thinking, and fancy will not be "urged into unusual activity under the necessities of a capacious understanding."

But there will be all the more reason for keeping it active by other means. We may be able to think accurately in abstract terms, but if we are to speak vigorously, our thoughts must take form and colour, must clothe themselves in flesh and blood, so that they can be seen and handled by the people who are listening to us. It may not be necessary to be constantly creating new imagery and new forms of expression to convey our meaning; if the common language of common men will serve our turn, we should use it.

As I have said, every word that stands for a spiritual idea was at first a picture and a poem. In the case of most words of this class, the image stamped upon them by the fancy of the poet has worn away and become undistinguishable, like the impression on a coin which has been passing from hand to hand for a generation: — the colours have faded from the canvas, and have left vague and blurred outlines where there was once a picture. If your imagination is vigorous, you will so use these words as to restore to the worn coin the sharpness of the original impression, and to the canvas the brilliance and the richness of the original colouring. The difference between vivid and languid speaking depends very largely upon the extent to which the imagination contributes in this way to the expression of thought. The imaginative speaker instinctively rejects words, phrases, symbols, which are incapable of being animated with vital warmth. He rejects them as a tree rejects withered leaves and dead wood. His style is alive in every fibre of it.

Imagination has another function which perhaps young preachers are in some danger of forgetting. In the investigation of truth we are anxious to work in the dry light of the logical understanding. We make it a matter of conscience to give to every argument its just weight, and not more than its just weight; to follow every line of evidence as far as it will legitimately lead us, and no farther. There is an intellectual integrity which to the scholar is everything that commercial integrity is to the merchant and judicial integrity to the judge. When men leave the university they are apt to suppose that the same laws which should govern the search for truth have authority in the propagation of it. They have a suspicion that their intellectual honesty will be compromised if they set an argument on fire with imagination and passion.

But imagination is a most legitimate instrument of persuasion. It is an indispensable instrument. The minds of men are sometimes so sluggish that we cannot get them to listen to us unless our case is stated with a warmth and a vigour which the imagination alone can supply. There are many, again, who are not accessible to abstract argument, but who recognise truth at once when it assumes that concrete form with which imagination may invest it; they cannot follow the successive steps of your demonstration, but they admit the truth of your proposition the moment you show them your diagram. Then, again, there are some truths—and these among the greatest—which rest, not upon abstract reasoning, but upon facts. Imagination must make the facts vivid and real.

Further—in a country like this there are large numbers of persons to whom it is unnecessary to offer any proof of the great articles of the Christian faith, although they are living in the habitual neglect of Christian duty. That there is a living God; that He abhors sin and loves righteousness; that the Lord Jesus Christ is the Son of God; that He died for them, and that He will come again to judge the living and the dead, they believe. But these awful and glorious truths, though they have a place in the intellect, exert no influence on the heart, the conscience, and the will. They inspire no wonder; they alarm no fear; they kindle no hope; they quicken no affection; they fail even to excite the faintest moral interest. All life has gone out of them. But imagination is akin to emotion—much nearer akin than the logical understanding—and in such cases imagination may do something to bridge the gulf between the speculative and the active powers; may fulfil the office which Bolingbroke attributes to history, and "set passion on the side of judgment, and make the whole man of a piece."

There are some verses in Mr. Tennyson's "In Memoriam" which remind us of another reason why the Christian preacher, above all other public speakers, should cultivate this faculty.

> Though truths in manhood darkly join
> Deep-seated in our mystic frame,
> We yield all blessing to the name
> Of Him that made them current coin.
>
> For wisdom dealt with mortal powers,
> Where truth in closest words shall fail,
> When *truth embodied in a tale*
> Shall enter in at lowly doors.

227

And so the Word had breath, and wrought
With human hands the creed of creeds,
In loveliness of perfect deeds,
More strong than all poetic thought.

Which he may read that binds the sheaf,
Or builds the house, or digs the grave,
And those wild eyes that watch the wave
In roarings round the coral reef.

Nor is it merely at "lowly doors" that "truth embodied in a tale" finds easier entrance than truth which appears in the form of abstract propositions. God, who knows as we cannot know the mystery of our nature, has revealed Himself to mankind in a supernatural history. The revelation which we have to illustrate, and which furnishes the very substance of all our preaching, is not a series of theological dogmas or ethical principles; it is in the main a record of how God has dealt with individual men, with nations, and with the human race. Above all, it is the story of the earthly life, the death, the resurrection, and the ascension into heaven of our Lord Jesus Christ—God manifest in the flesh.

What is commonly described as an historical imagination, is indispensable to us if we are to form a right judgment on the historical contents of Holy Scripture. "Our view of any transaction," says Archbishop Whately, "especially one that is remote in time or place, will necessarily be imperfect, generally incorrect, unless it embrace something more than the bare outline of the occurrences; unless we have before the mind a lively idea of the scenes in which the events took place, the habits of thought and of feeling of the actors, and all the circumstances of the transaction; unless, in short, we can in a considerable degree transport ourselves out of our own age and country and persons, and imagine ourselves the agents and spectators. . . . To say that imagination, if not regulated by sound judgment and sufficient knowledge, may chance to convey to us false impressions of past events, is only to say that man is fallible. But such false impressions are even *much the more* likely to take possession of one whose imagination is feeble or uncultivated."

If the imaginative faculty is too sluggish to make the facts which are the vehicles of a large part of Divine revelation real and alive to us, we shall read two-thirds of the Old Testament and a third of the New with very languid interest; we shall fail to discover the truths and laws which the facts illustrate, and our hearts will remain untouched by the story. Even the epistles—and the epistles which are most exclusively doctrinal—will fail to convey to us their true meaning, unless we are able, by an effort of the imagination, to reproduce to ourselves the circumstances, the habits of thought, the moral and spiritual perils of the people to whom they were written, and the personal character and idiosyncrasies of the apostolic writers. If we are to understand the Epistle to the Galatians, we must become, while we read it, members of one of the Galatian Churches, with our minds imperfectly liberated from heathenism, and impressed by the confident claims of those who profess to be truer representatives of the new faith than St. Paul, from whom we first heard the gospel of Christ. We must know St. Paul as the Philippians knew him, and we must love him as they loved him, if we are to understand the Epistle to the Church at Philippi. There is hardly a page of Holy Scripture which will not become more intelligible to us if we read it with an active imagination.

Something to Do

1. What metaphor does Dale use to show the difference between using metaphor for embellishment or for enlightenment? How might he have carried the metaphor further?

2. Would Dale have agreed with Emerson's views of words and pictures?

3. According to DeQuincey, Burke, and Dale, how are we supposed to think about abstract things?

4. What images does Dale use to discuss "sharpness of imagination"?

5. How is imagination useful in persuasion?

6. What does Dale mean by "historical imagination"? How might Dale respond to "narrative theology" and "narrative preaching"?

19

"Imagination Bodies Forth"
Halford E. Luccock

A TEACHER OF preachers rather than the minister of one church, Halford Edward Luccock (1885–1960) taught preaching at Yale Divinity School and wrote books that still inspire and instruct. He gave the Lyman Beecher Lectures in 1953, which were published in 1954 by Harper as *Communicating the Gospel*. He published twenty-seven books and numerous articles, as well as over 600 letters for the "Simeon Stylites" column in *Christian Century* magazine, the precursor of the "Eutychus and His Kin" columns in *Christianity Today*.

Luccock was a master of the metaphor with the ability to make his readers and listeners see pictures and want to respond to what they saw. "The aim of preaching," he said, "is not the elucidation of a subject, but the transformation of a person" (*Communicating the Gospel,* p. 125).

Developing a Christian Imagination

This selection is from *In the Minister's Workshop* by Halford E. Luccock, pp. 112–17. Copyright 1971 Mary W. Luccock. Used by permission of the publisher, Abingdon Press.

"Imagination Bodies Forth"

Practically all of the preceding chapter could have been logically included under the head of the preacher's use of the imagination. So much that is penetrating and helpful has been written on that theme, it is so large a part of the rich tradition of preaching, that nothing to be said here can have any remote claim to freshness. A few practical words of reminder are set down to give the theme a setting in the whole.

Using the image-making faculty in preaching is a means of helping people to see. And that is a primary purpose of sermons. At the beginning we may boldly transfer from fiction to preaching the classic words of Joseph Conrad: "The novelist's purpose is by the power of the written word to make you hear, to make you feel, . . . before all, to make you see." "Before all, to make you see"—that is a preacher's purpose, too. There is no way of accomplishing it unless the preacher's mind thinks in visual images and on occasion paints pictures.

Out of hundreds of suggestive definitions of imagination take Wordsworth's as something to work on:

It is the faculty of brooding upon some conception until it begins to take shape and color, to spring up and to dilate, to put forth signs of life and to dilate, and so to clothe itself in words and images and trains of thought, which are as truly expressive of its real nature as the human face and body are expressive of the human personality which informs them.

In those words the poet has described an incarnation. The idea becomes flesh and dwells among us—"begins to take shape and color, . . . and so to cloth itself." Unless there is some real incarnation of ideas into pictures there is no full salvation of preaching. For the purpose of preaching is not to make people see reasons, but

232

visions. To say this is not to join the Nazis (or the extreme Barthians, for that matter) in their disparagement of reason, but merely to put first things first in preaching. It was not the conclusion of a syllogism which arrested Paul on the Damascus Road and turned his life in a new direction, but a vision: "Suddenly there shone from heaven a great light round about me." Where there is no vision in the pulpit, the people perish.

Imagination plays a vital part in a preacher's life in two senses: first, in helping him to project himself into the experience of others and, second, in helping him to put the truth into images, which people can see and hence feel.

The first sense is not our immediate theme and need only be mentioned. Nothing is more central to a genuine ministry than the faculty of feeling one's way into the lives of others—what General "Chinese" Gordon called "creeping under the other man's skin." It is more than sympathy; it is *empathy*, the imaginative projection of one's consciousness into another's being, the ability to see with his eyes, to feel with his nerves. Walt Whitman, writing of his days as a volunteer nurse in Washington hospitals during the Civil War, expressed it, with characteristic grandiloquence but with truth, no doubt, "I *become* the wounded man." Keats had empathy to a remarkable degree. That was one reason he gave up the study of medicine. He was too physically affected by illness. He wrote of himself, "If a sparrow come before my window, I take part in its experience and pick about the gravel."

It is the other sense of imagination, that of putting the truth into images, which concerns us here.

One of the most helpful of all the rules of thumb which can be given is this: Turn the ear into an eye. No rule can be universal in its application to a profession, and that one certainly is not. There are many occasions when the habit of writing and speaking in pictures is a cheap and easy escape from the discipline and duty of hard, straight thinking. A beautiful illustration is a vain thing for safety when there is need for an argument to be carried home in clear, direct words. This must be granted. Yet the rule of thumb has real wisdom for many occasions; for when the truth is put in pictures and images which make one see as well as hear, not only is the immediate impression greater, but the memory lasts longer. This is particularly true in what can be called an eye-minded generation.

Developing a Christian Imagination

People in our mechanized world take in so much of all they get through the eye. The heyday of the picture magazine makes one wonder whether the next generation may not find that reading anything longer than a picture caption brings on prostration and a splitting headache. Indeed, until the advent of the radio the ear was rapidly disappearing as one of the organs of sense. Recently, also, the craze for jazz and swing has been an aid to the ear in its rivalry with the eye, aided by the amazing spread of interest in the best in music. And of course the advent of the sound-track moving picture played a timely part in saving the ear. In the days of the silent movies, multitudes became so accustomed to seeing that they became very poor listeners. Complaints that they could not hear from a pulpit or platform were common, and very often they were merely an excuse to cover a sense of hearing that was growing atrophied from disuse.

Yet for all the rescue-party work of the radio, the increased interest in music, the sound motion picture, ours is still so largely an eye-minded world. No one who seeks to arouse conviction by means of words should ever forget it. This is often forgotten by those who gather at the wailing wall and lament the trend of the crowds away from church, as though it were only religious services which were having a hard time today. The hard fact is that anything which depends entirely or largely on the ear for its attendance and acceptance is having a hard time. The lecture platform, the political speech (without benefit of radio), are hardly hot spots in the present scene. Even the radio tries, often feverishly, to "turn the ear into an eye." The sports broadcasts, descriptions of current events, radio dramas, and operas—"horse," "soap," and Metropolitan, all three—bring as much of visual sensation as can be brought with words. (Even the prayers, particularly at broadcast outdoor services, sometimes tell the Lord, and the distant listeners, how the scene looks, who is there, and what they are doing.)

Some implications of all this stand out rather clearly. One is aside from our present interest, but well worthy the attention it is receiving from leaders and thinkers in the field of worship. It is in the question: What can be done to deepen and enhance the effect of worship by acts of worship ministering through the eye, particularly in churches roughly grouped as nonliturgical? That deserves continued exploration and reverent experiment. (Incidentally, the candle-

234

light service, while along this fruitful line, is surely not to be the sum total of our visual aid to worship.)

But here we are concerned with the word from the pulpit. Simply stated, turning the ear into an eye means bringing to the presentations of truth the aid of sense perception in all the ways possible, by images, pictures, narrative, thus breaching two gaps, eye and ear, into the walls of man's soul. For most people, general statements, with which we must deal if we are preaching the Christian gospel, must not only be stated clearly but pictured. Pictures were man's first language, in the caves of the Cro-Magnon man, in the tombs of Egypt, and in the buried palaces of Crete. In every age man's most impressive language has been that which visualizes and makes the reader see. The Elizabethan power of the visualization of abstract ideas was a wonderful achievement worth a lifetime's effort by the preacher. Not only Shakespeare but many of his contemporaries could personify conceptions and platitudes that were centuries old and make them walk on the stage as concrete things. Thus the dramatists took phrases and ideas that were almost in the sleep of death and infused them with emotion and touched them into life.

A minor but real service of thinking in images and visual pictures is that it stimulates a liveliness of mind and speech which a man needs desperately if he is not to be an itinerant performer, setting off the same set of fireworks in a different place each week, but is to preach to the same congregation for five or ten years. A habit of earnest, solemn exhortation may rob the mind of its last trace of sprightliness and agility. Mark Twain once gave good counsel to a friend: "Take your mind out and dance on it; it's getting all caked up." The imagination is a dance of the mind. It helps to dispel the miasma of dull solemnity which hangs over too much preaching. It is no wonder that the minds of the congregation get all "caked up" if the preacher's mind has hardened and solidified. Christopher Morley speaks to the same point with an attractive visual imagery when he says: "It was a fine day for flying kites; I had no kite to fly, so I flew my mind instead."

Another real asset of the mind flown as a kite is that it embodies the sound military strategy of creeping up on an enemy on the line of least expectation. It may seem strange to call a congregation an enemy, but in a real sense it is—an enemy to be captured as well as a friend to be loved. When a preacher ceases entirely to think of an audience as a speaker's natural enemy, to be engaged with all the strategy and resources he can summon, and with whom the struggle is always in doubt, he loses a saving fear and sinks back into a dangerous complacency. The frontal, direct attack on a congregation, even though employing the loud guns of command and dogmatic assertion, is often far less effective than an indirect approach through the imagination, in which the enjoyment of the picture opens the mind to the entrance of the truth. The guards of the mind are lowered and sometimes disarmed.

One way in which the powers of imagination may be increased is by reading in books of imagination. A preacher's mind needs much travel in that realm of gold. To employ DeQuincey's distinction, he needs more of the literature of power to balance the large amount of the literature of knowledge which he must study. He needs books with color and fire and music in them so that his mind and his speech do not become strangers to what it is in language which has given it lasting power over men; otherwise he will begin to speak in an alien jargon and think in unfamiliar terms. The tragedy often is that the more a man studies, the worse he gets; his mind becomes subdued to what he works in, and the textbook style of language hardens on him like a shell. He becomes a literary and vocal crustacean. The preacher who is too busy to read poetry, fiction, drama, and the naturalists is too busy. While he is busy here and there with Kant or John Dewey or Karl Barth or Karl Marx or other Olympians, the opportunity of speaking for God to people in their native tongue is gone.

A word on the training in theological seminaries naturally follows from this. Few men with ten years experience in parish preaching week after week would disagree with the statement that seminary courses fail much more on the side of art than on the side of theological and biblical and sociological content. The seminaries give four fifths of their attention to training men to preach to one fifth of their audience, that is, to the one fifth of the congregation which can follow an abstract train of reasoning. In most congregations, the estimate of one fifth is a gross overestimate. The theological and biblical loading, of course, must not be left undone. But to it should be added more attention to the power to carry truth to people through the development of imagination. It is a great mistake in aeronautics to build transport planes to carry a load greater than the wing power. The average student leaves the seminary with more load than wing power to carry it.

Something to Do

1. What is your response to Luccock's statement, "For the purpose of preaching is not to make people see reasons, but visions"?

2. According to Luccock, what are the two roles of imagination in preaching?

3. This book was published before the widespread use of television. What does Luccock think about the "conflict" between the "eye" and the "ear"? How do you think he would respond to the challenge of the "video generation"?

4. How can deepening corporate worship help us in preaching the Word?

5. "The imagination is the dance of the mind." What does Luccock mean by this statement and how do you respond to it?

6. Luccock mentions "literature of power" and "literature of knowledge." What kind of reading does he suggest for the people who want to expand their imagination?

7. Would his 1954 assessment of seminary training be true today? What changes could our ministerial training schools make that would strengthen the minister's pulpit work?

20

"With Many Such Parables: The Imagination as a Means of Grace"
Leland Ryken

THE 1989 W.H. GRIFFITH THOMAS Lectures at Dallas Theological Seminary were delivered by Dr. Leland Ryken, Professor of English at Wheaton College. His theme was "The Bible as Literature."

I recommend Dr. Ryken's books to you as helpful tools in studying the Bible and learning to appreciate good literature: *The Christian Imagination* (Grand Rapids: Baker, 1981); *How to Read the Bible as Literature* (Grand Rapids: Zondervan, 1984); *The Liberated Imagination* (Wheaton, Ill.: Harold Shaw, 1989); and *Triumphs of the Imagination* (Downers Grove, Ill.: InterVarsity, 1979).

This lecture was originally published in the October–December issue of *Bibliotheca Sacra* (vol. 147, #588), pp. 387–98, and is used by permission of Dallas Theological Seminary.

"With Many Such Parables:
The Imagination as a Means of Grace"

The a... of this article is to explore a heresy that rules vast segments of evangelical Christianity. That heresy is to defend a neglect of the imagination and the arts on the ground that believers must be busy in God's work, *assuming that God's work is never artistic.* Yet the Bible itself, to say nothing of the creation in which humankind lives, shows that God's work is partly artistic.

One of my colleagues has several times conducted an informal poll in his art classes. He asks how many students can say that in their families any of the arts was talked about and regarded as important. The percentage of such families is exceedingly small. Then when he inquires into the matter more precisely, he finds that in the overwhelming number of cases either the families in which the arts are considered important are non-Christian families, or the affirmation of art is something that preceded conversion to Christianity.

Of all people on the face of the earth, Christians have the most reason to value the arts and the imagination. The title of this article speaks of the imagination as a means of grace. This does not mean that participating in the arts makes a person more acceptable to God or that the arts explicitly recall God's saving acts. Instead it suggests that the imagination is a means by which God can reveal His truth and beauty and people can respond with due appreciation.

The Doctrine of Creation and the Artistic Enterprise
In countering the heresy that God's work excludes involvement in the arts, three great biblical principles may be addressed. The first is the doctrine of Creation. The Bible begins by stating that God created the world. That world is beautiful and artistically pleasing, as is known simply by looking around and as the Bible confirms.

God looked at what He had created, and, "behold, it was very good" (Gen. 1:31). The psalmist wrote that the creation proclaims God's handiwork (Ps. 19:1), implying that handiwork has value. In the Garden of Eden God made to grow "every tree that is pleasing to the sight and good for food" (Gen. 2:9). This is a double criterion — one artistic, the other utilitarian. The conditions for human well-being have never changed since that moment. Can a person justify the time spent reading a novel or writing a poem or visiting an art

240

gallery? In a Christian scheme of things, the answer is yes.

God also created people in His own image (Gen. 1:26). What does this mean? At this point in the biblical record nothing is yet known about the God of providence or redemption or the covenant. The one thing known about God is that He creates. In its immediate narrative context, therefore, the doctrine of the image of God in people emphasizes that people are, like God, creative. A well-known evangelical, when serving as a referee for one of my book manuscripts, wrote a marginal comment about "the trivial view that God's image in people is a matter of creativity." Is this the impression a person gets when reading Genesis 1? The comment is in fact an evidence of the very heresy just mentioned.

What does the image of God in people say about the arts? It affirms human creativity as something good in principle, since it is an imitation of one of God's own acts and perfections. Abraham Kuyper once wrote, "As image-bearer of God, man possesses the possibility both to create something beautiful, and to delight in it."[1] Christian poet Chad Walsh has said that the artist "can honestly see himself as a kind of earthly assistant to God . . . carrying on the delegated work of creation, making the fullness of creation fuller."[2] This applies equally to those who are not themselves creative artists but who delight to enter into the creativity of others. And it stands as a rebuke to those who disparage God's gift of creativity in people.

This then is one foundation for thinking Christianly about the arts: the Christian doctrine of Creation assures mankind that human creativity can be honoring to God. God Himself created a world that is artistically beautiful and delightful as well as utilitarian.

The Value of Beauty and Artistry

A second biblical principle is that works of art have value in themselves, simply as objects of beauty and artistry. For one thing, the Bible makes no division of art into sacred and secular.[3] Art has equal value in an everyday setting and in worship. The Bible includes not only songs sung in worship at the temple but also ones sung in the everyday circumstances of work without direct reference to anything religious (Num. 21:16-18; Isa. 16:10; 52:8-9). The Song of Solomon is a collection of love lyrics that keeps the focus on human love and does not explicitly bring God or spiritual values into the picture. The Bible records a patriotic elegy by David about national heroes that does not mention God (2 Sam. 1:17-27).

As an extension of this unwillingness to divide art into sacred and secular, the Bible also refuses to make the value of artistic form depend on religious content in works of art. Consider the many references in the Psalms and elsewhere to instrumental music without accompanying words. Can this be legitimate, even in worship? In Psalm 150 musical sound alone is said to praise God when it is offered to Him as an act of worship.

The descriptions of the visual art that adorned the Old Testament tabernacle and temple are a gold mine of information about the arts, and one of the important things learned is that the art God prescribed for these religious places was not always specifically religious in its content. There was a wealth of realistic or representational art that symbolized nothing specifically religious. The pillars of the temple were decorated with pomegranates and lilies (1 Kings 7:15-22), and the stands for the brass lavers with lions, oxen, and palm trees (vv. 29, 36). Given the stereotyped notions of "sacred art" that often prevail in Christian circles, this might seem out of place. As the Old Testament worshipers stared at the lampstand, they saw, not angels and cherubim, but things of natural beauty—flowers and blossoms.

What should one make of this exuberance over the forms of nature in the most holy places of Old Testament worship? Above all it completely undercuts any sacred-secular dichotomy for art. What God created is a suitable subject for the artist. Since God made the flowers and sky, they are worth painting or carving.

Most surprising of all, given current stereotypes, was the presence of abstract or nonrepresentational art in the tabernacle and temple. Nonrepresentational art means art that represents nothing beyond itself, like a Persian tapestry. As the Old Testament worshipers approached the temple, they saw two gigantic freestanding pillars over 25 feet high. These monoliths had no architectural weight-bearing function. They did not resemble anything in created nature. They were simply beautiful and suggested by their very size and form the grandeur, stability, and power of God. They also made the worshipers feel small as they stood beside them, and this, too, made a religious statement in a purely artistic, nonverbal way.

The artistic imagination is free to be itself. What it produces under the guidance of God is good in itself. The robe of Aaron indicates

242

that. The embellishment of Aaron's priestly garment was "for glory and for beauty" (Exod. 28:2). Beauty and artistry are worthy in themselves.

Some of the art in the Old Testament was realistic, but there was no requirement that it had to be so. The decorations on Aaron's garment included blue pomegranates. What's so unusual about that? In nature there *are* no blue pomegranates. An intriguing artifact in the temple is the molten sea (1 Kings 7:23-26). It was a huge circular basin 45 feet in circumference and holding up to 10,000 gallons of water. Under the brim were engravings of gourds. The whole grand design rested on the backs of 12 statuesque oxen. Nowhere in the real world can one find a sea held up on the backs of oxen. It is an utterly fantastic conception, all the more delightful for its imaginary qualities.

Some of the literature in the Bible is equally fantastic. In a single short chapter of Zechariah, for example, readers learn about a flying scroll that destroys the wood and stone of houses, a woman named Wickedness sitting inside a cereal container, and two women with wings like those of a stork who lift the container into the sky. As Schaeffer wrote, "Christian artists do not need to be threatened by fantasy and imagination. . . . The Christian is the really free person . . . whose imagination should fly beyond the stars."[4]

An additional reason for believing that works of art have value in themselves emerges from what the Bible says about the vocation and gifts of the artist. Two key passages in Exodus describe how God called and equipped the artists who worked on the tabernacle (Exod. 31:1-11; 35:30–36:2). God called the artists, filled them with His Spirit, inspired them with artistic ability, and stirred them up to do the work. The impression gained from these passages is that the artist's calling is a glorious calling. Unlike what often happens in Christian circles today, the artist's vocation was not regarded as suspect or second best.

This, then, is a second way in which to think Christianly about the arts: the Bible affirms that the artistic imagination and its creations have value in themselves, not simply for the religious or ideational content they may contain. The arts do not need to be defended, as people throughout history have felt obliged to defend them, as something other than art. They have integrity for what they are in themselves. Christians find a place for the arts as an aid *to* worship, but not often as an act *of* worship. Yet 91 out of 107 references to music in the Psalms specify God as the audience of music.[5] The principle that emerges from this is significant for the arts: anything offered to God can become an act of worship. This means that artistic experiences, whether as creators or participants, can be an act of worship—a means of grace.

The value of the nonutilitarian and the dignity of the concept of leisure must also be acknowledged. The Christian community lacks an adequate theory of leisure and play. Regarding recreation, including the arts, as frivolous or ignoble, Christians often sink to mediocrity by default. Yet the wise use of leisure time is part of the stewardship of life.[6] No one could have lived a busier life than Jesus did during the years of His public ministry. Yet He did not reduce life to continuous work or evangelism. He took time to enjoy the beauty of the lily and to attend dinners.

Truth and the Imagination

The Bible, then, endorses artistic creativity and encourages Christians to believe that artistic form and beauty have value in themselves as gifts from God. This might be viewed as the nonutilitarian side of the artistic imagination. But the imagination is useful as well as delightful. This leads to the question of truth in art, or the imagination as a vehicle for expressing truth. This too is a value of the arts. The imagination can express truth in its own unique way for the glory of God and the edification of people.

What is this unique way of expressing truth? Such truth as the arts express is conveyed by means of the imagination. The imagination *images forth* its subject matter. It does not work primarily by abstractions or propositions but by concrete images and experiences. As Chesterton put it, "Imagination demands an image."[7] The arts take concrete human experience rather than abstract information as their subject.

Can the imagination express truth? Look at the example of the Bible. The Bible is overwhelmingly literary in its form. The one thing that it is *not* is what we so often picture it as being—a theological outline with proof texts attached. When asked to define "neighbor," Jesus told a story. He constantly spoke in images and metaphors: "I am the light of the world"; "You are the salt of the earth." The Bible repeatedly appeals to the intelligence through the imagination. The prominence of music and visual art in the worship described in the Bible has already been noted. If it is doubted that truth can be embodied in visual, nonpropositional form, look at baptism and communion. They use physical images that allow people to experience spiritual realities.

It is therefore not surprising that Dorothy Sayers links the imagination with Christian theology. In a famous essay on artistic theory, she wrote,

> Let us take note of a new word that has crept into the argument by way of Christian theology—the word *Image.* Suppose, having rejected the words "copy," "imitation," and "representation" as inadequate, we substitute the word "image" and say that what the artist is doing is *to image forth* something or the other, and connect that with St. Paul's phrase: "God . . . hath spoken to us by His son, the . . . *express image* of His person."—Something which, by being an image, *expresses* that which it images.[8]

"Imaging forth" is exactly what the Bible repeatedly does. Its most customary way of expressing God's truth is not the sermon or theological outline but the story, the poem, the vision, and the letter, all of them literary forms and products of the imagination. Think of how much biblical truth has been incarnated in character and event. To this can be added the poetry of the Bible, including the heavy incidence of image and metaphor in the prose of the New Testament.

The point is not simply that the Bible allows for the imagination as a form of communication. It is rather that the biblical writers and Jesus found it impossible to communicate the truth of God without using the resources of the imagination. The Bible does more than sanction the arts. It shows how indispensable they are.

That the imagination is a vehicle of truth is known also from sources other than the Bible. An earlier article referred to the discovery of recent brain research that shows that the two hemispheres of the human brain respond to stimuli and assimilate reality in different ways.[9] The left hemisphere is active in logical thinking, grasping abstract propositions, and dealing with language. The right hemisphere is dominant in processing visual and other sensory experiences, in seeing whole-part relationships, in grasping metaphor and humor, and in experiencing emotion. The arts and the imagination are essentially right-brain media. Believers need to express and receive God's truth with the right brain as well as the left.

In Western culture at large, and perhaps especially in the evangelical subculture, the tendency is overwhelming to assume that truth is conceptual and propositional only. But the arts, with their emphasis on imagination, show that there is another type of truth, or a whole other way by which people assimilate and know the truth. Suppose a person is assembling an appliance. If the directions include a good picture, he may not even use the written instructions.

It is a fallacy to think that one's world view consists only of ideas. It is a world picture as well as a set of ideas. It includes images that may govern behavior even more than ideas do. At the level of ideas, for example, a person may know the goal of life is not to amass physical possessions. But if his mind is filled with images of fancy cars and expensive clothes and big houses, his behavior will likely follow a materialistic path. A person might say that God created the world, but if his mind is filled with images of evolutionary processes, he will start to think like an evolutionist. Someone may know that he should eat moderately, but his appetites override that knowledge when his mind is filled with images of luscious food. The imagination is a leading ingredient in the way people view reality. They live under its sway, whether they realize it or not. Advertisers seem to grasp this better than people do in the church.

The Uses of the Imagination in Teaching and Preaching

Thus far three biblical principles have been suggested to combat the assumption that doing God's work excludes a commitment to the imagination and the arts. Those principles are the doctrine of Creation, the Bible's endorsement of art as having value in itself, and the Bible's example in confirming that the imagination is one means by which people can know and express the truth. What are some ways these principles may be applied to Christians and especially to teachers and preachers?

In view of the Bible's endorsement of the arts, Christians need to affirm artists and their work much more than they typically do. They need to show from the pulpit and the Sunday school podium and by their conversations and actions that they believe the arts to be important. Everyone has an imagination. Some Christians have sat in the pew for years and never been told that their God-given imagination is good. Art, music, and literature deserve a more prominent place in churches than they currently have. They deserve to be in the bulletin and church services, and Sunday school classes. It would be helpful to have artists' nights when church members display their own visual art or photography, read their own poems or stories, and perform music. Too little of artists' gifts is seen in churches today.

All this is in sharp contrast to what is found in the worship described in the Bible, where the arts were flaunted to a degree almost unheard of today. The idea of the *beauty* of holiness does not mean much in contemporary worship, and one of the reasons for the attractiveness of high church worship to some evangelicals is that their aesthetic inclinations are either starved or offended in evangelical churches.

There is no reason why the burden for artistic expression within the church should rest solely on the minister. Most churches have a core of people who are interested in the arts. They are the logical people to tap as resources for making the artistic imagination a vital part of church life.

Many Christians have been guilty of a great abdication. They cannot all be artists, but they can all respect and participate in the art that others create. The Christian church must be active on every front in society—in science, in economics, in education, in politics, in the arts, in the media. God gave His followers a cultural command as well as a missionary command. They should not set these up as rivals. To relinquish the presence of believers in any cultural area only weakens the Christian voice in the culture as a whole and makes evangelism all the more difficult.

The attitude of Christians toward the arts says something about the God they proclaim, and often the wrong signal is sent to the unsaved. A missionary who wrestled with the issue of how beauty related to her life in a foreign culture came to this conclusion: "I believe my attitude toward beauty and order, as reflected in my home and lifestyle, says much to the people around me about the God I serve. Therefore, I want to reflect . . . something of the artistry, the beauty, the order of the one I'm representing, and in whose image I've been made."[10]

Developing a Christian Imagination

Christians also need to acknowledge more fully that the imagination is a leading means by which to express the truth. Turning from the pages of the Bible to the evangelical subculture today, one cannot help but be struck by the contrast in this regard. The theological abstraction and outline have replaced the imaginative boldness of the writers of the Bible. People no longer trust the power of metaphor or paint on canvas or musical sound to express the truth. Jesus, however, did not distrust the imagination. He told stories and spoke in metaphor.

The non-Christian world has a better grasp of the power of the arts to persuade people than the Christian community does. For every "Chariots of Fire," there are hundreds of movies that express an untruthful or immoral view of life. Christians need to believe that a painting or piece of fiction can be as truthful to life and to the Christian view of life as a sermon or religious article can be. "Chariots of Fire" is as truthful an expression of Eric Liddle's Christianity as is a biography of him. This is not to suggest that believers displace anything with art, music, and literature. Rather, the point is that these too are ways in which God's truth and beauty can be communicated. The Bible itself communicates the truth in all possible ways. And it does so with obvious artistry. Christians need to lay to rest the heresy that God's work is never artistic.

A final application has to do with the sermon. As a modern-day Puritan who believes in the primacy of the sermon in worship, I find the state of the sermon in evangelical churches alarming. It is in deep trouble in most churches. This is concealed from view because churchgoers accept listening to the sermon as part of the duties of attending church. They theorize that as long as a church is filled with people listening to sermons, the sermon must be flourishing as an institution. But sitting dutifully through the sermon is not the same as being excited by it or strongly impacted by it. The average churchgoer finds something lacking in sermons and feels mildly guilty about not being as interested in sermons as he or she would like to be. It must be remembered that the visual media have transformed what audiences expect in a sermon. Contemporary preaching has captured the minds and sometimes the emotions of people, but not their imaginations.

One problem is the excessive tendency toward theological abstraction in contemporary preaching. If the imagination is a valid

248

means of communicating God's truth, then the Christia
needs to be imaged forth more than it is. A good starting
preach on literary parts of the Bible. There is no defensible reason
why preachers should gravitate so naturally to the most abstract
parts of the Bible, especially the Epistles. The stories and poems and
visions of the Bible are important too.

And when preachers choose a literary text in the Bible, it is important to approach it as literature. A story or poem asks that the readers and hearers enter a whole imagined world and walk around inside it. It conveys its truth by getting the readers to share an experience. Reliving the story or the thought process of the poet should be the first item on the agenda of Bible expositors. To do this will require them to rethink their concept of a three-part sermon. Instead of imposing three propositional generalizations on the text and dipping into the text for supporting data, they must first relive the story or poem. Then they can deduce the principles and apply them to the lives of their listeners.

When expositors make an application, they need to rely on their imagination — their ability to picture the truth in concrete terms. The imagination allows them to identify with people and experiences beyond themselves. Identifying with things "out there" is not something that comes easily to preachers. The voice of authentic human experience with its suffering and longing is not as common as it should be in contemporary preaching. The exceptions to that stricture are the preachers who rather quickly achieve popularity and become celebrities. But the ability to identify with actual human experience is within the reach of every preacher or teacher and needs only to be cultivated.

Expositors tend to look on sermon or lesson preparation in terms of doing research for a lecture or paper. They should view it more like writing a story or poem. According to the usual model, the preacher or Bible teacher spends time reading Bible commentaries and finding illustrations for generalizations. But as poets and fiction writers go about their composition, the key ingredients in their process are memory, observation of life, introspection, reading, and imagining.

Paradoxically the ability to identify with the person in the pew and to picture the truth concretely might begin with introspection. Imaginative writers are not afraid to look within and assume that

249

what they find there is of universal interest and insight. The minister or teacher who sits down to breakfast and who transports children to music lessons or Little League games has the same tensions and triumphs, the same anxieties and longings, that ordinary people have. Not to tap this source is a failure of both nerve and imagination, and it leaves congregations with abstracted theology as their Sunday diet.

Observation is of course needed to supplement introspection. The way to empathize with people is to observe their pain and triumphs, their longings and fears. Pressed for time as they are, preachers can develop a network for gaining insight into how a biblical passage applies to real life. The most efficient means of doing this is to assemble a small group Bible study that studies the passage on which the next sermon will be based. The application part of the sermon is too big a task for one person to produce alone.

In addition to needing more imaging of the truth from the pulpit and Sunday school podium, more innovation is also needed. One of the functions of the imagination is to defamiliarize what has become overly familiar. Its task is to state the timeless truth in perpetually fresh ways. People are temperamentally resistant to change and experimentation. It is easy to forget that in its original setting the Bible was a subversive book. Its writers and speakers challenged conventional assumptions and conventional ways of stating things. Preachers and teachers need to be more daring and imaginative, knowing beforehand that some experiments will work better than others.

What form might such innovation take? Expositors might profitably follow the model of the Bible itself. The Bible takes every possible approach to the truth, much of it literary and artistic. Could some of the street drama of the Old Testament prophets serve as a model? Jeremiah once wore a yoke on his neck as a message to the people. On another occasion he exposed a garment to the elements until it had decayed in order to symbolize the spiritual state of his nation.

What prevents us from trying brief dramatic vignettes and visual imagery as part of a sermon? Equally attractive is the possibility of impersonating a biblical character, either directly or in a pretended interview. The Bible consistently appeals to the right side of the brain as well as the left. There is no reason why sermons and Sunday

250

school lessons cannot feature more visual and aural resources than they customarily do.

And what about the prominence given in the Bible to narrative or story? One of the most universal human impulses can be summed up on the four words, "Tell me a story." Among the findings of two people who made a study of successful American companies was the conclusion that "we are more influenced by stories (vignettes that are whole and make sense in themselves) than by data."[11] There is every reason for Bible communicators to tap into the story quality of both the Bible and the Christian faith. It is possible to make use of the strengths of narrative preaching without casting an entire sermon in narrative form. But more than the conventional two-minute anecdote is needed to illustrate a generalization. A story is needed that invites the hearers to enter a whole world of the imagination and that incarnates the truth instead of simply illustrating it.

Fiction too has an amazing ability to defamiliarize both biblical material and everyday reality. It uses dislocation to create new angles of vision. It removes hearers from the familiar world so they can see that world with greater clarity. The classic example of this in the Bible itself is the parable Nathan told to David (2 Sam. 12:1-15). By entering a fictional world, David was completely disarmed. Having entered this world of the imagination, he looked out of it to the world of his own life. This is how the imagination works: it first removes the hearers from immediate reality to send them back to it with renewed insight. There is nothing wrong with telling a story that does not carry all its meaning on the surface. Jesus told fictional stories that partly concealed the truth in order to reveal it by delayed action to the thoughtful listener.

To sum up, all people, including Christians, need the truth and beauty that the imagination can impart. That truth and beauty are needed during the week, and on Sunday. The nature of truth is such that it can never be adequately expressed or experienced only as an abstraction or as a set of facts. Truth also requires the story, the poem, the paint on canvas, the sound of music.

Notes

1. Abraham Kuyper, *Calvinism* (Grand Rapids: Eerdmans, 1943), 142.
2. Chad Walsh, "The Advantages of the Christian Faith for a Writer," in *The Christian Imagination,* ed. Leland Ryken (Grand Rapids: Baker, 1981), 308.
3. For a fuller discussion of this and related points, see Leland Ryken, *The Liberated Imagination: Thinking Christianly about the Arts* (Wheaton, Ill.: Harold Shaw, 1990).
4. Francis A. Schaeffer, *Art and the Bible* (Downers Grove, Ill.: InterVarsity, 1973), 61.
5. Dale Topp, *Music in the Christian Community* (Grand Rapids: Eerdmans, 1959), 13.
6. For an elaboration of a Christian view of leisure, see Leland Ryken, *Work and Leisure in Christian Perspective* (Portland, Ore.: Multnomah, 1987).
7. G.K. Chesterton, "The Soul in Every Legend," in *The Man Who Was Chesterton,* ed. Raymond T. Bond (Freeport, N.Y.: Books for Libraries, 1902), 37.
8. Dorothy L. Sayers, "Towards a Christian Aesthetic," in *The New Orpheus,* ed. Nathan A. Scott (New York: Sheed and Ward, 1964), 13.
9. Leland Ryken, " 'I Have Used Similitudes': The Poetry of the Bible," *Bibliotheca Sacra* 147 (July-September 1990): 260–61.
10. Margaret Ho, "Reflecting a God of Beauty," *Eternity,* November 1982, 29.
11. Thomas J. Peters and Robert H. Waterman, Jr., *In Search of Excellence: Lessons from America's Best-Run Companies* (New York: Harper and Row, 1982), 61.

Something to Do

1. How does the author relate creation to artistic enterprise?

2. What is the place of the artistic in Scripture?

3. How do the writers of Scripture reveal their use of imagination? Do we have the authority to follow their example?

4. What is the "great abdication" of which many Christians are guilty? Do you agree with Dr. Ryken?

5. What counsel does Dr. Ryken give concerning handling "theological abstraction"? How do you respond to his suggestion that preparing a sermon is like writing a story or a poem?

21

"Serving Appetizing Meals: The Use of Word Pictures in Preaching and Teaching the Bible"

Mark S. Wheeler

MARK S. WHEELER is singles pastor at Crossroads Baptist Church, Bellevue, Washington. He is a graduate of Talbot School of Theology and Dallas Theological Seminary.

This article appeared in the *Christian Education Journal,* vol. 12, no. 2, pp. 57–73, copyright 1991 by Scripture Press Ministries.

"Serving Appetizing Meals:
The Use of Word Pictures in Preaching and Teaching the Bible"

A constant source of complaint is that what is preached or taught within the church or the Christian school is often not translated into daily living. In conjunction with this, what is being taught or preached is often not even retained in the memory long enough to be of any effect on the individual's life. Westerhoff indicates that this is at least partly due to the fact that churches and Christian schools have bought into what he refers to as the "schooling-instruction paradigm."[1] This phrase refers to the phenomenon where the student comes to be instructed and the teacher does the instructing. Often, this takes the form of the teacher pouring from his mug into the pupil's jug. It is as if the teacher or preacher were to back up the dump truck of his accumulated knowledge and were to dump the entire contents upon the student. When instruction is done in this fashion, it is amazing that anything is retained at all.

There are many things that can be done to enhance the teaching-learning process. They would include everything ranging from the use of words to the use of a variety of methods to simplification of the lesson plan to feedback from the teacher to the stressing of process content and on and on and on. There is literally no end to the suggestions as to how to improve the student's retention of the material being taught. However, it is not within the scope of this research to examine all of these areas. Rather than doing a survey of all of these methods, this research will attempt to focus on one of them, namely, the use of *word pictures*.

It is the opinion of this author that one of the most important areas of preaching and teaching, and also one of the most neglected, centers around the use of word pictures. Oftentimes, teaching and preaching is simply a recapitulation of what the teacher or preacher has read in a book or commentary. The same words are used, the same ideas are mentioned, and even the same outline is used.

Penner points out that while this lack of style can dull a listener's senses, word pictures can be used to enhance communication. He says,

Good language style is a tremendous aid in communication because it holds the attention of the listener, by firing his imagination with vivid word pictures, revealing the unknown through analogies, quickens the understanding and stirs the mind into action. On the other hand, a lack of style wearies the listener with boredom, because it is devoid of variations and becomes insipid, flat and colorless.[2]

What many teachers and preachers fail to realize is that there is a major difference between a written style of language and a spoken style of language. These differences grow out of the fact that one style is intended for the eye and the other for the ear. The reader may absorb at leisure; the hearer must take it on the wing. The reader proceeds at his own pace while the listener must keep up with the pace of the speaker. The reader has the opportunity to pause to think or to reread. He can even consult a dictionary, if necessary. The listener must move ever onward. If he pauses to question and think, he will be left behind.

The major difference between written and spoken style can be summarized in this way: "Written style must be ultimately intelligible to the reader. Spoken style must be instantly intelligible to the hearer."[3] It has been said that the first thirty seconds of a conversation or speech are crucial.[4] Spoken words and ideas must have clarity if they are to be understood. Concerning this, Dr. Howard Hendricks has often said, "If it's a mist in the pulpit, it will be a fog in the pew." Good communicators must use every advantage they can from the moment they begin to speak.

The purpose of this research, then, is to examine how words can be used to enhance the clarity of a spoken message. Specifically, the research will focus on how "word pictures"[5] can be used to enhance not only the clarity of a message but also the retention of that message.

The format of this research will be as follows: first, a definition of word pictures will be presented. This will be followed by a brief discussion of the philosophy behind the use of this technique. This will be seen through a review of the secular literature on this subject. Also, a review of the teaching method of Jesus Christ will enable the reader to see how He employed word pictures in His teaching style. The research will conclude with a discussion of how to develop the art of using this technique.

Definition

The phrase "word picture" refers to the technique of using words to create mental images. A word picture can be as short as a one-word metaphor or as long as a story or parable. It is through the power of words that a speaker has the ability to indirectly stimulate many kinds of sensations. The use of imagery consists of "describing experiences and events in specific, pictorial, and vivid language in order to evoke bright mental images. Pictorial language involves the selection of words designed to evoke sensory reactions from a person as if the person were actually experiencing an event."[6] Smalley and Trent add to this by defining an emotional word picture as "a communication tool that uses a story or object to activate simultaneously the emotions and intellect of a person. In so doing, it causes the person to experience our words, not just hear them."[7] While these definitions have different elements in them, their common denominator is that this technique is designed to help the hearer "experience" the words rather than simply hearing them.

Imagery refers to words which describe sensations. The types of imagery that have been identified refer to the sensations of sight, sound, taste, smell, touch, physical movement, and internal activity. Words can be used to create mental pictures of each of these sensations. Visual images help an audience to see the events being described. Auditory images help an audience to imagine the sound of the events. Gustatory images enable an audience to imagine the taste of what is being described. Olfactory images help an audience imagine the smell of events. In addition, tactile images refer to the feel of what is described. Kinesthetic images allow an audience to sense motor activity. Finally, organic images enable an audience to sense activity which occurs inside people. This technique "describes sensory experiences in such precise and vivid detail that members of the audience react as if they were in the presence of and responding to the immediate event."[8] Studies have shown that word pictures not only activate our emotions, but they also physically affect us.[9] That is, when we hear a story about either a real or imaginary event, our five senses are triggered almost as if we experienced the event ourselves.[10]

The phrase "word picture" is generally used to refer specifically to those words which describe an activity of the senses. For the purpose of this research, it will be broadened to include other aspects of language such as figures of speech and stories. The justification of this broadening is that stories and figures of speech (if they are any good) are composed of words which are pictorial in nature. In order for a story or a figure of speech to capture the attention of the listener, it must paint a mental picture which is instantly intelligible.

Literature Review

The technique of using word pictures is based on the presupposition that man thinks in images, or rather, a succession of images. Paivio concluded that in memory, man uses two coding systems, the pictorial and verbal. He refers to this as "bimodal coding."[11] This is the same conclusion that was reached by Bandura in his studies in the area of modeling.[12] He points out that in the retentional process, there are also two coding systems, the imaginal and the verbal.

The thrust of Paivio's theory is that a word having an image representation is stored with both a verbal and an image code and that the word can be retrieved using either code. Research conducted by Groninger and Groninger supported Paivio's theory.[13] In their study, they tested pupils twice at three-week intervals using encoding sets of (a) spelling, (b) defining, and (c) image description. The results showed significant congruence effects for imagery sets using concrete words and significant congruence effects for definition sets using abstract words.

The ability to think in images is not affected by age, visual impairment, or hearing impairment. Fullerton used a syllogistic reasoning task to assess the ability of two adult age-groups to use imagery. He discovered that older adults are able to use imagery as a control process when it is combined with a contextual framework while young adults are more likely to use imagery as a strategy in and of itself.[14]

Zimler and Keenan conducted experiments comparing congenitally blind and sighted adults and children on tasks that presumed to involve visual imagery in memory. In all three experiments, the blind subjects' performances were remarkably similar to the sighted. Both groups recalled more high-imagery pairs than the others.[15]

Bonvillian conducted a study which examined 40 deaf and 20 hearing students' free recall of visually presented words varied systematically with respect to signability (words that could be expressed by a single sign) and visual imagery. The results indicated that for deaf students, recall was better for words that had sign-language equivalents and high-imagery values. For the hearing students, recall was better for words with high-imagery values, but there was no effect of signability.[16]

It is because man thinks in images that word pictures are so effective. The use of this technique accomplishes two major tasks in communication:

> (1) It enhances the impressiveness of a message, and (2) it intensifies and clarifies experience. Language is impressive when an expression sticks in a listener's memory. Words that refer to sensory experiences call up in the listener's mind precise pictures of the details of people and their actions. Experiences become clear and intense when they stir the emotions, when the descriptions arouse joy, shame, pity, compassion, disgust, or wrath. People respond more keenly to scenes, experiences, and situations of which they can visualize the happenings and consequences clearly.[17]

When a person experiences an event, the memory of that event is recorded in vivid sensory impressions that lead to attitudes or predispositions to behave in particular ways. The more intense and dramatic the event is, the more enduring the attitude and feeling. The event is locked into a person's memory.

When an experience is reconstructed with a striking description, it creates a profound sense of reality and inspires a belief in the experience in a way similar to reenacting the experience itself. This is due to the fact that our emotional and sensory responses are the same whether the experience is real or imagined. Thus, when an experience is described in concrete, specific, colorful, sensory language, it may be imagined more dramatically than a real experience. This is due to the fact that people tend to react to words with almost the same intensity as they react to real experiences.[18]

Word pictures are primarily effective because of their vividness. This is the *"sine qua non"* of spoken style."[19] They stimulate the brain, causing it to work faster and expend more energy than while reading or listening to conventional words.[20] To illustrate, when one reads a page of his favorite novel and an equal amount from the encyclopedia, he'll find reading the novel much faster, and for good reason.

"Serving Appetizing Meals"

A speaker's choice of words has a profound effect on the vividness of the message. The words that he chooses should be words which are specific, simple, and effective. They should also be words which possess shades of color or tone, that have an atmosphere, and that have nuances. They should also be words which are familiar to the vocabulary of the listener.

Many people have advocated the superior force and clarity of short, familiar words. Billy Sunday, a famous evangelist, treated the subject this way:

> If a man were to take a piece of meat and smell it and look disgusted, and his little boy were to say, "What's the matter with it Pop?" and he were to say, "It is undergoing a process of decomposition in the formation of new chemical compounds," the boy would be all in. But if the father were to say, "It's rotten," then the boy would understand and hold his nose. "Rotten" is a good Anglo-Saxon word and you don't have to go to the dictionary to find out what it means.[21]

There are many other things which affect the vividness of a message. However, only figures of speech, illustrations, and stories will be mentioned. According to Bullinger:

> A figure denotes some form which a word or sentence takes, different from its ordinary and natural form. This is always for the purpose of giving additional force, more life, intensified feelings, and greater emphasis. Whereas today "Figurative language" is ignorantly spoken of as though it made less of the meaning, and deprived the words of their power and force. A passage of God's Word is quoted; and it is met with the cry, "Oh, that is figurative"—implying that its meaning is weakened, or that it has quite a different meaning, or that it has no meaning at all. But the very opposite is the case. For an unusual form (figura) is never used except to add force to the truth conveyed, emphasis to the statement of it, and depth to the meaning of it.[22]

Wilson and Arnold indicate that figures of speech will help to brighten up a prosaic, unimaginative lecture. They state:

Figures of speech are forms of expression which serve to inten-
sify meanings. They make their points indirectly by stating
things vividly in terms of something else. They are not literally
meant or interpreted. They enhance ideas by making them
more graphic and appealing. Like all comparison, contrasts,
and exemplifications, figures of speech are especially useful in
translating the unknown into terms of the known.[23]

In summary, figures of speech have the ability (1) to make communication more vivid and colorful, (2) to make communication
more powerful and forceful, and (3) to illustrate the similarity between two dissimilar things.[24] It should also be noted that while
figures of speech can add force and clarity to one's message, they
can also be abused through excessive use. Sometimes a literal statement would serve equally well or better than a figurative one. Also,
figures of speech can be abused when they paint a distorted image.
This is commonly referred to as a "mixed metaphor."

There are many types of figures of speech. A listing of the most
common would include simile, analogy, metaphor, contrast or antithesis, personification and apostrophe, synecdoche, metonymy,
and antonomasia, and irony and allegory.[25]

Concerning metaphors, Reynolds and Schwartz write:

Metaphors are necessary building locks of language in that they
allow ideas that were previously inexpressible to be expressed,
frequently in a vivid, compact form. . . . The use of metaphors
in didactic discourse is considered not only a sign of linguistic
elegance, but a sign of linguistic efficiency as well.[26]

In their study, they discovered that metaphor can affect the processing of written language. They point out that there is an increased memorability for passages when the concluding statement is
expressed metaphorically rather than literally. Also, not only are the
concluding metaphors themselves recalled better than the equiva-
lent literal sentences but there is also an increase in memory for the
preceding context.

Another type of figure of speech is anthropomorphism. This figure
involves giving human qualities to nonhumans. A study conducted
by Blanchard and McNinch showed that for word learning, anthro-

pomorphic cues resulted in enhanced learning rates when compared to illustrated and no-picture cues.[27] In addition, the anthropomorphic cues helped the students retain a significantly greater proportion of the words when compared to the other two cue conditions.

In addition to figures of speech, illustrations can also aid in making a message or lesson more clear and vivid. In essence, illustrations are the salt of the speech. They give it a pungent and wholesome flavor. They translate the abstract into the concrete, the obscure into the vivid. Illustrations are especially important when dealing with a mixed group, which is generally what the average audience is. Abstract ideas which can be understood by one group may be meaningless to the others. The normal common ground for a whole audience is the concrete.

In his book, *The Art of Illustrating Sermons,* Ian Macpherson lists 17 benefits of using illustrations. They (1) make the meaning plain; (2) promote persuasion; (3) cause the discourse to come alive; (4) add beauty and increase the popular appeal; (5) spice them with variety; (6) keep the message as short as possible; (7) facilitate rhetorical repetition; (8) "earth" a message, keeping it tied to common things; (9) preserve a proper balance in the divisions; (10) make transitions smooth; (11) appeal to the classes of the hearers; (12) establish a rapport between speaker and listener; (13) give the listener a mental breathing-spell; (14) aid memory; (15) enforce a point by indirection; (16) touch the heart; and (17) lead to change.[28]

Illustrations can also be effective in helping people remember when they paint a bizarre picture. O'Brien and Wolford showed that regarding word recall, subjects who formed the more bizarre images were better able to recall the items on an unexpected test 15 weeks later. Their study concluded that bizarre imagery facilitates recall on both an immediate and delayed test, but particularly on a delayed test.[29]

Another aspect of word pictures is the use of stories in teaching. According to Livo, these are even more effective when shared orally. She says:

Words can be read silently—it is only when they are shared orally that they come to life.

The mental imagery storytelling evokes creates a theatre of

the mind. The listener must create scenes and people from the storyteller's paint box of words. Thus storytelling requires an active involvement of both storyteller and listener, and becomes an excellent teaching medium.

In our electronic media age, it is easy to forget that storytelling gives meaning to our lives. It incorporates the blood-and-guts feelings and doings of real people. Stories bring us closer to the human heart and its symbolic condition.[30]

She goes on to point out that there are at least five benefits or rewards of becoming a storyteller. They are:

It provides a much needed opportunity for adults and students of all ages to interact on a very personal level. It develops an awareness of and sensitivity to the thoughts and feelings of listeners. It stimulates imagination and visualization. It helps develop poise. It improves discrimination in choice of books and stories, and fosters increased knowledge of good books.[31]

In describing the use of story in teaching religion, Lee says that "at bottom, a story is primarily a cognitive experience which invites the listeners to vicariously participate in the events narrated in the story. Because a story is a cognitive invitation to a vicarious experience, it tends to be one of the most effective kinds of verbal pedagogical devices."[32]

Concerning the use of stories, the question should also be asked as to whether stories are only effective for children or whether they can be used with adults as well. Livo indicates that they are good for all ages. Kieran Egan also believes that stories are an effective educational device for all ages.[33] He points out that for them to be effective, they need to be structured differently and used differently depending on the age-group.

In addition to locking thoughts into one's memory, word pictures also serve as a catalyst for change.[34] Concerning this, Wilson and Arnold wrote: "While we may customarily think of imagery as a poetic device, it can also be employed by oral communicators to fill out details and to arouse or engage the feelings of audiences—an engagement which, in turn, provides bases for positive or negative attitudinal and valuative judgments."[35]

Scriptural Review[36]

During His three and a half year ministry, a variety of teaching methods were used by Jesus Christ. Oftentimes, His ministry and methods are compared and contrasted with those of the rabbis. Part of the reason for the difference is that Christ had an itinerant ministry. The rabbis could gather their pupils around them to give sustained instruction. But Jesus could not use those same methods. His purpose was to adapt His teaching to make the most of the passing opportunity.

While Jesus did make use of sustained discourse (Sermon on the Mount, Matt.5–7, eschatological discourse, Matt. 24–25), His general method was to impart His teaching more concisely. In order to do this, great skill was required to impress knowledge on fleeting occasions. The major way that Christ did this was through the use of figurative language or word pictures. "Jesus used figures of speech to convey truth as a masterful artist might use particular colors to paint a masterpiece which reflects the artist's inner vision of the world around him."[37]

Guthrie comments on this subject by saying:

> It would seem that Jesus aimed to implant in the memory of His hearers unforgettable illustrations which, reflected upon, would convey spiritual truth. His teaching abounds in metaphors so memorable that many of them have passed into common speech (e.g., "whited sepulchers"). The form in which Jesus expressed His teaching varied considerably. Sometimes an event gave rise to an epigram which summarized His comment on an important theme, as His remark about the tribute money, in which He urged men to render Caesar's things to Caesar and God's things to God (Matt. 22:21). Sometimes the teaching followed naturally from the event, as when a healing illustrated the necessity for faith or the superiority of spiritual healing over physical healing.[38]

In His ministry, Jesus used word pictures to instruct, to exhort, and to confront. The use of word pictures in the teaching of Jesus takes on a greater significance when one realizes that Jesus had only the medium of words at His disposal to communicate spiritual truth. Harcus notes that the Jews would not allow any image or picture of sacred things, but permitted verbal word-pictures through the medium of the ear.[39] Thus, due to the artistic limitations imposed upon Him by His Jewish culture, Jesus was limited to verbal communication.

Jesus used a variety of methods and figures of speech in His teachings. Stein discusses 13 that he feels are among the most important and most often used.[40] They include overstatement, hyperbole, pun, simile, metaphor, and proverb. Also included are riddle, paradox, *a fortiori,* and irony. He also discusses Jesus' use of questions, parabolic or figurative actions, and poetry.

Among the most important of these teaching methods employed by Jesus are His use of verbal and visual illustration. This was often done through the use of simile or metaphor. On many occasions, Jesus used figures of speech drawn from the body to convey spiritual truth. Guthrie comments on this by saying:

> Physical blindness illustrated the far more serious blindness of the soul (John 9:39-41). Political bondage pointed up the bondage of the soul (John 8:31-36). Jesus keenly observed common things and aptly used them to illuminate His teaching. The ubiquitous sparrow could claim the heavenly Father's love (Matt. 10:29). Splinters in eyes illustrate obstructions to spiritual discernment (Matt. 7:15); grass demonstrates the transiency of life (Matt. 6:50); and trees, the secret of true growth (Matt. 7:17-18). Such illustrations impressed themselves on the mind more vividly than abstractions can.[41]

Perhaps the most well-known of all the word pictures used by Jesus is the parable. Pentecost defines the parable by saying that it is "a literary device and is used to teach by means of transference. In order to make it possible to discover truth in an unknown realm, something familiar is transferred from the known realm to the unknown realm."[42] In contrast to an allegory, which may or may not be true to life, a parable is always true to life. Pentecost goes on to compare the two by saying that "transference in an allegory is in ideas, whereas in parables transference is always through a historical reality."[43] Thus, it becomes imperative that a student understand the historical context in order to interpret the parable.

Much of the discussion concerning parables hinges on the reason why Christ used parables. In response to the disciples' questions as to why He spoke in parables, Christ replied that He used parables first to reveal truth to some men and, second, to hide truth from other men (Matt. 13:11-15). Christ recognized that He was speaking to a mixed audience. There were those who had or would believe and needed instruction, and there were those who had already rejected Him. Rather than attempt to separate the two, He constructed His teaching in such a way that those who had believed would understand, and those who had rejected, even though they heard, would not understand.

By using parables, Christ recognized that the parables offered a means of capturing the imagination even when the hearers' understanding is unenlightened. Once rooted in the memory, the parable might later lead to a fuller grasp of the basic truth. Yet the parabolic form has no significance to those whose minds are already closed to the truth.

Pentecost goes on to explain:

> Believers have the key to knowledge and can interpret His teaching. Unbelievers do not possess that key and, therefore, cannot understand His word. The one who has the key of knowledge will use that key to gain more knowledge, but the one who does not have that key will lose such knowledge as he once possessed. This was the explanation Christ gave the disciples as to why He used parables in His teaching.[44]

The essence of a parabolic method of teaching demands an uncomplicated plot. Generally, characters come on the scene without overlapping each other. This can be seen in the parable of the prodigal son (Luke 15), where the father, the younger son, and the elder son all come into focus at various points in the parable. Scenic details are reduced to a minimum and are unessential to the interpretation. Generally, the characteristics of the subjects are left to be inferred from their actions or words.

In only two parables did Jesus supply His own interpretation (Matt. 13:18-23, 36-43). In both of these parables, the parable of the sower and the parable of the tares, the progress of the kingdom is in mind, and both show the importance of more than one detail of the parable. The basic principle of interpretation centers around a comparison between the physical and the spiritual worlds.

The teaching of Jesus had a living quality to it. He was never dull, as amply demonstrated by the variety of the forms He used for communicating truth. His aim was to capture the attention of His listeners in order to implant ideas to stimulate further progressive thought. Jesus did not allow Himself to fall into any kind of a stereotyped pattern. Whatever rhetorical device He used was employed as an instrument and was never allowed to dominate the teaching. It is this variety of methods that brought unparalleled freshness to His teaching.

It has been said that the wide range of a teacher's illustrations reveals much about the teacher. In the case of Jesus, it points to a mind keenly aware of its environment, a readiness to note insignificant things to illuminate profound truths. He evidently loved the countryside since He often drew His verbal pictures from it. He referred to aspects from the carpentry trade, from merchants, and from fishermen. He used a great variety of illustrations to communicate to His contemporaries.

How to Use Word Pictures

As has been shown thus far, word pictures are an effective tool for the communicating of truth. They enable a message to be more vivid, powerful, and memorable. Because of this, there is a greater possibility that whatever is communicated will be retained and that there will be a resulting change in the life of the listener. This is the whole reason for using this technique in the communication of biblical truth.

In general, it should be remembered that word pictures go beyond the simple, albeit vivid, description of something. Imagery is not only description, it includes colorful, sensory language to create mental pictures. Thus, skillful application of the technique uses words to evoke images. This is developed in two basic ways: (1) Create an image by building a description of an event word by word. Reconstruct the experience, step by step, as it unfolds. (2) Translate the description into figures of speech—into similes and metaphors. The more dramatic and unusual the comparison, the more vivid the image that is evoked. In addition to that, the more striking the comparison, the more vivid the image.

Minnick lists five ways that the fidelity and vividness of an experience can be increased.[45] He says that the experience should be compared with other experiences. This could be accomplished through the use of simile or metaphor. He also suggests that the experience be narrated and described with an abundance of details. He indicates that it is best to use terms which are familiar to the audience. Furthermore, he maintains that fidelity and vividness of the experience can be increased through the use of multisensory words in the description. Finally, he suggests that complex experiences be reduced to simple dimensions. He points out that fewer than six major points of a 15 minute radio show are retained by the ordinary listener.

In regard to the art of illustrating sermons, Mark Littleton has eight suggestions.

1. Don't waste time getting into the story. Get in and get out.
2. Make sure the people know what you're illustrating.
3. Make sure your illustration doesn't overshadow your point.
4. Be excited about the illustration.
5. Make sure it's believable and true.
6. Make sure people will identify with the illustration.
7. Be sure of your facts.
8. Be visual.[46]

In regard to the use of stories, it is important that the story be examined to see if it contains the essential elements of a story. According to Brown, there are six elements of a good story.[47] The first is an introduction which arouses the curiosity of the reader. Second, there must be action. The story must go somewhere. This is also referred to as a plot. Third, there should be some sort of conflict or suspense. Difficulties will present themselves or problems will arise. Fourth, there should be a climax. This is where the matters come to a head. The fifth element is the conclusion where the problems are solved. The final element is where the readers relax. This refers to the aspect of making sure that all the loose ends are tied up and that the initial curiosity of the listener is satisfied.

Probably the best description of how to create a word picture is found in Smalley and Trent's book, *The Language of Love*. They suggest seven steps to follow in creating and using word pictures.[48] The first and most important is to establish a clear purpose. Word pictures can be used to clarify thoughts and feelings, to move a relationship to a deeper level of intimacy, to praise or encourage someone, or to lovingly correct someone's behavior. After deciding on a purpose, one must then study the other person's interests. The word picture will be more effective if the other person can relate to or identify with the picture. The picture is then drawn from four areas: nature, everyday objects, imaginary stories, and past memories. The fourth step is to practice or rehearse the story. Step five involves choosing a convenient time without distractions in which to present the picture. Since not every picture is effective the first time it is presented, one must not give up, but keep trying and practicing. The final step is to "milk" the word picture. Expand the picture and use it to clarify concerns and feelings. These steps can be used regardless of whether the medium is a metaphor, an illustration, a story, or some other form of word picture.

Exercises
In order to develop skill in this technique, one must understand different types of imagery, how to describe an event or a person, and how to construct vivid descriptions. At first blush, some individuals may feel somewhat self-conscious in trying to vividly describe an experience. Most people are inclined toward the use of abstract language, rather than toward the use of concrete details. However, word pictures can only be painted through the use of words that represent individual, unique characteristics and attributes. The completion of the following exercises will start the reader on the first step toward mastery of using the technique of word pictures.

A person is walking down the street. Make a list of 15 terms that describe the action using the following sensations:

Visual (sight)

1. glistening	2. staggered	3. ambled
4. reddish	5. slunk	6.
7.	8.	9.

Auditory (sound)

1. crash	2. zing	3. crackle
4. whine	5.	6.
7.	8.	9.

Gustatory (taste)

1. salty	2. dusty	3. bitter
4. sweet	5.	6.
7.	8.	9.

Olfactory (smell)

1. pungent	2. stale	3. flowery
4. rain-fresh	5.	6.
7.	8.	9.

Tactile (feel/touch)

1. gravelly	2. burning	3. sticky
4. dry	5.	6.
7.	8.	9.

Kinesthetic (motor activity)

1. shoving	2. running	3. backbreaking
4. pulsating	5.	6.
7.	8.	9.

Organic (activity occurring inside people)

1. hunger	2. dizziness	3. faintness
4. fear	5. passion	6.
7.	8.	9.

Taking this list of terms, write a short description of the person walking down the street. Use as many or as few of the terms as is necessary. After completing the description, translate it into figures of speech—into similes and metaphors. Remember, similes and metaphors represent comparisons of events that are quite dissimilar. In other words, one type of phenomenon is compared with an entirely different type. For example, the person in the description above might be characterized, upon seeing a fiery-red automobile, as "moving across the lawn like a great stallion leaping a hedge." On the other hand, the automobile's undercoating might be described as "rough as sandpaper." The motor beneath the hood was "the color of burned toast." The more dramatic and unusual the comparison, the more vivid the image that is evoked. To create similes, use the term "like" to make the connection between those experiences being compared. To create a metaphor, simply omit the expression of likeness.

In creating similes and metaphors, comparison may be made of likenesses in attributes such as size, shape, structure, color, texture; or in likenesses of behavior; or in likenesses of operation. The more striking the comparison, the more vivid the image. For example, one might describe the puppy as standing like a Little League pitcher after a 31–0 defeat, or the football player as a lean wolf fed on raw meat.

Conclusion

Word pictures are an effective tool for use in the preaching and teaching of the Bible. They have been used throughout Scripture as God communicated to His people. They were used very effectively by Jesus Himself. They are a device which educators are just beginning to recognize as having great merit for inclusion in the teaching process. This technique ought to be used more in teaching and preaching. It is effective for any subject.

Since this is a device which can aid in the retention of material, it should be used with material that is especially important to be learned. Thus, it goes without saying that it should be employed in teaching and preaching the Bible. Biblical content is more than simply material to be learned. It is material which has the potential and the ability to change lives. Thus, word pictures should be used in the communication of biblical content so that that content will be retained long enough to change the life of the individual.

Notes

1. John H. Westerhoff, III, *Will Our Children Have Faith* (New York: Seabury, 1976).
2. Jon G. Penner, *Why Many College Teachers Cannot Lecture* (Springfield, Ill.: Charles C. Thomas, 1984), 165.
3. W.N. Brigance, *Speech Composition* (New York: Appleton-Century-Crofts, 1937), 200.
4. Leonard Zunin, *Contact: The First Four Minutes* (New York: Ballantine, 1975).
5. In the literature, several different terms are used to describe this technique. They include "pictorial language," "extended metaphors," or simply "figurative language." "Word pictures" seems to be both a simpler and more descriptive term and is found in books such as Gary Smalley and John Trent, *The Language of Love* (Pomona, Calif.: Focus on the Family, 1988) and articles such as Carol Huber, "The Logical Art of Writing Word Pictures," *IEEE Transactions on Professional Communication* (March 1985): 27–28. Thus, for this reason it will be used in this paper.

6. R.W. Pace, B.D. Peterson, and M.D. Burnett, *Techniques for Effective Communication* (Reading, Mass.: Addison-Wesley, 1979), 283.

7. Smalley and Trent, *Language of Love*, 17.

8. Pace, Peterson, and Burnett, *Techniques*, 284.

9. G.R. Potts, "Storing and Retrieving Information about Spatial Images," *Psychological Review*, 75 (1978): 550–60; and Z.W. Pylyshyn, "What the Mind's Eye Tells the Mind's Brain: A Critique of Mental Images, *Psychological Bulletin* 80, no. 6 (1973): 1–24.

10. Among other studies, see Albert Mehrabian, "The Silent Messages We Send," *Journal of Communication*, July 1982.

11. A. Paivio, *Imagery and Verbal Processes* (New York: Holt, Rinehart and Winston, 1971).

12. See Albert Bandura, "Analysis of modeling processes" in *Psychological Modeling*, ed. Albert Bandura (Chicago: Aldine-Atherton, 1971), 1–62; and *Aggression: A Social Learning Analysis* (Englewood Cliffs, N.J.: Prentice-Hall, 1977).

13. L.D. Groninger and L.K. Groninger, "Function of Images in the Encoding-Retrieval Process," *Journal of Experimental Psychology: Learning, Memory, and Cognition* (July 1982): 353–58.

14. A.M. Fullerton, "Age Differences in the Use of Imagery in Integrating New and Old Information in Memory," *Journal of Gerontology* (May 1983): 326–32.

15. J. Zimler and J.M. Keenan, "Imagery in the Congenitally Blind: How Visual Are Visual Images?" *Journal of Experimental Psychology: Learning, Memory, and Cognition* (April 1983): 269–82.

16. J.D. Bonvillian, "Effects of Signability and Imagery on Word Recall of Deaf and Hearing Students," *Perceptual and Motor Skills* (June 1983): 775–91.

17. Pace, Peterson, and Burnett, *Techniques*, 284.

18. Pylyshyn, "What the Mind's Eye Tells the Mind's Brain," 22.

19. Brigance, *Speech Composition*, 218.

20. Robert Hoffman, "Recent Research on Figurative Language," *Annals of the New York Academy of Sciences* (December 1984): 137–66.

21. W.C. Minnick, *The Art of Persuasion* (New York: Houghton Mifflin, 1968), 200.

22. E.W. Bullinger, *Figures of Speech Used in the Bible* (Grand Rapids: Baker, 1968), v–vi.

23. John F. Wilson and Carroll C. Arnold, *Public Speaking as a Liberal Art*, 2nd ed. (Boston: Allyn and Bacon, 1968), 303.

24. D.J. Partie, "Figurative Language in the Teaching of Christ: Its Purposes and Its Interpretation" (Master's thesis, Talbot Theological Seminary, 1978).

25. E. Rogge, and J.C. Ching, *Advanced Public Speaking* (New York: Holt, Rinehart, Winston, 1966), 137–48. Regarding a definition of these concepts, simile, analogy, and metaphor are all used in comparisons. Contrast or antithesis is self-explanatory. They are used to show contrasts. Personification gives life to inanimate objects while apostrophe gives the impression that the author is addressing someone who is not alive at the time. Synecdoche, metonymy, and antonomasia all refer to the act of substituting one word for another. Synecdoche substitutes the part for the whole, metonymy the whole for the part, and antonomasia the name of a more familiar person or place for a less familiar person or place.

26. R.E. Reynolds and R.M. Schwartz, "Relation of Metaphoric Processing to Comprehension and Memory," *Journal of Experimental Psychology* (June 1983): 452.

27. J. Blanchard and G. McNinch, "The Effects of Anthropomorphism on Word

Learning," *Journal of Educational Research* (November/December 1984): 105–10.

28. Ian Macpherson, *The Art of Illustrating Sermons* (Grand Rapids: Baker, 1964), 13–33.

29. D.J. O'Brien and C.R. Wolford, "Effect of Delay in Testing Retention of Plausible Versus Bizarre Mental Images," *Journal of Experimental Psychology: Learning, Memory, and Cognition* (March 1982): 148–52.

30. N.J. Livo, "Storytelling: An Art for all Ages," *Media & Methods* (September 1983): 25.

31. Ibid., 25.

32. James Michael Lee, *The Content of Religious Instruction* (Birmingham, Ala.: Religious Education, 1985), 55. To back up his thought, Lee refers the reader to two books and three articles. The books are John Shea, *Stories of God* (Chicago: Thomas More, 1978); Sallie McFague TeSelle, *Speaking in Parables* (Philadelphia: Fortress, 1975). The articles are Michael Benton, "Children's Response to Stories," in *Children's Literature in Education* 10 (Summer 1979): 68–85; Brian Sutton-Smith, Gilbert Botvin, and Daniel Mahoney, "Developmental Structures in Fantasy Narratives," in *Human Development* 19 (January 1976): 1–13; Brian Sutton-Smith, "Importance of the Storytaker: An Investigation of the Imaginative Life," in *Urban Review* 8 (Summer 1975): 82–95. After reading two of the articles and after examining the books, it was concluded by this author that they do indeed back up what Lee is claiming. However, they were not found to be of enough help to be included in detail in this paper.

33. Kieran Egan, *Educational Development* (Oxford: Oxford Univ. Press, 1979).

34. See Smalley and Trent and their discussion on how word pictures can be used to strengthen relationships.

35. Wilson and Arnold, *Public Speaking*, 293.

36. For the purpose of this study, only the life of Jesus will be considered. It is recognized that figures of speech and word pictures occur throughout the Bible. These are used extensively in the ministry of the prophets, the writers of the Gospels, and the writers of the New Testament. It is also well-known that the Psalms, Proverbs, Song of Solomon, and the rest of the Old Testament poetical books are filled with figures of speech. However, due to the limitations of both time and space, only the figures of speech and word pictures used in the ministry of Christ will be considered in this paper.

37. Partie, "Figurative Language in the Teaching of Christ," 23.

38. Donald Guthrie, "Jesus" in *A History of Religious Educators,* ed. Elmer L. Towns (Grand Rapids: Baker, 1975), 18.

39. A.D. Harcus, "Why the Parabolic Method? *Expository Times,* 1951, 5–7.

40. R.H. Stein, *The Method and Message of Jesus' Teachings* (Philadelphia: Westminster, 1978).

41. Guthrie, "Jesus," 21–22.

42. J. Dwight Pentecost, *The Words and Works of Jesus Christ* (Grand Rapids: Zondervan, 1981), 211.

43. Ibid., 212.

44. Ibid.

45. Minnick, *Art of Persuasion*, 200.

46. Mark R. Littleton, "Raisins in the Oatmeal: The Art of Illustrating Sermons," *Leadership* (Spring 1983): 66–67.

47. J.P. Brown, *The Storyteller in Religious Education* (Boston: Pilgrim, 1951).

48. Smalley and Trent, *Language of Love*, 48–67.

Something to Do

1. In the title and first paragraph, what images of teaching and preaching does the author use? How do you respond to them?

2. What various kinds of images are there? How do they help the learner?

3. Where do "illustrations" fit into the scheme of visual images? Are all stories illustrations?

4. What is a parable? How does it differ from stories in general?

5. Did you do the exercise the author suggested? What did you learn about yourself?

22

"Bruce"
Eugene H. Peterson

EUGENE H. PETERSON is the founding pastor of Christ Our King Presbyterian Church in Bel Air, Maryland, where he served for twenty-nine years. Currently he is Professor of Spiritual Theology at Regent College in Vancouver, British Columbia. I find his books stimulating and instructive, among them *Run With the Horses* (Downers Grove, Ill.: InterVarsity, 1983), *A Long Obedience in the Same Direction* (Downers Grove, Ill.: InterVarsity, 1980), *Earth and Altar* (Downers Grove, Ill.: InterVarsity, 1985), and *Answering God: The Psalms As Tools for Prayer* (San Francisco: Harper and Row, 1989).

This selection is from *Under the Unpredictable Plant* (Grand Rapids: Eerdmans, 1992), 167–72. Used by permission.

"Bruce"

Thirteen four-year-old children sat on the carpet of the sanctuary at the chancel steps on a Thursday morning in late February. I sat with them holding cupped in my hands a bird's nest from the previous season. I talked about the birds on their way back to build nests like this one and of the spring that was about to burst in on us. The children were rapt in their attention.

I love doing this, meeting with these children, telling them stories, singing songs with them, telling them that God loves them, praying with them. I do it frequently. They attend our church's nursery school and come into the sanctuary with their teachers every few weeks to meet with me. They are so *alive*, their capacity for wonder endless, their imaginations lithe and limber.

Winter was receding and spring was arriving, although not quite arrived. But there were signs. It was the signs that I was talking about. The bird's nest to begin with. It was visibly weedy and grey and dirty, but as we looked at it we saw the invisible—warblers on their way north from wintering grounds in South America, pastel and spotted eggs in the nest. We counted the birds in the sky over Florida, over North Carolina, over Virginia. We looked through the walls of the church to the warming ground. We looked beneath the surface and saw the earthworms turning somersaults. We began to see shoots of color break through the ground, crocus and tulip and grape hyacinth. The buds on the trees and shrubs were swelling and about to burst into flower, and we were remembering and anticipating and counting the colors.

I never get used to these Maryland springs and am taken by surprise every time all over again. I grew up in northern Montana, where the trees are the same color all year long and spring is mostly mud. The riotous color in blossom and bloom in Maryland's dogwood and forsythia, redbud and shadbush catches me unprepared every time. But this year I was getting prepared—and getting the children prepared—for all the glorious gifts that were going to be showering in on us in a week or so. We were looking at the bare bird's nest and seeing the colors, hearing the songs, smelling the blossoms.

There are moments in this kind of work when you know you are doing it right. This was one of those moments. The children's faces were absolutely concentrated. We had slipped through a time warp and were experiencing the full sensuality of the Maryland spring. They were no longer looking at the bird's nest; they were *seeing* migrating birds and hatching chicks, garlanded trees and dewy blossoms. Then, abruptly, at the center of this moment of high holiness, Bruce said, "Why don't you have any hair on your head?"

The spell was broken. Spring vanished. Reality collapsed to a vireo's empty nest and a pastor's bald head. Why didn't Bruce see what the rest of us were seeing—the exuberance, the fecundity? Why hadn't he made the transition to "seeing the invisible" that we were engrossed in? All he saw was the visible patch of baldness on my head, a rather uninteresting *fact*, while the rest of us were seeing multidimensioned *truths*. Only four years old, and already Bruce's imagination was crippled.

It usually doesn't happen this early. Childhood, naturally rich in imagination, has a built-in immune system to the cultural poisons that destroy it. But sometimes the immune system, unsupported by stories and songs, succumbs to the poison gas of television.

And why didn't Jonah see grace and salvation in Nineveh? All he saw was a city full of sinners destined by his prophecy for doom. Why didn't he see mercy and grace and salvation?

We who are made in the "*image*" of God have, as a consequence, *imag*-nation. Imagination is the capacity to make connections between the visible and the invisible, between heaven and earth, between present and past, between present and future. For Christians, whose largest investment is in the invisible, the imagination is indispensable, for it is only by means of the imagination that we can see reality whole, in context. "What imagination does with reality is the reality we live by."[1]

When I look at a tree, most of what I "see" I do not see at all. I see a root system beneath the surface, sending tendrils through the soil, sucking up nutrients out of the loam. I see light pouring energy into the protoplast-packed leaves. I see the fruit that will appear in a few months. I stare and stare and see the bare branches austere in next winter's snow and wind. I see all that, I really do—I am not making it up. But I could not photograph it. I see it by means of imagination. If my imagination is stunted or inactive, I will only see what I can use, or something that gets in my way.

Czeslaw Milosz, the Nobel-prize-winning poet, with a passion for

Christ supported and deepened by his imagination, comments on how the minds of Americans have been dangerously diluted by the rationalism of explanation. He is convinced that our imagination-deficient educational process has left us with a naive picture of the world. In this naive view, the universe has space and time—and nothing else. No values. No God. Functionally speaking, men and women are not that different from a virus or bacterium, specks in the universe. It is by means of imagination that we pack in the glory.

Milosz sees the imagination—and especially the religious imagination, which is the developed capacity to be in reverence before whatever confronts us—as the shaping force of the world we really live in. "Imagination," he said, "can fashion the world into a homeland as well as into a prison or a place of battle. It is the invisibles that determine how you will view the world, whether as a homeland or as a prison or place of battle. Nobody lives in the 'objective' world, only in a world filtered through the imagination."[2]

A major and too-little-remarked evil in our time is the systematic degradation of the imagination. The imagination is among the chief glories of the human. When it is healthy and energetic, it ushers us into adoration and wonder, into the mysteries of God. When it is neurotic and sluggish, it turns people, millions of them, into parasites, copycats, and couch potatoes. The American imagination today is distressingly sluggish. Most of what is served up to us as the fruits of imagination is, in fact, the debasing of it into soap opera and pornography.

Right now, one of the essential Christian ministries in and to our ruined world is the recovery and exercise of the imagination. Ages of faith have always been ages rich in imagination. It is easy to see why: the materiality of the gospel (the seen, heard, and touched Jesus) is no less impressive than its spirituality (faith, hope, and love). Imagination is the mental tool we have for connecting material and spiritual, visible and invisible, earth and heaven.

We have a pair of mental operations, Imagination and Explanation, designed to work in tandem. When the gospel is given robust and healthy expression, the two work in graceful synchronicity. Explanation pins things down so that we can handle and use them—obey and teach, help and guide. Imagination opens things up so that we can grow into maturity—worship and adore, exclaim and honor, follow and trust. Explanation restricts, defines, and holds down;

278

Imagination expands and lets loose. Explanation keeps our feet on the ground; Imagination lifts our head into the clouds. Explanation puts us in harness; Imagination catapults us into mystery. Explanation reduces life to what can be used; Imagination enlarges life into what can be adored.

But our technological and information-obsessed age has cut Imagination from the team. In the life of the gospel, where everything originates in and depends on what we cannot see and is worked out in what we can see, Imagination and Explanation cannot get along without each other.

Is it time to get aggressive, time for the Christian community to recognize, honor, and commission its pastors as Masters of the Imagination, joining our poets, singers, and storytellers as partners in evangelical witness? How else is Bruce going to hear the gospel when he grows up—hear Isaiah's poetry and Jesus' parables, see John's visions and Jonah's plight? It will be sad if when he is forty years old and enters a congregation of worshiping Christians and ministering angels all he sees is a preacher's bald head.

Notes

1. David Ignatow, *Open between Us* (Ann Arbor: Univ. of Michigan Press, 1980), 28.
2. Milosz, in an interview published in the *New York Review of Books,* 27 February 1986.

Something to Do

1. Do you ever give children's sermons? Do you find them easy or difficult to prepare and deliver? What makes them difficult or easy for you?

2. Why is childhood "rich in imagination"?

3. What destroys the child's imagination?

4. How do you respond to Peterson's quotation from David Ignatow, "What imagination does with reality is the reality we live by"? How does this statement affect our view of preaching and teaching the Bible?

5. In what sense is the recovery of the imagination a part of our ministry as teachers and preachers? How do we go about doing this?

6. Review the selection and make a list of the forces that the author sees destroying imagination in today's society. How can we counteract them? How does the church fit in?

23

"Jesus the Subversive"
Eugene H. Peterson

FROM *The Contemplative Pastor*, by Eugene H. Peterson (Grand Rapids: William B. Eerdmans, 1993), 32–33. Copyright 1989 by *Christianity Today* and used with permission.

"Jesus the Subversive"

Jesus was a master at subversion. Until the very end, everyone, including his disciples, called him Rabbi. Rabbis were important, but they didn't make anything happen. On the occasions when suspicions were aroused that there might be more to him than that title accounted for, Jesus tried to keep it quiet—"Tell no one."

Jesus' favorite speech form, the parable, was subversive. Parables sound absolutely ordinary: casual stories about soil and seeds, meals and coins and sheep, bandits and victims, farmers and merchants. And they are wholly secular: of his forty or so parables recorded in the Gospels, only one has its setting in church, and only a couple mention the name God. As people heard Jesus tell these stories, they saw at once that they weren't about God, so there was nothing in them threatening their own sovereignty. They relaxed their defenses. They walked away perplexed, wondering what they meant, the stories lodged in their imagination. And then, like a time bomb, they would explode in their unprotected hearts. An abyss opened up at their very feet. He *was* talking about God; they had been invaded!

Jesus continually threw odd stories down alongside ordinary lives (*para*, "alongside"; *bole*, "thrown") and walked away without explanation or altar call. Then listeners started seeing connections: God connections, life connections, eternity connections. The very lack of obviousness, the unlikeness, was the stimulus to perceiving likeness: God likeness, life likeness, eternity likeness. But the parable didn't do the work—it put the listener's imagination to work. Parables aren't illustrations that make things easier; they make things harder by requiring the exercise of our imaginations, which if we aren't careful becomes the exercise of our faith.

Parables subversively slip past our defenses. Once they're inside the citadel of self, we might expect a change of method, a sudden brandishing of bayonets resulting in a palace coup. But it doesn't happen. Our integrity is honored and preserved. God does not impose his reality from without; he grows flowers and fruit from within. God's truth is not an alien invasion but a loving courtship in which the details of our common lives are treated as seeds in our conception, growth, and maturity in the kingdom. Parables trust our imaginations, which is to say, our faith. They don't herd us paternalistically into a classroom where we get things explained and diagrammed. They don't bully us into regiments where we find ourselves marching in a moral goose step.

There is hardly a detail in the gospel story that was not at the time (and still) overlooked because unlikely, dismissed because commonplace, and rejected because illegal. But under the surface of conventionality and behind the scenes of probability, each was effectively inaugurating the kingdom: illegitimate (as was supposed) conception, barnyard birth, Nazareth silence, Galilean secularity, Sabbath healings, Gethsemane prayers, criminal death, baptismal water, eucharistic bread and wine. Subversion.

Something to Do

1. How does the author define the word "subversive"? Why does he claim that our Lord's ministry was "subversive"? Do you agree?

2. Why does he say that parables are "secular stories"? How can we use the "secular" today to teach the truth?

3. What effect did parables have on our Lord's listeners? What effect do they have to contemporary listeners? What is the difference and why?

4. Comment on: "Parables trust our imaginations, which is to say, our faith." What is the connection between imagination and faith?

5. What is the ministry of "the commonplace" and how do we make it work as we preach and teach the Word?

Bibliography

For a more extensive bibliography, see my *Preaching and Teaching with Imagination: The Quest for Biblical Ministry* (Wheaton, Ill.: Victor, 1994), 383–89.

Achtemeier, Elizabeth. *Creative Preaching.* Nashville: Abingdon, 1980.

Brueggmann, Walter. *Finally Comes the Poet: Daring Speech for Proclamation.* Minneapolis: Fortress, 1989.

————. *The Prophetic Imagination.* Philadelphia: Fortress, 1978.

Beuchner, Frederick. *Telling the Truth: The Gospel as Tragedy, Comedy and Fairy Tale.* San Francisco: Harper and Row, 1977.

Caird, G.B. *The Language and Imagery of the Bible.* Philadelphia: Westminster, 1980.

Egan, Kieran, and Dan Nadaner, eds. *Imagination and Education.* New York: Teachers College Press/Columbia Univ. Press, 1988.

Frye, Northrop. *The Educated Imagination.* Bloomington, Ind.: Indiana Univ. Press, 1964.

Hawkes, Terrance. *Metaphor.* London: Methuen, 1972.

Johnson, Mark. *Moral Imagination: Implications of Cognitive Science for Ethics.* Chicago: Univ. of Chicago Press, 1993.

Kearney, Richard. *The Wake of the Imagination.* Minneapolis: Univ. of Minnesota Press, 1988.

Kittay, Eva Feder. *Metaphor: Its Cognitive Force and Linguistic Structure.* Oxford: Clarendon, 1987.

Lakoff, George, and Mark Johnson. *Metaphors We Live By.* Chicago: Univ. of Chicago Press, 1980.

McFague, Sallie. *Metaphorical Theology*. London: SCM, 1983.

May, Rollo. *The Cry for Myth*. New York: W.W. Norton, 1991.

Minear, Paul S. *Images of the Church in the New Testament*. Philadelphia: Westminster, 1977.

Ryken, Leland. *The Christian Imagination*. Grand Rapids: Baker, 1991.

Siegelman, Ellen Y. *Metaphor and Meaning in Psychotherapy*. New York: Guildford, 1990.

Troegar, Thomas H. *Imagining a Sermon*. Nashville: Abingdon, 1990.

Wilson, Paul Scott. *Imagination of the Heart*. Nashville: Abingdon, 1988.